*Music at Oxford
in the Eighteenth and
Nineteenth Centuries*

Music at Oxford in the Eighteenth and Nineteenth Centuries

Susan Wollenberg

OXFORD
UNIVERSITY PRESS

OXFORD
UNIVERSITY PRESS

Great Clarendon Street, Oxford, OX2 6DP
Oxford University Press is a department of the University of Oxford.
It furthers the University's objective of excellence in research, scholarship,
and education by publishing worldwide in

Oxford New York

Athens Auckland Bangkok Bogotá Buenos Aires Cape Town
Chennai Dar es Salaam Delhi Florence Hong Kong Istanbul Karachi
Kolkata Kuala Lumpur Madrid Melbourne Mexico City Mumbai Nairobi
Paris São Paulo Shanghai Singapore Taipei Tokyo Toronto Warsaw
with associated companies in Berlin Ibadan

Oxford is a registered trade mark of Oxford University Press
in the UK and certain other countries

Published in the United States
by Oxford University Press Inc., New York

British Library Cataloguing in Publication Data
Data available
Library of Congress Cataloging-in-Publication Data
Wollenberg, Susan
Music at Oxford in the eighteenth and nineteenth centuries / Susan Wollenberg
p. cm
Includes bibliographical references (p.) and index.
1. Music–England–Oxford–18th century–History and criticism.
2. Music–England–Oxford–19th century–History and criticism. I. Title
ML286.8.O9 W65 2001   780'.9425'7409033–dc21   2001033820
ISBN 0-19-316408-6

1 3 5 7 9 10 8 6 4 2

Typeset by Figaro, Launton, OX26 5DG
Printed in Great Britain
on acid-free paper by
Biddles Ltd.,
Guildford & Kings Lynn

For my mother,
and in memory of my father

Preface

The history of music in Oxford is of such evident potential interest that it is surprising to find that it has never before formed the subject of a book. There have been partial, excellent, accounts of individual topics; in this regard the work of C. F. Abdy Williams and J. H. Mee particularly should be mentioned. When I was first asked to contribute to the *History of the University of Oxford* I assumed that a narrative of the history of its music would already exist in published form. The realization that this was not so was accompanied by an increasing awareness of the rich materials extant on which such a history might be based.

This is not the place to indulge in reminiscences of the delights of sampling the relevant contents of college and university archives in a variety of circumstances and locations. The acknowledgements below pay tribute to the expert and enthusiastic guidance of the many librarians and archivists who helped me in my searches.

Any attempt to put together a history of music in Oxford must be made in the wake of the late George Thewlis, indefatigable chronicler of Oxford's musical past. His aims were far more extensive than those of the present book; the voluminous notes he collected form an invaluable and inspiring source. At the same time they show the difficulties of constructing a comprehensive survey.

It has seemed to me that a chronicle, or calendar, format would not best suit the kind of commentary and analysis of trends which I wished to present here. What follows is thus designed as a selective, rather than attempting an exhaustive, account of the subject. It covers a specific and central period chosen for both practical and historical reasons; and it is my hope that it may serve to stimulate further exploration of the diverse areas of enquiry that are touched on here—whether concerning the choral tradition, concert life, individual personalities, or other aspects.

Although the emphasis is on music in the University and colleges, these were certainly not the sole sources of musical activity. Attention is also given to aspects of music in the city and its environs. But it is important to recognize that 'town and gown' combined and overlapped (perhaps in music more easily than in some other areas). Personnel were shared between city and university, and audiences were drawn from both spheres: the advertisements for musical events constantly referred to 'the Ladies and Gentlemen of the University and City, and of its vicinity' (*JOJ*, 28 October 1820), or some similar formula.

As Rosamond McGuinness has remarked,[1] certain classes of (printed) source material are not necessarily all, or altogether, true. They may not present the complete picture, or they may be inaccurate in the information they give. (However, as Basil Lam once said, uncertainty is a reason for using more sources, rather than not using them at all.) Concert advertisements and printed programmes may represent only what was intended, rather than what actually took place. Nevertheless such documents show the general taste and repertoire at the particular time and place. Where corroborated by critical reports after the event, or, in the case of programmes, annotated with handwritten comments, their informational value may be greatly increased.

Given an advisable measure of caution in approaching and assessing the sources, the manuscript and printed records of Oxford's musical life offer the chance not only to evaluate some of the developments and achievements over a broad span, but also to capture some of the more momentary detail that can evoke the character of a particular event or stage in a musical history. In relation to Oxford, official publications (such as the *University Gazette* and *University Calendar* for the nineteenth century) and formal records, for example of committees and ceremonial, contain a solid core of data. Beyond this, a vast range of manuscript and printed material potentially gives context and adds detail. In drawing together as much of all this as is feasible, it is not necessary always to avoid what has been dubbed by one reviewer the 'easy craft of storytelling'. Sometimes simply telling the story is the best approach to a particular topic; and of course, even in just telling, one is inevitably selecting and commenting. Cyril Ehrlich has observed that 'always in social history, tedious research

[1] R. McGuinness, review of *R. M. A. Research Chronicle*, 22 (1989), ed. J. Milsom, *ML* 71 (1990), 97.

and counting is a necessary preliminary to useful generalization',[2] and I can assert that while never finding this research too tedious, I have certainly done my share of counting.

The hazards of this kind of enterprise are well expressed by Mee and his colleagues, and I cannot resist the temptation of quoting their words here: 'We venture to say that the difficulty of obtaining accuracy in dealing with such great numbers of statements of facts as are involved in the following pages can only be fully appreciated by those who have made the attempt.'[3]

To sum up, then: this book aims to distil the documentary and musical evidence relating to a rich period in the history of Oxford's music, and to provide a repository of references which may enable readers to follow up a particular item or area of research. It is not designed primarily as a critical study of the music itself, although much of the repertoire is deserving of attention; and I should like to preface the book with an acknowledgement of the intrinsic musical attractions to be found in the works of eighteenth- and nineteenth-century British composers. I confess that I began my research with no particular brief for British music of this period, but soon became aware of how unjustly it had been treated (or neglected) in the literature (although recent studies, especially those of Temperley on the nineteenth and Johnstone and Fiske on the eighteenth century, have done much vital pioneering work of rehabilitation).

As Edmund Fellowes emphasized, it is desirable to cultivate an open-minded attitude to concert life, and music-making generally, of the past in Britain: 'there was much excellent amateur playing and singing in Victorian days, and taste for the best class of music was by no means lacking. Evidence of this latter point is provided by some of the concert programmes of mid-Victorian days . . .'. Fellowes was clearly sympathetic to the music of the period, writing with regret (in 1946) that it was 'increasingly becoming the fashion to disparage the music and musicians of Victorian days'.[4] Nor has eighteenth-century British music been immune from such discouraging attitudes.

---

[2] C. Ehrlich, review of R. Leppert, *Music and Image: Domesticity, Ideology and Socio-Cultural Formation in Eighteenth-Century England* (Cambridge, 1988 [1989]), *ML* 71 (1990), 254.

[3] Buck, Mee, and Woods, *Ten Years*, editorial preface.

[4] Fellowes, *Memoirs*, 7 (source of both quotations).

At times in my reading of the secondary literature, it seemed as if Geor-gian, and even more, Victorian, music was being blamed simply for being itself, of its time and place, instead of being fairly assessed (as we now try to assess earlier music) on its own terms and in its proper context. Although I had approached the subject of music in Oxford primarily in search of his-torical information from the sources, I earned in the course of my research the bonus of a purely aesthetic response to the fine examples of the music itself that I encountered.

In charting the general trends in Oxford's musical life, I found that indi-vidual figures emerged distinctively from their background: the irascible and corpulent Philip Hayes; the versatile and inventive Malchair, and his close friend Crotch; the learned and dedicated churchman, Ouseley; and I felt that these, and others, merited, in addition to their place in the narra-tive of events and developments, some separate space in which their achievements could be surveyed. Hence the chapters on 'Personalities' (Chapters 6 and 11), alongside those on the concerts, ceremonies, and aca-demic contexts in which they helped Oxford's music to flourish.

The boundaries between chapters are not rigidly drawn: for instance, the seventeenth-century musical scene in Oxford is treated to some extent in the Introduction (Chapter 1), but also appears in the discussion of later topics where it is of particular relevance, as in the academic context (Chapter 2) and concert life (Chapter 4). Chronologically, although the main focus is on the eighteenth and nineteenth centuries—when a par-ticularly richly developed musical life flourished in Oxford—notice has been taken both of related matters concerning the last decades of the seventeenth century (the time of Dean Aldrich) on the one hand, and on the other, of the period up to the start of the First World War, and beyond (Chapter 12) when various nineteenth-century initiatives came to fruition.

While the division of chapter topics is accompanied by potentially a considerable amount of overlap, the chapter titles reflect their main focus. 'Music in an Academic Context' (Chapters 2 and 7) covers degrees and related musical matters: in Chapter 2, this includes consideration of the Encaenia and Commemoration celebrations, but because of the new emphasis on music's academic status in nineteenth-century Oxford, Chapter 7 is concerned with the formal aspects of its development. 'Music

5 Wollenberg, 'Malchair', 41.

in the University and City' (Chapters 3 and 8) receives correspondingly differing treatment. In Chapter 8 (on the nineteenth century) the university and civic musical culture, including ceremonial use, is considered generally, while in Chapter 3 on the eighteenth century a variety of occasions for music other than Encaenia is discussed. The chapters on concert life (Chapters 4 and 9) are more directly concerned with specific concert series and institutions, and with issues of venues, performers, and repertoire. The traditional duality of University and colleges allows for separate consideration of college music-making (Chapters 5 and 10).

This book has been many years in gestation: a host of other tasks and preoccupations have intervened in the process of researching and writing it. To quote Malchair: the 'leisure howers of many years were employed in forming this collection, ney, necessary busness was at times incrotched uppon when the fitt of collecting Grew Violent.'[5] In my case the 'necessary business' unavoidably encroached on the opportunities for collecting and recording the material of this book. But the notion of a 'Violent' attachment to the process of accumulating it rings very true.

During its preparation I have seen the wider subject of university history grow in prominence and develop into a discipline in its own right, with its own journal (*History of Universities*), conferences, articles, and books. This welcome growth has also acted as a stimulus to my work, as has the notable development of studies in the social history of music in general, and of concert life in particular (for example in the work of Cyril Ehrlich, and of Simon McVeigh). A number of people gave me invaluable assistance at particularly difficult times, and I am enormously grateful to them.

The following have earned my warm thanks for their tireless help in providing advice on the subject and access to the sources: the staff of Cecil Sharp House Library, London; Centre for Oxfordshire Studies, Central Library, Westgate, Oxford; Library of Christ Church, Oxford (Janet McMullin); Oxford, Bodleian Library, especially Colin Harris (Modern Papers), Peter Ward Jones, Robert Bruce (Music Room) and their colleagues; Oxford University archives, Bodleian Library; Oxford University Music Faculty Library (John Wagstaff and colleagues); Library of the Royal College of Music, London; University of Birmingham, Special

Collections; the current and former archivists of Balliol College (John Jones), Christ Church (Judith Curthoys), Magdalen College (Brenda Parry-Jones; Robin Darwall-Smith), New College (Caroline Dalton), Pembroke (Aidan Lawes) and Queen's College, Oxford (John Kaye); and Roger Highfield, H. Diack Johnstone, Roy Judge, E. D. Mackerness, H. J. Marx, Philip Olleson, Harold Pollins, Steven Tomlinson (of the Bodleian Library), Brian Trowell, and the family of the late George Thewlis. Thanks are also due to Susan Waters and Hilery Bronfen, who typed early drafts of various chapters; and to Jane Bolton, who heroically took on at a late stage the task of producing the complete typescript. It has benefited greatly from Mary Worthington's copy-editing skills, and I am grateful to her and to the editorial staff of Oxford University Press for their enthusiastic work on the production of the book. Bruce Phillips, formerly of Oxford University Press, gave vital support when the book was first mooted.

I am indebted to all those who granted permission to reproduce items from their collections as illustrations; and to the following for permission to quote from material in their archives: Cheshire County Council; the Governing Body of Christ Church; the President and Fellows of Magdalen College; the Warden and Fellows of New College; the Master and Fellows of Pembroke College. For research funding in support of this book I thank the following: The British Academy; the Board of the Faculty of Music, University of Oxford; and Lady Margaret Hall, Oxford.

My editors for the *History of the University of Oxford*, Dame Lucy Sutherland and, later, Leslie Mitchell for volume v, and Michael Brock and Mark Curthoys for volume vii, gave me much encouragement in my research; and my fellow contributors, John Caldwell (on late medieval Oxford and the sixteenth century) and Penelope Gouk (on the seventeenth century) were generous in sharing the fruits of their researches with me. Frederick Sternfeld, my much-missed mentor, originally steered me in the direction of the subject. I acknowledge gratefully the kind efforts of all those colleagues and friends who thought of me when they encountered items of interest relating to Oxford, and communicated their finds to me. Mark Curthoys and Simon McVeigh generously gave time to reading and commenting on chapters in draft and John Caldwell read the whole, and made various helpful suggestions. Esther Schmidt provided, in the final stages, valuable research assistance. Last, and definitely not least, I record my gratitude to my family: Lionel, Michael, and Anne, for their patience, interest, and humour as they encouraged me to persevere with this project.

Contents

List of Plates

List of Figures

List of Music Examples

Abbreviations

A	Alto
B	Bass
BLR	*Bodleian Library Record*
CCA	Archives of Christ Church, Oxford
Ckc	King's College, Cambridge (Rowe Library)
CUMS	Cambridge University Musical Society
DNB	*Dictionary of National Biography*
EO	*Encyclopaedia of Oxford*, ed. Hibbert
EM	*Early Music*
GM	*Gentleman's Magazine*
Grove	Grove, *Dictionary of Music and Musicians*; refers in the text to one of the dictionaries, with date as identification (e.g. *Grove* (1994)), and specific (abbreviated) title given in footnote (e.g. *NGCDM*)
HCM	Minutes of Hebdomadal Council (held in University Archives)
HCP	Hebdomadal Council Papers (held in University Archives)
HUO	*History of the University of Oxford*
JAMS	*Journal of the American Musicological Society*
JOJ	*Jackson's Oxford Journal* (in footnote references; abbreviated in text to *Journal*)
MCA	Magdalen College Archives, Oxford
MGG	*Die Musik in Geschichte und Gegenwart*
ML	*Music & Letters*
MMR	*Monthly Musical Record*
MQ	*Musical Quarterly*
MT	*Musical Times*
NCA	Archives of New College, Oxford

NG	*New Grove Dictionary of Music and Musicians* (1980); *NG2* refers to 2nd rev. edn., 2001
NGCDM	*Grove Concise Dictionary of Music*
Ob	Oxford, Bodleian Library
Och	Library of Christ Church, Oxford
OCMC	Oxford and Cambridge Musical Club
OCMS	Oxford Chamber Music Society
OHEM	*Oxford History of English Music*
OHS	Oxford Historical Society
OLMS	Oxford Ladies' Musical Society
Ouf	Music Faculty Library, Oxford
OU Gazette	*Oxford University Gazette*
OUMC	Oxford University Musical Club
OUMU	Oxford University Musical Union
OUOC	Oxford University Opera Club
PCA	Archives of Pembroke College, Oxford
PMA	*Proceedings of the Musical Association*
PRMA	*Proceedings of the Royal Musical Association*
QCA	Archives of Queen's College, Oxford
RAM	Royal Academy of Music
RCM	Royal College of Music
RCO	Royal College of Organists
RMARC	*R. M. A. Research Chronicle*
S	Soprano
T	Tenor
UA	University Archives (Bodleian Library, Oxford)
UAMS	University Amateur Musical Society
UOC	University of Oxford Commission

Bibliographical Note and University Terms

Within the text and in the footnotes, references giving either short title or partial details only indicate items listed in the bibliography, where the full reference will be found. The bibliography covers specialized items relating to the subject, and more general items where these are relevant; it does not purport to be a bibliography of eighteenth- and nineteenth-century British music.

The University calendar was divided into four terms: Michaelmas, Lent (or Hilary), Easter, and Act (Trinity). Salmon (*The Present State of the Universities* (1744), 268) has Michaelmas term as 10 October to 17 December; Hilary or Lent term as 14 January to the Saturday before Palm Sunday, Easter term as the tenth day after Easter to the Thursday before Whit Sunday; and Trinity or Act term as the Wednesday after Trinity Sunday to after the Act (degree ceremonies).

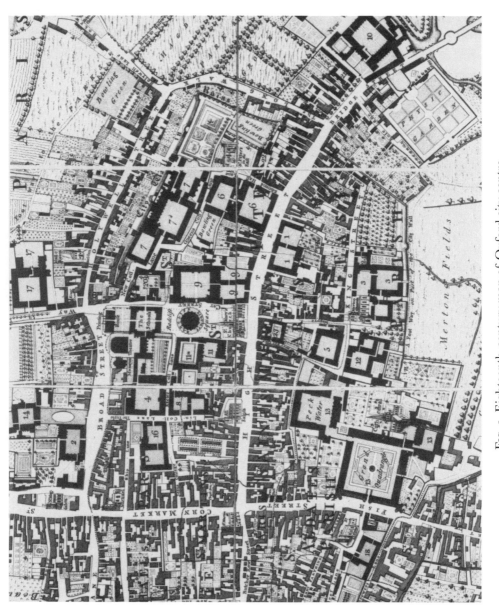

Fig. 1 Eighteenth-century map of Oxford city centre

PART I

The Eighteenth Century

I

Introduction: The Tradition
before *c*.1660

Oxford's history can be traced back as far as the year 912. Parts of its early fortifications are still visible today in the remains of the city walls (some of which were incorporated into the colleges) and the castle tower, built for William the Conqueror in 1071. The two great Augustinian priories of St Frideswide's and Oseney Abbey, dating from 1122 and 1129 respectively, promoted an environment of learning which contributed to the development of the university towards the end of the twelfth and beginning of the thirteenth centuries: the appointment of a chancellor of the university was first mentioned in a document of 1214.[1]

From the earliest period there are reports of both private and sociable music-making within the university community. It was written of Robert Grosseteste (Chancellor of the University *c*.1224) that:

> He loved moche to here the Harpe,
> For mans witte yt maketh sharpe.
> Next hys chamber, besyde his study,
> Hys Harper's chamber was fast the by.

---

[1] For the general history of the university see V. H. H. Green, *A History of Oxford University* (London, 1974); and *The History of the University of Oxford*, 8 vols. (Oxford, 1984 ff.). Generally on Oxford's musical history see Wollenberg, articles 'Oxford' in *NG2*, and *MGG*. These are the chief sources of the information presented here.

And Chaucer's Nicholas, the poor 'Clerk of Oxenford', possessed, according to the *Miller's Tale*, a psaltery,

> On which he made a nightes melodye
> So swetely that al the chamber rang:
> And Angelus ad virginem he sang.

In 1381 three harp makers were documented in Oxford; a variety of musical instruments, including harps and lutes, appeared among fifteenth- and sixteenth-century inventories of the goods of university members. Informal musical gatherings included the medieval college custom of singing around the fire in hall after supper on festivals and special occasions. Formal provision for music existed in the various college statutes; New College (1379), the first of the three major choral foundations, had a statutory allocation (to be retained whatever the college's financial position) of ten chaplains, three clerks, and sixteen choristers, with an *informator choristarum* first documented in 1394–5. An element of training occurred specifically in the founder's statutes for the Queen's College (1340) with the prescription of thirteen chaplains and two clerks to give instruction in plainsong and polyphony to the 'poor boys'. The second of the major choral foundations to be established, Magdalen College (1458), was provided with four chaplains, eight clerks, sixteen choristers, and their *informator*. Evidence of the latter's function in composing chapel music for the choir survives in the work by Richard Davy (*informator* 1490–2) preserved in the Eton choirbook, with the inscription 'hanc antiphonam composuit Ricardus Davy uno die collegio magdalene Oxoniis'.

At Cardinal College (1525) on the site of St Frideswide's, the third of the great choral establishments to be founded, Wolsey provided for thirteen chaplains, twelve clerks (one of whom was to serve as organist), sixteen choristers, and an *informator*. In 1546 the old priory church of St Frideswide's was designated Christ Church Cathedral, henceforth functioning—uniquely—as both diocesan cathedral church and college chapel for Henry VIII's refounded college of Christ Church (or *Aedes Christi*). Also in 1546 Henry VIII established the cathedral school for the free education of the choirboys, together with a complement of fee-paying pupils.[2]

---

[2] On Oxford's later role as refuge for King and court in the 1640s see Ch. 4 below.

Degrees in music (B.Mus., D.Mus.) had been awarded at Oxford from at least the late fifteenth century. These belonged to a distinct category separate from the BA and MA obtainable after four, and then a further three, years' study of the liberal arts. Some thirty candidates took music degrees (the majority B.Mus.) in the period up to 1535, among them Hugh Aston (1510) and Robert Fayrfax (incorporated D.Mus. from Cambridge in 1511, the earliest recorded mention of the doctorate). The candidates were expected to have spent a substantial number of years in the study of music (which could be external to the university) and to compose a mass, or mass and antiphon, customarily performed during the degree ceremony. A series of distinguished composers supplicated for the Oxford degree of B.Mus. during the later sixteenth and early seventeenth centuries, including John Bull and John Munday (1586), Thomas Morley and John Dowland (1588), Giles Farnaby (1592), Thomas Weelkes (1602), Thomas Tomkins (1607), and Richard Dering (1611). The D.Mus. was granted to, among others, John Sheppard (1554), *informator* at Magdalen College. A glimpse of the splendour attached to the Oxford degrees in the seventeenth century is provided by Christopher Gibbons (son of Orlando) who in 1663 was 'nominated by the King for the degree of D.Mus. at Oxford University'; this was conferred in July 1664, and Wood related that the music for the occasion was performed 'with very great honour to himself and his faculty'.[3]

Although the Puritan proscriptions had disrupted the choral tradition in Oxford, as elsewhere, the college resources either remained or were restored after 1660. In 1663 a 'large and stately organ' was fitted up in New College chapel; the organ of Magdalen College chapel, removed on Cromwell's orders to Hampton Court, was returned to the college after the Restoration; and the organ in use at St John's College until 1768 was the same as before the Restoration.[4] Music teaching is documented in Oxford at this time; Wood took lessons on the violin from one of the city waits, for which he paid '2s.6d. Entrance, and 10s. Quarterly', and Edward Lowe taught a young lady to play the virginals, preparing a manuscript collection of virginals pieces for her together with advice.[5]

3 *NG2* ix. 830, 'Christopher Gibbons'.
4 Wood, *History and Antiquities* (ed. Gutch), i. 199; ii. 271; and iii. 554. For the history of New College organ see also P. Hale in Buxton and Williams (eds.), *New College, Oxford*, 270–3.
5 Cf. Spink, *The Seventeenth Century*, 25.

All these elements of musical provision set the pattern for the diversity of music-making in Oxford throughout the following centuries. The medieval scholars also established a tradition of theoretical music in connection with the study of the seven liberal arts, whereby music was studied alongside arithmetic, astronomy, and geometry in the quadrivium. A series of theoretical treatises on music emanated from Oxford writers during the thirteenth to the sixteenth centuries. During this period, too, the *De musica* of Boethius (d. 524) was granted, and retained, its leading position in the Oxford curriculum: Boethius's text was specified in the MA regulations from at least 1431. This speculative element in Oxford's musical tradition was renewed in the seventeenth century by the work of a group of Oxford mathematicians and philosophers (Edmund Chilmead, John Wallis, John Wilkins, and their colleagues); Wilkins's Oxford group formed the nucleus of the early Royal Society (founded 1660).

When William Heather endowed the Professorship of Music at Oxford that bears his name, in 1627 (inspired by his friend Camden's similar foundation in History in 1622)[6] he recognized the dual strands of practical and theoretical music in his stipulation that the Choragus (later known as Professor), with a stipend of £13.6*s*.8*d*. per annum, should preside over weekly music practices during termtime (except in Lent), while the Lecturer in the science of music, at a yearly stipend of £3, should be responsible for theoretical instruction. This latter post fell into disuse in the course of the seventeenth century, but survived in the Music Lecture or Music Speech which formed part of the annual Act (degree ceremonies). Nevertheless Heather's endowment of the Professorship was a landmark event that put Oxford music 'on the map' for the future. A series of distinguished holders of the post during the seventeenth century included Richard Nicholson (1627–39), John Wilson (1656–61), Edward Lowe (1661–82), and Richard Goodson senior (1682–1718). The Heather Professor traditionally presided over the Music School (located in the Bodleian Quadrangle, where the inscription 'Schola Musicae' still stands over the

---

[6] See *HUO* iv. 345, 623–4. Heather himself in 1622 took the degrees of B.Mus. and D.Mus. at Oxford simultaneously (a practice later regarded as undesirable: see Ch. 2 below); it was thought that on the same occasion his Chapel Royal colleague and friend Orlando Gibbons took the D.Mus. at Oxford, having previously graduated Mus.B. at Cambridge in 1606 (*NG* vii. 354, 'Orlando Gibbons'), but doubt has been cast on this (cf. *NG2* ix. 833). On Gibbons's 'O clap your hands', evidently written for this occasion, see Caldwell, *OHEM* i. 369–70.

doorway), which housed Heather's collection of music books, portraits, and instruments: successive Professors arranged for refurbishments and added to the collection. As Hawkins (who worked there in preparing his *History of Music*) later described it, the 'music-school at Oxford' was 'the repository of a great number of books containing compositions of various kinds, some of them of great antiquity'.[7] Oxford by that time reflected and stimulated both the traditional antiquarian interests in music, and the development of the newer historical scholarship in the subject.

[7] Sir John Hawkins, *A General History of the Science and Practice of Music* (London, 1776), preface to vol. i; on the early holdings of the Music School see M. Crum, 'Early Lists of the Oxford Music School Collection', *ML* 48 (1967), and Ford, 'The Oxford Music School in the late 17th century', *JAMS* 17 (1964); generally on the early Music School see *HUO* iv. 625–6. Hawkins, *History* (2nd edn., London, 1875) refers (ii. 699) to ' "a rare Theorbo for singing to . . . with the Earl of Bridgwater's crest in brass just under the fingerboard" . . . given by Lawes to the Oxford Music School and survived until the middle of the nineteenth century' (quoted in Spink, *The Seventeenth Century*, 304).

2

Music in an Academic Context, I

The university musical scene in Oxford was enlivened during the eight-eenth century by two notable visits: those of Handel in 1733, and Haydn in 1791. Both these occasions were much discussed at the time and have been copiously documented since.[1] In both cases an honorary degree was involved: Handel, notoriously, refused the university's offer (for reasons which have been the subject of speculation); Haydn gracefully accepted, becoming henceforth 'Dr Haydn'.[2] Famously, specific works by these com-posers were associated with their visits: Handel's oratorio *Athalia* was premièred—very unusually for his oratorios, outside London—at the Sheldonian Theatre in 1733; Haydn's 'Oxford' Symphony (No. 92 in G major) was performed there in 1791 and, later, his canon 'Thy voice O Harmony' was sent to the university in recognition of the honour be-stowed on him. Nevertheless these compositions fulfilled expectations rather than requirements. It was in connection with the annual degree ceremonies of the Oxford Act that a specific musical tradition had devel-oped, in the form of musical 'exercises' and 'Act-music'. The exercises in composition were subject to statutory regulations, while the Act-music (incidental music for performance at the degree ceremonies, as distinct

---

[1] See especially Deutsch, *Handel*, and Robbins Landon, *Haydn*, vol. iii (*passim*).

[2] Further on these two occasions, see pp. 23 ff. below.

from the exercises in composition submitted by degree candidates) was governed by convention.[3]

Another traditional musical feature of the Act was the Music Lecture or Music Speech, originally intended by Heather as part of the regular duties of the Music Lecturer. By the late seventeenth century the Lecturer was elected annually for this specific purpose by the Proctors and Vice-Chancellor. The speech was characterized as a 'solemn lecture in English . . . with intervals of instrumental music' to be given on 'the Vesperies of the act every year' (Act Saturday) at the Music School.[4] During the late seventeenth century these events attracted a crowded audience. A standard was set for the Restoration period by the celebrations of May 1660 when, as Wood reported, 'there was a most excellent musick-lecture . . . in the public school of that facultie' (with Wood performing a part on the violin). The illustrations were directed by Edward Lowe, organist of Christ Church (deputizing for the Professor of Music, John Wilson) and 'all . . . carried very well, and gave great content to the most numerous auditory. This meeting was to congratulate his majestie's safe arrival . . .'. In noting that the school was 'exceeding full', Wood observed that the gallery at the end of the school was full of the female sex'. And finally, 'after all was concluded, Mr. Low and some of the performers . . . retired to the Crowne Taverne, where they dranke a health to the king'.[5]

While the Music Speech contributed (notionally at least) to the intellectual debate on the subject, combined with musical illustrations, the Act-music provided a practical demonstration of composition and performance for ceremonial use. Most surviving Act-music dates from the period 1669–1710, when the Act particularly flourished.[6] (The origins of the Encaenia and Commemoration celebrations held annually in the summer were connected with the transfer of the Act ceremony from the University Church of St Mary to the newly built Sheldonian Theatre in

---

[3] The statutory public performance of music exercises had traditionally been incorporated into the ceremonies of the Act.

[4] It was later 'remov'd from the Musick-School to the [Sheldonian] *Theatre* by Act of Convocation': Ob, MS Top. Oxon e. 214.

[5] 24 May 1660; quoted in Mee, *Music Room*, pp. viii–ix from Wood, *Life and Times*, ed. Clark, i. 316. Wood further documented the licentiousness of some of the Music Speeches, as in 1693 when 'Mr Smith was very baudy among the women' (*Life and Times*, iii. 427, quoted in Thewlis, Notes, ii. 256).

[6] Relevant music is preserved in Ob, MS Mus. Sch. collection (listed in *Summary Catalogue*, v); and in Och (see Trowles, 'Musical Ode', ii. 10–25 and *passim* for details of sources). Perhaps because of their ephemeral nature, these works have survived only patchily.

1669.[7]) The nature of this music, conceived very much as a 'pièce d'occasion', enabled it to make a substantial contribution to the development of occasional genres such as the Ode, which Trowles has described as an important early form of 'large-scale secular choral music' in England.[8] Trowles traces over twenty musical odes composed for Oxford during the period *c.*1669–1710.[9] These varied between Latin and English settings. Distinguished additions to this essentially choral and orchestral genre included Matthew Locke's *Descende coelo* (1673) and John Blow's *Awake, awake my lyre* (*c.*1676). Local composers were also featured. The Heather Professor took general responsibility for the provision of Act-music; compositions arranged, if not originated, by the professors themselves included *O qui potenti* and *Carminum praeses* (*c.*1700 and *c.*1706 respectively) by Richard Goodson (senior).[10]

Texts at this time were probably composed specially for the occasion, perhaps by some official of the university, and might contain suitable topical references.[11] These texts were characteristically set with a mixture of instrumental overtures, symphonies, and dance movements, together with solo song, vocal ensembles, and choruses. Henry Aldrich (Dean of Christ Church 1689, Vice-Chancellor 1692–5), an enthusiastic supporter of this as of other aspects of university and college musical life, contributed Act-music in several years. So too did his colleague at Christ Church, Sampson Estwick.[12] In 1693, for example, the poem *Britannia* (possibly written by Anthony Alsop of Christ Church) was recited by Samuel Lennard,

[7] See *EO* 129–30 ('Encaenia'). Benjamin Rogers's Ode for the dedication of the Sheldonian Theatre (in July 1669, when Rogers, who was *Informator choristarum* at Magdalen College, 1665–86, received the degree of D.Mus.: the music is lost) commemorated this occasion (cf. Trowles, 'Musical Ode', ii. 117). Organ-playing was a feature of the Encaenia; for the original ceremony an organ was borrowed from Worcester (the Vice-Chancellor's accounts recorded the 'setting up the organ at the Act and returning it': see Wood, *Life and Times*, iv. 71, n. ii. 165). In 1671 the Sheldonian acquired its own 'Father Smith' organ (periodically replaced since). Among Lord Crewe's benefactions to the University was an endowment to cover organ-playing at Encaenia.

[8] Trowles, 'Musical Ode', abstract.

[9] Ibid. i. 42–8.

[10] See below on authorship (n. 11 refers).

[11] For example making mention of royal personages, as in Estwick's Oxford Act Ode to the Queen ('O Maria, O diva') and *Carminum praeses*, which exists in a version implying performance during William III's reign (on the uncertainty over Goodson's authorship, cf. Trowles, 'Musical Ode', ii. 14–15; *NG2* (i. 339) attributes it to Aldrich). Goodson's 'Janus, did ever to thy wond'ring eyes' (1705) and 'Ormond's Glory, Marlborough's Arms' (*c.*1702) were written for University celebrations commemorating the military successes of the Duke of Marlborough at Blenheim and in the War of the Spanish Succession.

[12] On Estwick's career, see Ch. 5 below. For his works, see Trowles, 'Musical Ode', ii. 70–2.

followed by a performance of Aldrich's setting of selected verses from it.[13] The musicality of the poetry was an important factor. During the eighteenth century, Oxford writers contributed to the poetic development of the Ode; and, as Trowles remarks, 'the importance which Warton and Collins placed on the musical qualities of poetry was doubtless a major reason why composers repeatedly selected their poems for musical setting'.[14]

With the shift in focus of the music included in the Encaenia, under the influence of developments in the new genre of English oratorio and in concert repertoire during the eighteenth century, 'the performance of odes was now usually confined to special occasions' such as the installation of a new Chancellor at Encaenia: odes were composed for a handful of such occasions between 1759 and 1810 by the Heather Professor of Music, with texts usually by the Professor of Poetry.[15] A high point was reached with William Hayes's setting of *The Passions*, with poetic text by William Collins, performed for the Commemoration in July 1750 and signalled by Trowles as 'the first large-scale choral work by a composer other than Handel to receive a public performance in Oxford'.[16] Hayes's odes of 1759, 1763, and 1773 marked the installation of successive Chancellors of the University: first Lord Westmorland, then the Earl of Lichfield, and finally Lord North. The work performed in July 1759 was characterized in the *Gentleman's Magazine* as 'an ode suited to the occasion and set to music by Dr Hayes';[17] in this and other cases the occasional context led to an element of musical pastiche, with borrowings from previous odes. An Oxford tradition can be perceived in the mixing of myth, early history, and more recent Oxford history in Thomas Warton's poem of Hayes's 1751 Ode for Music (*Where shall the Muse*); similar tendencies appear in the work of Benjamin Wheeler (Warton's successor as Professor of Poetry), seen in Hayes's 1773 setting of *Daughters of Beauty*.[18]

---

[13] Trowles, 'Musical Ode', i. 40; ii. 13–14.

[14] Ibid. i. 18 (and *pace* Fiske in Johnstone and Fiske, *The Eighteenth Century*, 243). Joseph Warton was brother of the Oxford Professor of Poetry, Thomas Warton; both wrote Odes. William Collins published Odes in the 1740s.

[15] See Trowles, 'Musical Ode', i. 62.

[16] Ibid. i. 65. Heighes, 'Hayes' (iii. 52) notes its revival at the Three Choirs Festival, 1760 (see also Johnstone and Fiske, *The Eighteenth Century*, 239 for an appreciative account of the work).

[17] Quoted in Trowles, 'Musical Ode', i. 68 (from *GM* 29 (1759), 341).

[18] For discussion of these works see Trowles, 'Musical Ode', i. 62–70.

Philip Hayes continued the tradition in two odes written for specific university occasions. The *Ode on the King's Visit to Oxford, on his Recovery* (1785) commemorated the visit of George III, Queen Charlotte, and their children to Nuneham and Oxford, when Hayes 'at their entrance into the Theatre and during the Ceremony entertained their Majesties with overtures on the organ'.[19] For the installation of the Duke of Portland as Chancellor in 1793 Hayes set to music words by the Professor of Poetry, Robert Holmes. It was on this notorious occasion that the hazards inherent in the packing of the Sheldonian Theatre with a characteristically overcrowded and over-excited audience became apparent, when Hayes's Ode for the Encaenia was interrupted and only half of it performed.[20] Trowles speculates that this Ode may possibly never have been heard in full.[21] It represents the genre at a somewhat over-extended stage in its history, displaying a very protracted and disunified cantata-type form.[22]

Throughout the eighteenth century the ode continued to flourish in Oxford in an academic context, as one of the forms favoured for the exercises in composition submitted for the degrees of B.Mus. and D.Mus. Unlike other subjects in which degrees were awarded, music in eighteenth-century Oxford was largely detached from the main academic activities of lectures and tutorials.[23] The traditional scientific and philosophical approach to musical education in the universities (enshrined in music's place in the quadrivium alongside arithmetic, astronomy, and geometry) was losing its power, and it was not until the following century that moves were made to replace it with a more modern style of curricular musical instruction. Supplicants for degrees in music were not required to follow taught courses in residence at the university: the B.Mus. candidate could simply matriculate shortly beforehand under the aegis of an Oxford college (most popularly Magdalen, in the eighteenth century) in order to take the degree. While this meant that the university had little control over

---

[19] Ob, MS Top. Oxon d. 247, p. 162 (12 Sept. 1785). Because the autograph of Hayes's Ode is dated 17 November 1785, Trowles suggests that the work was possibly written after the event as a commemorative piece ('Musical Ode', i. 71). Heighes, 'Hayes' (iii. 168) notes that the full title is found only in a 19th-cent. hand.

[20] Ob, MS Top. Oxon d. 174, fo. 238.   [21] Trowles, 'Musical Ode', i. 72.

[22] Ob, MS Mus. d. 64.

[23] In an article from this time ('Fiddling considered', *The Student*, 1 (1750), 92) the practice of music was humorously regarded as a regrettable diversion from academic study: 'Must we not therefore with some concern see so many Students . . . destin'd to the common task of learning, debauch'd by Sound, neglecting LOCKE and NEWTON for PURCELL and HANDEL . . .'.

candidates' musical preparation, it also logically implied that musicians could obtain degrees confirming their expertise in their subject who would otherwise (perhaps for social, financial, or family reasons) have been unable to graduate from Oxford. Ages of candidates ranged widely, from William Crotch (B.Mus. 1794) aged 18 to Theodore Aylward (B.Mus. 1791) aged about 60: John Stanley (born January 1712) graduated B.Mus. in 1729, thus achieving the distinction of being probably the youngest Oxford B.Mus. of the century.[24]

The statutory requirements for the B.Mus. and D.Mus. consisted of the traditional exercises in composition: a 'Canticum' in five parts for the Bachelor's degree, and in six or eight parts for the Doctor's degree, was to be performed in the Music School 'tam vocibus quam instrumentis etiam musicis'.[25] Besides the specifications enshrined in the statutes, there were evidently unwritten 'rules', such as the expectation that the exercises would demonstrate fugal and contrapuntal technique: most eighteenth-century candidates laboured to produce evidence of these, some more impressively than others. In addition, the candidate for the B.Mus. must have spent seven years in the study or practice of music (producing testimonials to this effect), and in order to proceed to the D.Mus. (less commonly awarded in the eighteenth century) five further years of study must elapse. The statutes governing the award of the D.Mus. were very freely interpreted in the eighteenth century, especially with regard to the span of time between Bachelor's and Doctor's degrees, thus making nonsense of the idea of further study.

The practice of 'accumulated degrees' (followed earlier in William Heather's case) continued during the eighteenth century, whereby the two degrees were awarded simultaneously on production of one exercise. In an unusual case (and according to a widely circulated story) Samuel Arnold, whose oratorio *The Prodigal Son* was performed during the installation of Lord North as Chancellor in 1773, was offered the B.Mus. and D.Mus. degrees by the university; the Professor of Music, Dr Hayes, refused to judge Arnold's exercise (a setting of John Hughes's ode *The Power of Music*), deeming it unnecessary for the composer of *The Prodigal*

[24] For Crotch see esp. Ch. 6 below; Aylward was organist of St George's Chapel, Windsor, from 1788 and this appointment may have spurred him on to take the degree. Stanley's exercise, the cantata *The Power of Music*, is extant in Ckc, Rowe MS 7.

[25] Cited in Hawkins, *History*, ii. 349.

OXFORD.
RADCLIFFE INFIRMARY.

ON Tuesday the 6th of July will be held the Anniversary Meeting of the President and Governors of the Radcliffe Infirmary, when a Sermon will be preached in the Morning at St. Mary's Church, by the Right Reverend the Lord Bishop of Chester; and in the Service will be introduced a grand Te Deum, Anthems, &c.——After Sermon a Collection will be made at the Church Door, and in the Evening the favourite Oratorio of Judas Maccabæus' will be performed in the Theatre, for the Benefit of the Infirmary.

On Wednesday the 7th will be celebrated the annual Commemoration of Founders and Benefactors to the University, when the Right Hon. Lord North, as Chancellor of the University (attended by the Vice-Chancellor, Heads of Houses, Proctors, &c. in solemn Procession) will take his Seat in Convocation with the usual Formalities.

In the Evening there will be a grand Concert of Vocal and Instrumental Music, wherein will be introduced a Concerto Spirituale of Pergolesi, never performed in England.

On Thursday Morning the Noblemen and other young Gentlemen of the University, will recite in the Theatre, Compositions in Prose and Verse in Honour of the Celebrity; and in the Evening will be performed the new Oratorio of the Prodigal Son, composed by Mr. Arnold, as the Choral Music for the Term.

On Friday Morning the Academical Exercises in the Theatre will be continued, and the Celebrity closed in the Evening with a select Vocal and Instrumental Concert, consisting of favourite Songs by the principal Voices; and Solos, Concertos, and other capital Pieces on the Violin, Hautboy, Violoncello, French Horn, Bassoon, Clarionets, &c.

The principal Vocal Parts by Miss Linley, Signora Galli, Messrs. Norris, Meredith, Mathews, &c. the Gentlemen of the University Choirs, and the choice Chorus Singers from St. Paul's, Canterbury, Gloucester, and Worcester Cathedrals.

The Instrumental Part by Signor Jardini, supported by Messrs. Fischer, Crosdil, Punta, Eickner; the Performers of the Music-Room Band, and other capital Performers from the Queen's Band, the Opera-House, and Theatres.

The Whole conducted by Dr. Hayes, Professor of Music.

The Governors of the Infirmary are desired to meet at Half past Ten at the Radcliffe Library, and Service will begin at Eleven.——There will be an Ordinary at the Town-Hall at Two.

His Grace the Duke of }
MARLBOROUGH, } President.

Lord CHARLES SPENCER, }
Lord WENMAN, } Stewards.

FIG. 2. Advertisement for Commemoration performances, including Samuel Arnold's oratorio *The Prodigal Son* (*Jackson's Oxford Journal*, 29 May 1773)

Son to submit work formally for the degree.[26] By 1799 William Crotch warned that 'a Doctor's degree cannot in future be taken without previously taking a Bachelor's & afterwards a space of 5 years intervening between the 2 degrees. Such things have been permitted but the Vice Chancellor looks upon it as degrading to the honour of ye Profession . . .'[27]

Generally, because music was not taught and examined regularly within the university in the manner of other arts subjects, the work presented by candidates varied considerably in scope and quality. (On the other hand, many unsatisfactory and irregular happenings are recounted in connection with candidates, examiners, and tutors in the disciplines studied within the university.[28]) The peculiar position of music in relation to the 'mainstream' academic subjects was expressed in the status of music degree-holders. Doctors of Music were set apart from 'Doctors of Divinity, Physick and Law', and, as Hearne made clear, were not to be regarded as 'Doctors of a Faculty', nor were they entitled to vote in Convocation or admitted as members of Congregation 'unless they were first Masters of Arts'.[29] (Indeed these restrictions would hold true nowadays.)

Within the musical profession, the Oxford B.Mus. and D.Mus. carried a certain cachet. Where these degrees were possessed, they were often cited in concert notices and programmes, news reports, and publications (with the title 'Dr' used where applicable in referring to the musician concerned). Burney seems to have regarded his D.Mus. exercise (the anthem *I will love thee, O Lord my Strength*) as establishing his credentials as a serious composer, and conferring respectability on his efforts; he asked readers of his *History of Music* to excuse his egotism in citing his own work in order to rebut 'sinister assertions' that he ' "neither liked nor had studied Church Music" '.[30] (The acquisition of the degrees may also have helped those who, like Burney, aimed to supplement their income by taking musical pupils.)

The performance of the exercise remained an important element in the proceedings, as Burney's jubilant letter to his daughters on the occasion of his receiving the accumulated degrees reveals:

[26] See *NG* i. 616, 'Samuel Arnold'. The grandeur of this occasion was enhanced by the participation of a large band of over sixty players mingling Oxford performers and distinguished outsiders, headed by 'Signor Jardini': cf. *JOJ*, 29 May 1773.

[27] Och, MS 347/2, letter of W. Crotch to T. Busby, 15 Aug. 1799.

[28] See L. S. Sutherland in *HUO* v. 469–81.

[29] Hearne, *Remarks and Collections*, vi (1717–19), 298.   [30] Burney, *History*, iii. 329.

Oxford, Thursday June 22^d

past 2 o'clock

My dear Girls,

I know it will please you much to hear that the Performance of my Anthem is just
very well over, not one mistake of consequence—Barsanti did extreamly well, &
all was much applauded—I shall tomorrow have both my Degrees; (for I must
first take that of Batchelor of musick) with great unanimity & reputation—
Dr Hayes is very civil; & lends me his Robe with a very good Grace—Adieu—I
know not when I shall get Home.[31]

Besides bringing performers (for this performance Burney's young pupil
Jenny Barsanti made her professional début as a singer) candidates might
also have friends and relations present in the audience, as Burney did in
this case. Fanny Burney recorded, for example, that 'Mrs. & Mr. Pleydel
payed Papa the Compliment of going to Oxford purposely to hear his
Anthem'.[32]

Burney's anthem dispels any notion of dry academicism that might be
implicit in the concept of a degree exercise in composition. Although
Burney in his literary productions articulated strongly Handelian sympathies, this work chimes in more with his progressive views and his interest
in modern music: it makes reference to the new symphonic style, displaying dramatic power and skilful instrumentation. The opening sinfonia
forms a sharp contrast to the Baroque 'French overture' procedures
adopted by most candidates; Burney's expressive gestures here are more
akin to the style of C. P. E. Bach and Haydn than to the archaic pomp of
the Baroque overture (Ex. 2.1). Modernity is seen too in the choice of
obbligato instruments, with the use of clarinets in the aria 'The voice of
joy': possibly this was a compliment to Oxford's virtuoso clarinettists
William and John Mahon.[33] Burney's fine musical and literary sensibilities
are evident in such aspects of the work as the subtle phrasing of the vocal
line and sensitive word-setting. By this time, manuscripts of degree exercises (perhaps on William Hayes's initiative) were deposited more systematically in the Music School collection than hitherto. Doubtless some

[31] *Letters of Burney*, ed. Ribeiro, i. 52–3: letter to Esther and Fanny Burney, 22 June 1769. (See ibid., n. 1
for the critical acclaim bestowed on the work; Ribeiro's notes to this letter are generally very informative
on the various circumstances of the performance.)

[32] Ibid. i. 53, nn. 5–8 generally and n. 5 specifically.   [33] On the Mahons, see Ch. 4 below.

Ex. 2.1. Charles Burney, anthem, *I will love thee, O Lord my Strength*, D.Mus. exercise, 1769, No. [1], Sinfonia, bars 1–20 (Ob, MS Mus. Sch. Ex. c. 15, pp. 1–2)

[*editorial note: probably to be read as if from the treble clef]

remained there on the shelves, gathering dust, but Burney's anthem certainly did not sink into obscurity. Apart from its mention in his *History*, it was revived in performance on numerous occasions, as indeed Burney noted in the *History*: the work was given at Hamburg under the direction of C. P. E. Bach in 1773, and 'repeatedly performed at Oxford, after it had fulfilled its original destination'.[34]

The anthem *The Lord is King* by Thomas Norris, 'Performed in the Music School in Oxford Nov[r]. 12th 1765' for his B.Mus.[35] also transcends the general level of the music degree exercises in its confident, robust style, taking Handelian ideas over into more 'Classical' thought (with short phrases, varied use of dynamics and 'sonata form' influence on structure) and with its modern 'symphonic' manner (see Ex. 2.2): like Burney, Norris was a symphonist as well as a choral composer. His vocal and instrumental scoring here suggests some skilled performers (in particular, a good orchestra, presumably picked from the Holywell band). Norris himself was famed as 'a favourite singer at the weekly concerts in the Music Room' and as 'an excellent musician and master of several instruments'.[36]

The majority of supplicants for the Oxford degrees in music during the eighteenth century were organists and choirmasters in England's parish churches and cathedrals: several were connected with the Chapel Royal, such as Thomas Sanders Dupuis (B.Mus. 1790: 'Organist and composer to his Majesty') and the King's Band, as with William Parsons (B.Mus. 1790: Master of the King's Musick). They are well represented in Temperley's list of composers of 'original cathedral music . . . first-rate . . . both in quantity and in quality, [that] emanated from organists of the London foundations [and] the provinces'.[37] In keeping with the nature of their employment, most candidates chose, like Norris and Burney, to submit sacred anthems (usually to selections from psalm-texts in English) set for solo voices, chorus, and orchestra. These exercises thus created an occasion for the performance of orchestrally accompanied anthems, an important 'sub-class' of anthem which during the eighteenth century

---

[34] Burney, *History*, iii. 329; and cf. Scholes, *Burney*, i. 140 ff. Burney's exercise is in Ob, MS Mus. Sch. Ex. c. 15 (with printed programme).

[35] Ob, MS Mus. Sch. Ex. d. 94; Tenbury MS 880 (a second MS full score with added opening symphony, No. 1 of Norris's *Six Simphonies*, Op. 1, *c*.1772).

[36] *GM* (1790), 862; quoted in Shaw, *Succession of Organists*, 212. Norris's symphonies were published with a list of subscribers showing connections with high society and university figures, including the musical patrons Sir Watkin Williams Wynne, and the Earl of Abingdon.

[37] N. Temperley in Johnstone and Fiske, *The Eighteenth Century*, 364–5.

Ex. 2.2. Thomas Norris, anthem, *The Lord is King*, B.Mus. exercise, 1765, No. [1], bars 34–47 (Ob, MS Mus. Sch. Ex. d. 94, pp. 8–10)

*[all staves originally barred ¦ separately]   ** [word-setting identical, S & A bars 34–7; bars 42 /4–46]

[NB repeated g' ♯ (S) b.44$^{/3}$ follows end of line in original]

became associated with 'grand national ceremonies such as coronations, royal weddings and thanksgivings for victories' as well as with various festivals and private musical societies.[38] Handel's great anthems cast a long shadow over the century's productions in this genre. And in writing often in a Handelian manner, the producers of Oxford exercises were perhaps aligning themselves with the 'celebratory spirit of eighteenth-century Anglicanism, so closely allied to self-confident nationalism' represented, as Temperley suggests, by Handel's coronation anthems (notably *Zadok the Priest*) and 'Utrecht' and 'Dettingen' Te Deums, and other occasional works. In addition, the candidates' copious references to Handel's style and to Baroque musical gestures in general as late as the 1790s, paid tribute to Oxford's role as a centre for Handel performances and for the cultivation of 'ancient music'.[39]

The other main type of exercise, the ode, could be topical (carrying over this characteristic into the academic sphere from its usual generic associations), for example making reference to current military and political events. In the interim spanning Aldrich's death in 1710 and the notable revival of the Act in 1733, a rare highlight was constituted by the Act of 1713, when academic exercises composed by William Croft (organist of Westminster Abbey, and composer and Master of the children of the Chapel Royal) and Johann Christoph Pepusch were heard in Oxford. Pepusch's work seems to have been put in the shade on this occasion.[40] Croft in fact presented a double ode, 'With noise of cannon' and 'Laurus cruentas'; the '*English* part' certainly 'made a considerable impression . . . No doubt the topicality of a text celebrating the recently concluded Peace of Utrecht also helped—and so too possibly the fact that the words were by the Rev. Joseph Trapp (1679–1747), then a Fellow of Wadham College and the University's first Professor of Poetry.'[41]

The successful reception of Croft's 'With noise of cannon' was amply justified by the inherent strengths and quality of the work itself. It included some particularly fine and evocative bass solo writing in the best English

[38] N. Temperley in Johnstone and Fiske, *The Eighteenth Century*, 366 (from which the quotation that follows is also derived).

[39] On Handel in Oxford see further pp. 62–6 below. For more detailed musical discussion of the exercises see Wollenberg, *PRMA* (1981–2), 72 ff., and *EM* (2000).

[40] See Johnstone and Fiske, *The Eighteenth Century*, 90, for details of both contenders.

[41] Ibid. Both of Croft's odes were published under the title *Musicus Apparatus Academicus* (1715).

tradition (see Ex. 2.3) as well as an appropriate display of contrapuntal and fugal technique.[42] For the performance at the Sheldonian Theatre on 10 July 1713, as was customary later in the century, outsiders assisted (giving 'professional stiffening brought up from London').[43] Similar arrangements were made in Cambridge, notably in 1730 when on 6 July 'the new Senate House was officially opened with a performance of Maurice Greene's splendid setting of Alexander Pope's *Ode for Musick on St Cecilia's Day*', and when, 'like Croft and Pepusch at Oxford in 1713, Greene was accompanied by a large band of London professionals . . . and no fewer than eight vocal soloists from the choirs of St Paul's Cathedral and the Chapel Royal'. Greene's work also served as his D.Mus. exercise.[44]

When Handel visited Oxford in 1733 he too brought with him a band of performers, or as Thomas Hearne dubbed them his 'lowsy crew' of 'forreign fidlers'.[45] As an arch-Jacobite, Hearne was bound to disapprove of the Hanoverian composer (he also confused the source of Handel's royal patronage with his birthplace, describing him as 'one Handel, a foreigner (who, they say, was born at Hanover)'). It has been suggested that Handel's librettist Charles Jennens, who was present at the Oxford performances of *Athalia*, may have exploited the audience's capacity to appreciate the juxtaposition of Hanoverian ceremonial music with biblical themes of Jacobite resistance.[46] Handel's Oxford performances were well attended and set the pattern for the devotion of Oxford audiences to his music throughout the century. Hearne registered his objection to the high cost of tickets (actually half the London price) and programme-books for Handel's benefit performances at the Sheldonian Theatre ('his book (not worth 1*d.*) he sells for 1*s.*')[47] but other remarks suggest that Hearne did not attend these.

[42] See Trowles, 'Musical Ode', i. 50–2. Trowles comments on the copious references in the text to music ('The soul of music is the soul of peace') and the composer's lively response to the words, e.g. in *Laurus cruentas*: both these features recur in the 19th-cent. Oxford exercises (see Ch. 7, below).

[43] Johnstone and Fiske, *The Eighteenth Century*, 90. Trowles ('Musical Ode', i. 48) notes that two of Croft's band themselves received the B.Mus. degree while in Oxford; the organists John Isham and William Morley each composed an ode as an exercise.

[44] See Johnstone and Fiske, *The Eighteenth Century*, 90. In general the Cambridge tradition was even more fragmented at this period than in Oxford; cf. Trowles, 'Musical Ode', i. 54 ff.

[45] Hearne, *Remarks and Collections*, xi (1731–5), 224 ff.

[46] On the symbolism of Handel's oratorio librettos generally see Ruth Smith, *Handel's Oratorios and Eighteenth-Century Thought* (Cambridge, 1995); on *Athalia* specifically see Shapiro, 'Handel's Early English Oratorios', *ML* 74 (1993), 244.

[47] Hearne, *Remarks and Collections*, xi. 227.

Ex. 2.3. William Croft, Ode, *With Noise of Cannon*, from *Musicus Apparatus Academicus*, D.Mus. exercise, 1713, No. [2], pp. 11–13, bars 1–9, 12–22; 34–7

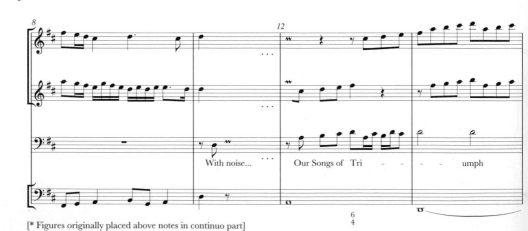

[* Figures originally placed above notes in continuo part]

[· · · indicates cut for the purpose of this example]

our Songs of Tri — — — umph shall re -

7 6

sound no more; no, no, no more; no, no, no more no, no, no

4 3# 8 7 6 5 6 6 5 6
[?6 5]

more our Songs of tri — — umph shall re-sound no more; ... Nor in our Verse shall war-like

7 5 7 6 7 6 [#] 7 6 4 3 7

[etc.]

Thun-der war-like Thun-der ro — — — — ar. [etc.]

7 6 7 7 6 7 6 7 6 6 * 5
4

[* 6/4 originally placed over minim]

It was with the intention of lending musical grandeur to the occasion that the Vice-Chancellor, Dr Holmes, conceived the plan of inviting 'Mr Handel' to take part in the proceedings of 1733. After the heyday of the Act in Aldrich's time it was noted more often for its non-occurrence (by order of special decrees passed each year). With its revival in 1733, as with any discontinued tradition, problems of procedure surfaced; as Hearne observed, 'Acts have been discontinued so long, that few are living in Oxford, that know the old method of proceeding'.[48] Hearne was critical of this attempt to re-establish the Act, complaining that the music under Goodson's direction at the Theatre on the Saturday was 'very poor' and that 'there was no Music Speech as ... formerly ... tho' none hath been since 1693'.[49]

Echoes of Hearne's sour remarks and his hostility to Handel resound throughout the text of 'The *Oxford* Act | A New Ballad-Opera | As it was Perform'd | By a Company of STUDENTS at *Oxford. London*: Printed ... 1733', possibly directly under his influence or even authorship.[50] The play opens with the Vice-Chancellor and one of the Proctors sitting at a table with a bottle of wine and glasses before them, conversing in a spirit of mutual congratulation, in which the former's dignified style and the latter's flattering deference are nicely differentiated:

(Act I sc. [i])

V-C   WELL, Mr. *Proctor*, I think we have manag'd this Publick Act exceeding well; it must redound very much to the Honour of the whole University in general, and to our Reputation in particular.

Pr   None but your worthy self, Sir, could have carried it through with so much Regularity and Decorum ...

V-C   ... The secret Pleasure that I receive from the Thoughts of it almost transports me. Come, Sir, Here's Prosperity to the University of *Oxford* [pouring out a glass of wine and drinking] may she for ever flourish ...

The anonymous author's sharp wit and confident delineation of character are further brought out in Act I scene [ii], set in Merton Walks, where Thoughtless, an '*Oxford* Scholar', is wandering, and ruminating ruefully on his fate. The student's devotion to musical entertainment is here satirically portrayed in the context of undergraduate life generally, and the

---

[48] Hearne, *Remarks and Collections*, xi. 231.   [49] Ibid. 232.
[50] Wordbook, with indications of songs, in Ob, MS Gough Oxf. 59.

speech is worth quoting at length to show the build-up to the quite vicious attack on Handel:

Th What an unfortunate, inconsiderate Dog am I, thus to have squander'd away all my ready Rhino, and tick'd with all that would trust, only to make a gaudy Appearance for four or five Days this Publick Act? Let me consider, (if the Reflection is not too bitter) what my Expences have amounted to this last Fortnight ... there's my *Midsummer* Quarteridge, which is Fifty Pounds, with which I should have paid off ... my Tutorage, my Taylor, Barber, Laundress, and other Creditors; but faith, 'tis all gone, and not one paid out of it: I sav'd it all, like a fool, to spend it extravagantly this Publick Act. D-mn the plaguy Act, and all that voted for it ... In the next Place, I have ate and drank my Library; poor Sir *Isaac*, faith, has contributed towards the Purchase of a Bottle of *Champaigne* to treat my Mistress with ... the Rascal had 'em of me at quarter value too; I am sure there were as many Books as cost me Twenty Pounds all gone for Five. In the next Place, there's the Furniture of my Room procur'd me some Tickets to hear that bewitching Musick, that cursed *Handel*, with his confounded *Orat[or]io*'s; I wish him and his Company had been yelling in the infernal Shades below

But the most biting satire is reserved for the portrait of the two dons, Pedant and Haughty, whose exchanges reveal an extreme aspect of the strong feelings with which this Oxford Act may have been viewed by senior members of the university. Again the effects are very cleverly, if cruelly, drawn, and echo the lament of young Thoughtless:

(Act II sc. i)   Paradise-Garden.

H Mr. *Pedant*, your Servant; what, I suppose your Morning Prayers are just finished too, and you come out for an Airing: 'Tis a fine Morning ...

P Very pleasant, Mr. *Haughty* ... [but] I have not rightly recover'd myself since the Act ...

H Our Cases run in a Parallel; nay, 'tis worse with me, for I question whether my gaping Herd of Creditors won't be for sequestring my Fellowship or not. I don't see what Occasion we had for this Act, unless it was to ruin us all ... no one has gain'd anything by it but Mr. *Handel* and his Crew.

P Very true; we had Fidlers enough here before, and by squandering away the Profits of our Fellowships, we not only endanger our Reputation, but our own dear Persons too ...

H ... the public Stock of the University is very much diminished too by these extravagant Expences: And as for the younger Sort ... There's my Pupil *Dick Thoughtless* says, this last Fortnight has stood him in above an Hundred Pounds;

and I question whether it may not be true, for *Dick*'s a generous young Fellow.

. . .

P   . . . But, Brother, I believe 'twill be better for us to part for the present, for fear of being nab'd; besides, I believe 'tis now Breakfast-time.

This sorry pair of characters are then linked up with the two high-ranking officials introduced at the opening of the play, to round off the tale of woe:

(Act III.)

(V-C's Lodgings. Enter V-C and Proctor)

V-C   . . . Do you hear any thing more concerning our Affairs? . . .

P   . . . Why, they tell me, Sir, that most of our College-Gates are beset with Bailiffs: *Haughty* and *Pedant*, two Senior Fellows, you know, are afraid to shew their Heads, and sent a very humble Message to-day . . . desiring that, if it were possible to save their Reputation, they might borrow thirty Pounds each . . . If you please, Sir, we will order your Beadle to convey them here . . . and then you may hear the Truth from their own Mouths.

V-C   . . . Pray ring the Bell, and order *John* to send for them.

(Enter H and P in disguise.)

V-C   Gentlemen, your Servant . . . Come, disburthen your Complaints . . .

H   . . . Sir, we can't conceive any Design in this Matter . . . unless it was to make us all poor.

V-C   How so Sir? Why you and Mr. *Pedant* are now considerably advanced in Years, and might very well have distinguished between the serious and ludicrous Part of this Entertainment . . . I dare say, if the Truth was known, most of your money was spent in Tickets to hear the *Oratorio*'s; I must confess a Crown each was rather too much; but had you been contented with a single one, without treating all your Acquaintance, that could never have hurt you.

H   Lord, Sir, you must excuse me; so many years can never have rolled over your Head and find you ignorant—that Musick has Charms to sooth the savage Soul, and much more rational Men; and as we ought to act according to that excellent Motto, *Manners maketh Man* [the New College motto], so you would not suppose us to be such Brutes as to engross all the Pleasure to ourselves, without complimenting our Friends with a Participation of it.

It is noticeable that the comments on the intrinsic value of Handel's music here are of a positive nature: specifically, its 'bewitching' qualities are stressed, and generally, music's therapeutic effect is recognized, as well as, quite simply, the 'Pleasure' to be had from this entertainment. The author acknowledged, through the mouth of the Proctor, that the Act also attracted some approving reactions from the press: 'the whole World speaks favourably of it; the publick Papers too give a very just and true Account of it, and ... in Terms much to our Advantage'.[51] Certainly the 1733 Act achieved its aim of recreating public interest in the event. It also constituted, in serving as a showcase for Handel's works, a high point in Oxford's musical calendar. Over a period of several days, Oxford audiences heard Handel's 'Utrecht' Te Deum and Jubilate, and Coronation Anthems, at the University Church of St Mary (on Sunday morning, 8 July); the oratorios *Esther* (on the evenings of Thursday and Saturday, 5 and 7 July), *Deborah* (on Thursday evening, 12 July) and *Athalia* (on Tuesday and Wednesday evenings, 10 and 11 July) at the Sheldonian Theatre; and *Acis and Galatea* at Christ Church on the morning of 11 July.

Handel seized the opportunity to make the maximum profits from his concerts during his stay in Oxford; in declining the university's proffered honorary degree, he may have felt some reluctance to pay the necessary fee (albeit a small one) or to be thus associated with certain other recipients of the D.Mus. (Greene, for example, at Cambridge) whom he considered inferior to himself. Whatever negative impressions may have been created by Handel's visit to Oxford, the magnetic charms of Handel's music continued to exercise their powerful effects on Oxford audiences throughout the remainder of the century. Subsequent Encaenia celebrations (and many other special occasions) were regularly marked by performances of Handel. Following the precedent of the 1733 Act, these often stretched over several days, taking on the appearance of a Handel festival. For the opening of the Radcliffe Library (now the Radcliffe Camera) in April 1749, *Esther*, *Samson*, *Messiah* (in its first Oxford performance), and anthems by Handel were heard on three afternoons, under William Hayes's direction; like the 1733 Act, this seems to have been an occasion simmering with political implications. As well as phrases in Handel that were taken as resonating with particular significance (notably 'Mercy to Jacob's Race, God save the King'), in an explosive speech given in Latin the Vice-Chancellor, Dr William King, expressed pro-Jacobite sentiments.[52]

[51] *The Oxford Act*, Act I sc. [i].

[52] See Kennicott's letter, printed in the *Bodleian Quarterly Record*, I/6 (1915), 165 (from Ob, MS Top. Oxon b. 43); also Peter Marr, 'The Life and Works of John Alcock (1715–1806)' (Ph.D. diss., University of Reading, 1978), 19–20; and *EO* 351 ('Radcliffe Camera').

At the 1754 Commemoration, when 'a Convocation was held in the
Theatre to commemorate the Benefactors to the University and to
receive . . . the Earl of Westmorland as its high Steward', the three days
from 3 to 5 July were used for performances of *L'Allegro, il Penseroso ed il
Moderato, Judas Maccabaeus*, and *Messiah* at the Sheldonian Theatre.[53] Later
in the century the influence of the great Handel Commemoration at
Westminster Abbey (1784) was clearly felt in Oxford, as the diary of Richard Paget of Magdalen College records:

1785   Wednesday, June 21st The Crewian Commem. at the Theatre.

In the evening Acis & Galatea by a very large & capital band . . . The Audience at
least 1000 . . . Thursday, the Messiah, and friday, a miscellaneous Concert by the
same powerfull band. The audience more numerous. The double drums &
double bassoon from Westminster Abbey, and the Keys of the Organ brought
down to the conductor's place, in front of the Orchestra, as at the Abbey.[54]

Acis and Galatea had endured as a recurrent feature of such occasions in
Oxford, although not always well appreciated by visitors to the city:

THE late solemnity of the instalment and commemoration at *Oxford*, afforded us
an opportunity of seeing that magnificent seat of the muses to the greatest advantage. We arrived there on *Tuesday* morning, and after providing ourselves with
lodgings, (which indeed was no easy matter to do) we went to view the public
entry of the chancellor . . .

    About four in the afternoon we went to the theatre, which is a noble and capa-
cious building in the form of a Roman D, and was at this time crouded with a
most splendid circle of ladies and gentlemen. Soon after the chancellor arrived,
accompanied by near an hundred doctors in their scarlet robes; and when he and
his company had taken their seats, the installation ode was performed by a
numerous band . . .

    Next morning, at ten o'clock, we again repaired to the theatre, where the audi-
ence appeared more numerous and more brilliant than the day before . . . then all
hurried home to their dinners to have the advantage of being early at the theatre
in the afternoon, where the company were detained from three to eight, hearing
that absurd composition called *Acis* and *Galatea*. Eight hours in the theatre in one
day I rather tho't unconscionable, and I don't doubt but many rosy faces I saw

---

53 Ob, MS Top. Oxon d. 247, p. 114 (2 July 1754). On the earlier 18th-cent. cultivation of Handel's
music in Oxford see Burrows, 'Sources for Oxford Handel Performances', *ML* 61 (1980).

54 Bristol University Library, Paget collection, DM 106/419 (June 1785), photocopy in MCA, MS 641.
Paget's description confirms the details as advertised in *JOJ* (18 June 1785).

there were of the same opinion, and would have wished for less music and more wine.[55]

Allowing for a degree of exaggeration, it seems nevertheless from this description that *Acis and Galatea* took much longer to perform than would be expected; possibly the habits of demanding encores, and performing entr'actes, both well documented in Oxford at this period, created at least part of the extra length. Paget in 1785 reported mockingly on one particular request for an encore involving Madame Mara, a regular member of the team of soloists booked to sing in Oxford at the Commemoration (and other concerts):

Wednesday & Thursday [21–2 June] there were very riotous proceedings in the Theatre, w[hi]ch originated from Mara's being unable to sing a long Song, in w[hi]ch she was (very absurdly) encored, Wednesday. Sufficient Apologies were made by Dr. Hayes & things went off tolerably well for the present. But Friday, a handle being made of Mara's sitting down in the chorusses, there was a most violent disturbance—Such a scene of noise & Confusion was surely never before exhibited in that place. Drunken gownsmen (for 'twas St. John's gaudey) & fainting women were carried off in Shoals. To complete the business, our wise V.C. put himself absolutely at the Head of the mob, by making a speech in w[hi]ch he said that "Madame Mara had given just cause of Offence"; so that we had a riot "by permission of the Revd & very worthy the V.[ice] Cha[ncello]r".[56]

In the period after 1733 the pattern for these summer celebrations was typically a series of concerts, ceremonies, and services held over several days in connection with the annual Infirmary meeting (after 1770, when Radcliffe's hospital was founded in Oxford; Cambridge held a similar event for Addenbrooke's Hospital), the Creweian Commemoration (of the benefactors to the university), and the Encaenia (incorporating the bestowal of honorary degrees). In 1788 these commemorative events were held on Wednesday, Thursday, and Friday, 25–7 June, with *Acis and Galatea* at the Sheldonian Theatre on the Wednesday, *Messiah* for the anniversary of the Radcliffe Infirmary on the Thursday, and a 'Grand Miscellaneous

---

[55] '*Account of the Encaenia* at Oxford', *GM* 33 (1763), 348–9. The 'gentleman on a journey' who provided this account, however, expressed no dissatisfaction with the subsequent performances, simply noting (p. 349) that 'on *Thursday* evening the oratorio of *Judas Maccabeus*, and on *Friday* evening that of the *Messiah*, were performed to a crowded and genteel audience'.

[56] Paget's diary (cf. n. 54). On Mara's career see *NG2* xv. 793–4 and Highfill, Burnim, and Langhans, eds., *Biographical Dictionary*, x. 77–87.

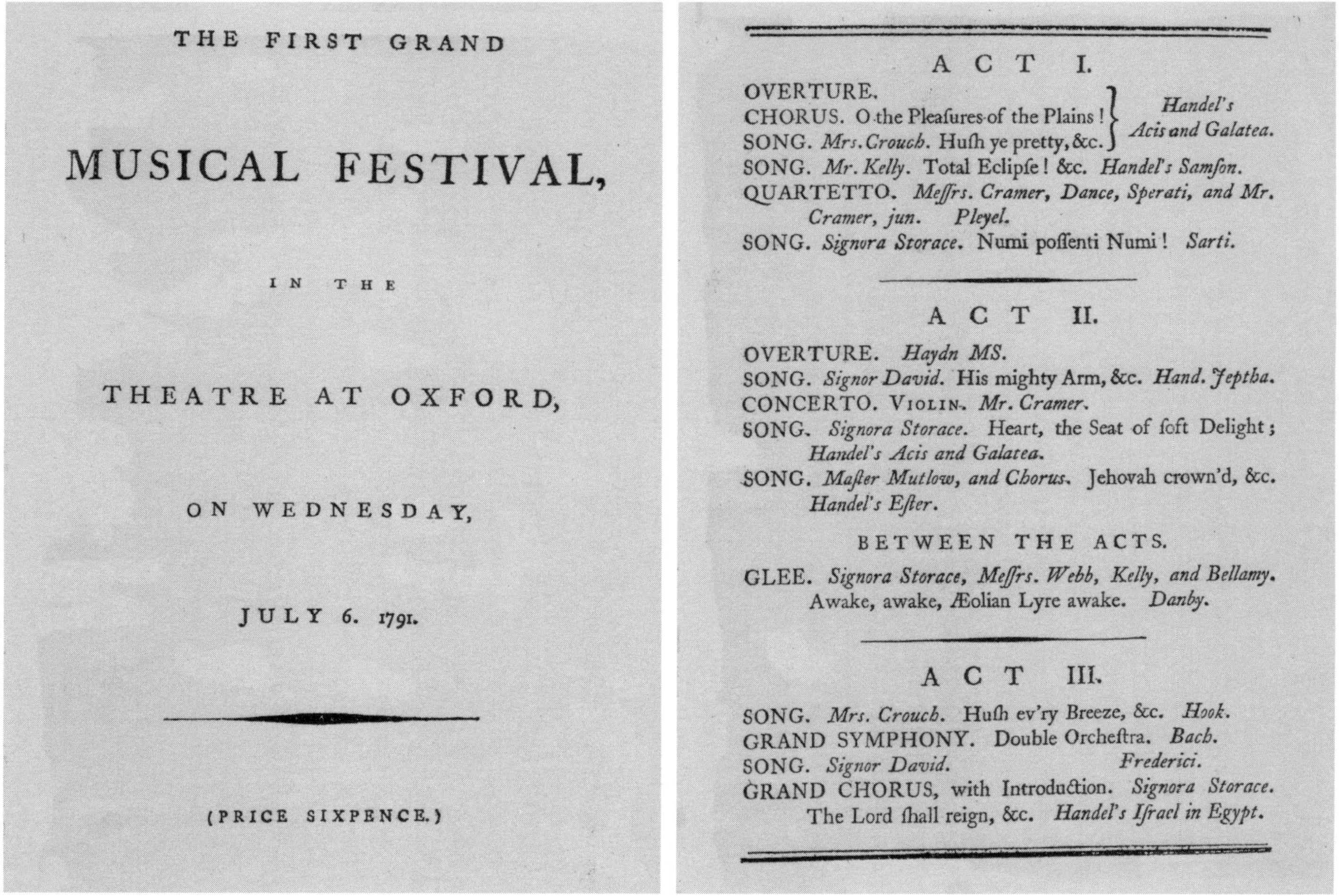

THE FIRST GRAND

MUSICAL FESTIVAL,

IN THE

THEATRE AT OXFORD,

ON WEDNESDAY,

JULY 6. 1791.

(PRICE SIXPENCE.)

ACT I.

OVERTURE.   *Handel's*
CHORUS. O the Pleasures of the Plains! } *Acis and Galatea.*
SONG. *Mrs. Crouch.* Hush ye pretty, &c.
SONG. *Mr. Kelly.* Total Eclipse! &c. *Handel's Samson.*
QUARTETTO. *Messrs. Cramer, Dance, Sperati, and Mr. Cramer, jun. Pleyel.*
SONG. *Signora Storace.* Numi possenti Numi! *Sarti.*

ACT II.

OVERTURE. *Haydn MS.*
SONG. *Signor David.* His mighty Arm, &c. *Hand. Jeptha.*
CONCERTO. VIOLIN. *Mr. Cramer.*
SONG. *Signora Storace.* Heart, the Seat of soft Delight; *Handel's Acis and Galatea.*
SONG. *Master Mutlow, and Chorus.* Jehovah crown'd, &c. *Handel's Esther.*

BETWEEN THE ACTS.

GLEE. *Signora Storace, Messrs. Webb, Kelly, and Bellamy.* Awake, awake, Æolian Lyre awake. *Danby.*

ACT III.

SONG. *Mrs. Crouch.* Hush ev'ry Breeze, &c. *Hook.*
GRAND SYMPHONY. Double Orchestra. *Bach.*
SONG. *Signor David.* *Frederici.*
GRAND CHORUS, with Introduction. *Signora Storace.* The Lord shall reign, &c. *Handel's Israel in Egypt.*

FIG. 3. Haydn's visit to Oxford, concert programme, 6 July 1791

Concert' at the Theatre on the Friday 'to commemorate the Founders and Benefactors'. Paget mentioned these in his diary as 'three very capital concerts at the Theatre for the benefit of Dr. Hayes . . . A great deal of company in Oxford this music meeting, and of the 1st rank. Many foreigners.'[57] During the 1789 festival (from Wednesday to Friday, 24–6 June) the commemoration concerts were enhanced by the singing of the Mozartian stars Signora Storace and Signor Benucci, enthusiastically acclaimed by a large audience and favourably reviewed in the press.[58]

Nancy Storace sang again in 1791 for the Commemoration when the customary 'three grand concerts in the Theatre' (Wednesday, Thursday, and Friday, 6–8 July) and the honorary degree ceremony on 8 July were graced by the presence of Joseph Haydn. Haydn had missed his scheduled first appearance in Oxford on 18 May 1791 when he was due to perform at a benefit concert for Mr Hayward, a member of the Holywell band. After a preliminary whetting of the audience's appetite by means of an advertisement in the local press to the effect that 'the celebrated Mr. HAYDN, from VIENNA, with two eminent Singers from London' had 'promised their Assistance' on this occasion (further 'Particulars' to be 'inserted in next Week's Paper'), the full announcement duly appeared the following week, specifying 'the HARPSICHORD by Mr. HAYDN, from Vienna, who comes entirely to serve this CONCERT, and is returning to London the next Morning'.[59] When Haydn was prevented by an opera rehearsal from travelling to Oxford that day, the audience broke into a riot. Both Hayward and Haydn printed an apology in the *Journal*, Haydn's in the form of an open letter to Mr Hayward in which he expressed the hope that 'as the University of Oxford, whose great Reputation I heard abroad, is too great an Object for me not to see before I leave England, I shall take the earliest Opportunity of paying it a Visit'.[60]

Haydn's hope was handsomely realized when—possibly at Burney's instigation—the university conferred on its distinguished visitor the honorary degree of D.Mus., at the July commemoration.[61] Having missed his entrance altogether on 18 May, Haydn arrived late for the proceedings on

---

[57] Paget's diary (cf. n. 54), June 1788.   [58] Ibid. (June 1789); *JOJ*, 26 June 1789.

[59] *JOJ*, 7 and 14 May 1791.   [60] Ibid. 28 May 1791.

[61] After his arrival in England in January 1791 Haydn became associated, through Salomon, with many of the musicians performing in London and Oxford; his first visit in London was to Burney. See particularly Landon, *Haydn*, iii. 88–95.

Wednesday, 6 July when his 'Oxford' symphony was due to be performed in the first of the 'three grand concerts' at the Sheldonian Theatre. As there was no time to rehearse the 'new' symphony, another work was substituted. The 'Oxford' symphony ('the new Overture of HAYDN, prepared for the occasion, and previously rehearsed in the morning') was, however, included in the second programme, on 7 July, 'and a more wonderful composition never was heard. The applause given to HAYDN, who conducted this admirable effort of his genius, was enthusiastic; but the merit of the work, in the opinion of all the Musicians present, exceeded all praise.'[62]

On Friday, 8 July at the traditional ceremony in the Theatre, Haydn, resplendent in academic dress and surrounded by a crowd of supporters, was presented for the honorary degree. And at the concluding concert, 'when Haydn appeared, and, grateful for the applause ... seized hold of, and displayed, the gown he wore as a mark of the honour that had in the morning been conferred on him, [he] met with an unanimous and loud clapping . . .'.[63] Unlike Handel, Haydn greatly valued the benefits of the Oxford degree, for which he noted he had to pay '1 ½ guineas for having the bell rung . . . and ½ guinea for the robe': altogether 'the trip cost 6 guineas', and he believed that it had brought him 'the acquaintanceship of the most prominent men and the entree into the greatest houses'.[64] This occasion, unlike some previous Commemoration celebrations, seems to have left the participants and observers generally well satisfied, presumably not least Dr [Philip] Hayes, presiding over the arrangements, to whom apparently the profits of the concerts accrued. For the university at large, and its cultivation of music in particular, the event was viewed as a sign of 'still . . . further strides towards perfection . . . Can anything exhibit the improved taste in that divine science so justly, as the degree just given to the modest Haydn by the University . . .'.[65]

[62] Landon, *Haydn*, iii. 90. The 'Oxford' symphony, No. 92 in G major, was not in fact a new work but one of a set of three symphonies written for Paris in 1788–9.

[63] Landon, *Haydn*, iii. 92.

[64] Hughes, 'Haydn at Oxford', *ML* 20 (1939), 248.

[65] An Oxford correspondent writing in the *European Magazine* (15 July 1791), quoted in Landon, *Haydn*, iii. 93.

3

Music in the University and City, I

By the late eighteenth century, the musical performances in Commemoration week represented a high point in Oxford's cultural and ceremonial calendar, involving large numbers of musicians and drawing great crowds. Life in Oxford at other times of year was rich in occasions for music. There is evidence that local musicians were linked with the early development of the St Cecilia's Day tradition in London in the late seventeenth century.[1] From 1693 these originally secular celebrations took in a religious element, with a choral service at St Bride's Church in Fleet Street and a sermon preached 'in defence of church music'.[2] In what seems to have been an extension of the London celebrations, Sampson Estwick, a chaplain of Christ Church, gave a sermon of this kind for St Cecilia's Day at a service in Christ Church on 27 November 1696 which was printed and dedicated to the stewards of the St Cecilia's Feast in London.[3] In 1707 St Cecilia's Day was marked in Oxford by a performance of Purcell's 'Hail, bright Cecilia' at St Mary's Hall (now Oriel College).[4] Trowles emphasizes the distinction between organized and definable events for the day itself

---

[1] For an account of this development see Trowles, 'Musical Ode', ch. 4, i. 75 ff.   [2] Ibid. i. 84.

[3] Sampson Estwick, *The Usefulness of Church-Musick* (London, 1696). Johnstone and Fiske, *The Eighteenth Century* (p. 461 n. 11) has a reference to William Dingley, *Cathedral Service Decent and Useful. A Sermon Preach'd before the University of Oxford . . . on Cecilia's Day, 1713* (Oxford, 1713).

[4] Trowles, 'Musical Ode' (i. 110) notes that the copy of the printed libretto in Ob names the performers.

and the general Cecilian vein that was cultivated in literature and music, suggesting that when this was detached from its original context, 'composers could expect audiences to remain receptive to "Cecilian" works'.[5]

Several Oxford odes from the eighteenth century belong in this latter category, including degree exercises such as John Alcock's 'Attend harmonious saint' (a partial setting of Joseph Addison's *Song for St. Cecilia's Day*: 'Perform'd for a Bachelor's Degree in Music in Act Term 1755').[6] Outside London, Trowles identifies 'the only substantial odes' in praise of music as those of Philip Hayes, in the late eighteenth century.[7] A series of four such works by Hayes included an Ode to British Harmony (1784) and an Ode for St Cecilia's Day which was connected with the day itself: the autograph manuscript is inscribed 'Perform'd at the [Music] School as my Professorial lecture for ye Term. on St Cecilia's day Nov. 22 1779'.[8] Hayes owned the autograph score of Blow's 1684 setting of the same poetic text (by John Oldham).[9] Apart from the Cecilian tradition, and the Installation Odes, a recurrent occasion for the performance of works in this genre was provided by the 'professorial lectures'. Philip Hayes delivered a series of these at the Music School in fulfilment of his professorial obligations, and in the spirit of Heather's original intentions.

Hayes's lectures seem to have been given primarily in the form of music rather than speech. Inscriptions along the lines of 'Perform'd as a lecture in the Music School' occur repeatedly in the autograph sources. The names of various performers marshalled by Hayes for these 'lectures' are noted in several of the scores. During the late 1770s and 1780s, Hayes as Heather Professor cultivated a circle of pupils and protégés linked with the Holywell concerts as well as with the more formal University performances at the Music School or the Sheldonian Theatre. Among them were several boy trebles and adult soloists drawn from the college chapel choirs, such as Master Clarke and the leading singers Thomas Norris (tenor) and William Matthews (bass). Another name recurring in the manuscript sources is that of the soprano Miss George, probably Hayes's pupil, who in 1780 was at the centre of his quarrel with the cellist Monro.[10]

5 Trowles, 'Musical Ode' i. 113.   6 Ob, MS Mus. c. 149.
7 Trowles 'Musical Ode', i. 126.
8 Ob, MS Mus. d. 68, fo. 101ᵛ. Heighes, 'Hayes' (iii. 159-60) notes that the *Ode on Lyric Poetry* (1782) was inscribed 'Perform'd as a lecture Nov. 21.-82. St. Cecilia's Day ...'.
9 See Heighes, 'Hayes', iii. 153 ff.   10 Cf. Ch. 4 below.

These works were periodically reused at the Music School, either in whole or in part. So the 1779 Ode for St Cecilia's Day was revived in December 1780 'at the opening of the Music School after ye Alterations', then in December 1786, and again in December 1787.[11] The 1780 revival was of particular significance. Where William Hayes had taken a special interest in the setting up of the Holywell Music Room in the 1740s, Philip Hayes in the 1780s made it his project to oversee a major programme of improvements to the Music School. During the eighteenth century a strong connection was forged between musical (notably choral) perform-ances and either charitable objects or fund-raising for specific purposes; Oxford's cultural life was regularly marked by such events. Hayes's ora-torio *Prophecy* (to a text anonymously compiled from biblical sources) was produced complete at one of three benefit concerts during the 1780 Com-memoration in the Sheldonian Theatre, in aid of the alterations to the Music School.[12] Hayes raised a total of £250, while the University gave £50. Donations were received from other sources, including Burney, and Hayes himself donated some of the furnishings, as well as some fine por-traits to add to the collection held at the Music School.[13]

A contributor to the pamphlet war provoked by the dispute between Hayes and Monro in 1780 had Tweedledee [Monro] addressing Tweedledum [Hayes] on the subject of 'your new Music School' in a 'DIALOGUE IN THE SHADES'.[14] This mention of the Music School occasions the lament:

> [*TWEEDLEDUM*]   Ah! Tweedledee! thy Words awake my Sorrow!
> Does some Impostor then my Visage borrow?
> Claims he my *new Improvements* as his own,
> And reaps that Harvest which myself had sown?

Reference is then made to his 'Plan', with 'a Cup-board to hold the V[ice]-C[h]an[cellor]' and 'such neat little Shelves for the P[rocto]rs',

---

[11] Ob, MS Mus. d. 68 (fo. 102).

[12] Ob, MS Mus. d. 71–3. As Heighes notes ('Hayes', iii. 174), the autograph score is dated 1778–9, and Hayes indicated that the first part was originally 'perform'd in the Music School as my Professorial lecture for the Term'.

[13] See Poole, 'The Oxford Music School Portraits', *The Musical Antiquary*, 4 (1912–13). Among the newly acquired portraits was one of Burney presented to the Music School 'at the request of Dr Hayes': cf. *Letters of Burney*, ed. Ribeiro, 322.

[14] Both characters are portrayed as deceased, Tweedledee having killed Tweedledum in a duel, and himself been executed.

> Such Seats for the Ladies, such Busts, such devices!
> So bepainted, becarv'd and begilded,
> Such sweet pretty Pillars, all par'd into slices -
> And my Orchestra—how I'd have fill'd it![15]

As Mee suggests, 'the main object of the author of this dialogue seems to have been to cast ridicule on the alterations in the fittings of the Music School effected by Hayes'.[16] But the mocking words serve to emphasize the role of the Music School as an official venue for performances comparable to the larger Sheldonian Theatre, in the presence of the Vice-Chancellor and Proctors.

Instrumentalists from the Holywell Band also participated in Hayes's Music School 'lecture' performances. Among the contribution made by both William and Philip Hayes to the genre of English oratorio was their joint production, *David*; in the autograph score, Act I is described as 'Perform'd Nov.r 28 as a music lecture 1781'. Besides the vocal soloists— Miss George, Mr Price (alto), Norris and Matthews—the performers noted on the manuscript included Malchair (violin 1), Mahon (violin 2) and Monro (cello).[17] The Music School also served still in the eighteenth century as the location for the statutory public performances of the degree exercises, including Philip Hayes's own; during William Hayes's professorship, Act I of Philip Hayes's masque *Telemachus* was put on at the Music School on 10 May 1763 as his exercise for the degree of B.Mus. (with Norris in the title role).[18]

Although no systematic academic teaching in music was made available in the University at this period, Oxford as a musical centre offered scholars important resources in the form of its library collections. By the later eighteenth century the Music School holdings had acquired the character of an archive, containing 'the FOUNDER's collection, and subsequent donations, as well as the Exercises of Proceeders to Musical Degrees'.[19] Both Hawkins and Burney worked at the Bodleian Library in preparing their histories of music. Burney also studied the Christ Church collection for the purposes of his *History*: 'through [Benjamin] Wheeler's

---

[15] Quoted in Mee, *Music Room*, 102; cf. Ob, MS Top. Oxon e. 48, fo. 22^v.

[16] Mee, *Music Room*, 102.

[17] On the various performers, and the Holywell Band in general, see Ch. 4 below.

[18] Further on the history of this work, see Heighes, 'Hayes', iii. 147.

[19] Wood, *History and Antiquities*, ed. Gutch, 889.

connection with Christ Church', he 'gained access to the musical library formed by Dr Henry Aldrich (1648–1710), and bequeathed to the college'.[20] This link was made in 1778, when Burney visited Oxford 'to run my Nose into Cobwebs, & consult the Learned'.[21] And in 1781 he instructed his son Charles: 'You may... say... that I have been working in the Bodleian & other Libraries at Oxford the last 3 summers successively. That I am very fond of Oxford, where I had my Degree, & where I have many Friends, &c &c—.'[22]

There was a strong Oxford tradition of antiquarian collectors of music, among them Narcissus Marsh, Aldrich, Goodson senior, Philip Hayes, and William Crotch. Philip Hayes, who annotated and edited music from various sources, was regarded at the time as an authority on Purcell manuscripts. It was with Philip Hayes's successor as Heather Professor, William Crotch, that the professorial lectures given at the Music School took on a new historical and aesthetic aspect in the wake of Burney's and Hawkins's *Histories*, and under the influence of Sir Joshua Reynolds's theories of art. The old scientific theory of music, and Hayes's cultivation of the musical performance as 'lecture', were here replaced by a wide-ranging investigation of the history of music from the ancients to the present day, passing from general considerations and an account of ancient and national music (Lectures I–IV) through chant and early church music, Renaissance polyphony, the 'invention of opera', and seventeenth- and eighteenth-century composers (among them the Scarlattis, Keiser, Lully, Corelli, Purcell, Bach, and Handel) in Lectures V–VIII, to the invention of the 'concert symphonie', Gluck, C. P. E and J.C. Bach, Mozart, Haydn, Clementi, and their contemporaries (Lectures IX–XII).[23]

In the accompanying *Specimens of Various Styles of Music*, Crotch's conscientious pedagogic approach was expressed in his avowed aim to

[20] *Letters of Burney*, ed. Ribeiro, 259 n. Further on the college libraries, see Ch. 5 below.

[21] Ibid. 259: letter to Mrs Thrale, 6 Nov. 1778.

[22] Burney was anxious to furnish his son with 'a little conversation ab[ou]t me & Oxford' for a prospective meeting with the Archbishop of York (formerly Dean of Christ Church): letter to Charles Burney, 25 Feb. 1781 (ibid. 320).

[23] Later excerpted in the *Substance of Several Courses of Lectures* (1831). Marsh provided witness to these occasions; 'Dr Crotch being now reading a course of lectures on music, I . . . went to one of them with Mr Nott, who was a subscriber; & was much pleased with his manner of delivering them as well as of elucidating examples of composition on the harpsichord organ etc.' *(The John Marsh Journals* (Feb. 1801), 728).

combine academic example with aesthetic and practical purpose, the intention being:

I.   To improve the taste, by introducing the performer to every kind of excellence . . .
II. To give a *practical* History of the progress of the Science.
III. To present in one work to the Student in Composition a great variety of matter for his study and imitation.
IV. To furnish performers in general with good subjects for practice, calculated for all stages of their progress . . .[24]

Volume II of the *Specimens* presents a veritable historical anthology of music ranging from 'Ambrosian Chant' and Guido to Handel and Pergolesi, with in between much Purcell, some Aldrich, Corelli, and Carissimi, among others. With over a hundred examples, all arranged for keyboard (for instance, a two-stave reduction, No. 21, of Orlando Gibbons's six-part anthem 'Hosanna to the Son of David') the collection is a testament to the range of Crotch's knowledge. In Volume III, J. S. Bach ('48', fugue II. ix) appears, as well as representatives of the modern keyboard style (Paradies, Schobert, C. P. E. Bach, Clementi), the Italian violin school (Geminiani, Tartini) and the Viennese Classical composers: Crotch's keyboard arrangement of Haydn's symphony No. 34 (complete) that forms the final item is particularly attractive. Through his lectures, his published writings, and his interests and enthusiasms (for example early music, Purcell, and J. S. Bach) Crotch 'brought his pupils into contact with a wide variety of music, and his scholarship became the basis for much musicological work in the future'.[25] In this, Crotch aligned himself with Burney, who at a time when 'music was no longer regarded as a serious topic of intellectual enquiry' was able 'by his work as a pioneer in the novel field of musicology. . . to reestablish a context for those who . . . understood music rather than merely performing it'.[26]

A special interest of Crotch was in folk music, and his work in this sphere seems to have been particularly influenced by his friend Malchair. In this field too, Crotch and Malchair, as collectors and compilers, were

[24] *Specimens*, [1].
[25] Rennert, Crotch, 47. On 'ancient music' see Weber, *The Rise of Musical Classics*. Irving ('Crotch on "The Creation" ', *ML* 75 (1994), 551) suggests that Crotch's lectures 'must have influenced a great many proponents of ancient music'.
[26] Rumbold, 'Music aspires to Letters', *ML* 74 (1993), 24.

pioneers.[27] 'Folk music' would not in fact have been a term likely to be used by Malchair or his disciple Crotch. What they collected and studied so painstakingly was regarded, and described, as 'national music'.[28] Both Crotch (in the *Specimens*) and Malchair (in his manuscript collections) documented carefully the extent and nature of the latter's energetic field-work: for example Malchair noted that his version of 'The Grand Duke of Tuscanys March' was 'as played by a Savoyard on a barrill Organ in the Streets at Oxford. November 30–1784'.[29] The music heard in 'the Streets at Oxford' in the late eighteenth century was thus lovingly preserved for posterity.[30] Besides the Grand Duke of Tuscany's March, they yielded such gems as *La Rochelle*, 'played by a Piedmontese Girl on a Cymbal in Oxford Streets December 22. 1784' (recorded in manuscript together with Malchair's instructions for reproducing the effect on the violin); an untitled tune (resembling 'Early One Morning') which Malchair tran-scribed from 'the Singing of a Poor Woman and two femal Children Oxford May 18, 1784'; a topical item, 'The Budget for 1785. Sung in the Streete July 21 – 1785—Oxon A Political Balad on Mr. Pit's Taxes'; a tune for 'flute a bec [recorder] and Tambour' which Malchair heard 'play'd in the Streets at Oxford Ash Wednesday Feb: 25, 1789'; and, finally, the lively 'Magpie Lane': 'I heard a Man whistle this tune in Magpey Lane Oxon Dbr. 22, 1789. came home and noted it down directely'.[31]

City Waits were documented in Oxford from medieval times. In the eighteenth century, references to the 'City Music' and 'City Drum' occur in the Lord Mayor's account books: an indication of their use comes in the description of 18 August 1806 when 'from the Town Hall the Mayor and his Brethren . . . went in procession to Magdalen Bridge . . . attended by a band of music'.[32] An annual occasion when folk music resounded (and

[27] See further discussion in Ch. 6 below; and in Wollenberg, 'Malchair'. Vol. I of Crotch's *Specimens* contains, besides the examples in the first section (Nos. 1–11) of 'the SUBLIME the BEAUTIFUL and the ORNAMENTAL in MUSIC' (matching the aesthetic classifications developed in his text), over 300 folk tunes; these range from 'Codiad yr Hedydd' ('The Rising of the Lark', No. 174) and 'Barbara Allen' (No. 145) to 'A Madras Boat Song Sung by the Steersman & Crew' (No. 325) and a 'Hindoo Hymn' (No. 341).

[28] Crotch, in the preface to his *Specimens* (p. 5), acknowledged his debt to 'Mr. Malchair, who has made National Music his study'.

[29] Cecil Sharp House Library, Malchair MS [QM], p. 58.

[30] Some of Malchair's tunes have been recorded recently on disc, by the group 'Magpie Lane'.

[31] Malchair, MS [QM], pp. 60, 42, 73, 82, and 88. For a version of 'The Budget' (1785) giving words and music see R. Palmer, *The Sound of History: Songs and Social Comment* (London, 1996), 238–9.

[32] Cf. Thewlis, Notes, iii. 509.

indeed still sounds) in the streets of Oxford was formed by the celebrations for May Morning. These were part of a widespread national tradition of May Morning festivities, richly documented in a variety of sources.[33] In Oxford the proceedings mingled aspects of secular and religious culture, folk and art music, and university and city. At some point during the eighteenth century, the Magdalen college grace, 'Te deum patrem colimus', in Benjamin Rogers's setting (known as the *Hymnus Eucharisticus*), was incorporated into the traditional singing of the choir at dawn on May Morning from the top of the great tower of the college. This became a fixed element in the ritual, merging with the older-established customs of greeting the Spring—Hearne in 1724 referred to the practice of blowing horns on the first of May 'to remind people of the pleasantness of that part of the year'—and the religious tradition of offering sung prayers on that date, which marked the Commemoration Day for Henry VII (d. 21 April 1509, buried 11 May), established as 'one of eleven such days during the year for various college benefactors'.[34] That the festive mood predominated in the eighteenth century is confirmed by John Pointer's description of the 'remarkable Custom' of 'having a Concert of Music upon the Top of the Tower, every May-day, at 4 o'Clock in the Morning'; while he referred to the opening item as 'a Mass of Requiem' for King Henry VII, he characterized the whole as 'a merry Concert of both Vocal and Instrumental Music, consisting of several merry Ketches, and lasting almost 2 Hours, and . . . concluded with Ringing the Bells'.[35] The weight of evidence suggests that 'concerts of the kind described by Pointer in 1749' continued until 'towards the end of the eighteenth century'.[36]

'Ringing the Bells' resounded through Oxford to mark special occasions, as in 1789, when Paget recorded:

Thursday Mar. 12th Malchair's benefit. After the Concert was over, "God save the King" was called for, and given 6 times over before the Company could be satisfied. Everybody stood while it was performing, & most of the Company

[33] See Judge, 'May Morning', *Folklore*, 97 (1986).

[34] Judge, 'May Morning', *Folklore*, 97 (1986), 30; 16. Judge (p. 16) suggests, following H. A. Wilson, that 1 May, falling between the dates of Henry's death and burial, may have been chosen 'for an initial solemn service as obit'.

[35] John Pointer, *Oxoniensis Academia* (London, 1749) and Ob, MS Rawlinson B. 405, fo. 137 (quoted in Judge, 'May Morning', 16).

[36] Ibid. 17.

joined in it. Next day the bells of the Colleges and Parish Churches rung all the Morning . . .

The climax came in the evening with 'an universal and very splendid Illumination, with fire works, drums beating, music playing, bells ringing, &c. &c.' (A few days later the University agreed in Convocation the 'Addresses to the King and Queen, on his Majestie's Recovery'; and 'God save the King' was heard again at the Music Room.[37])

The city churches, and the University Church of St Mary, were the scene of musical events for various special purposes: in April 1785 Philip Hayes directed a performance of *Judas Maccabaeus* at St Martin's Church (Carfax) in Oxford, when the 'charity children' sang and Mr Cross played the new organ.[38] The connection continued, and in 1786 and 1787 *Messiah* was given under Hayes's direction for Cross at St Martin's. As a performer, Hayes was periodically called on to 'open' new organs, not only in Oxford and the surrounding area but also elsewhere, including Canterbury Cathedral.[39] When the Duke of Portland and his procession attended the choral service at St Mary's (the University Church) in the year of his installation, 1793, they heard an anthem composed by Philip Hayes.[40] During the annual Commemoration week it became customary to hold a service at St Mary's for the benefit of the Radcliffe Infirmary; like the academic excercises, these occasions were a focus for the production of orchestrally accompanied anthems, such as Hayes's 1774 setting of Psalm 135 ('O praise the Lord').[41] The post of Heather Professor, while it had only a relatively weak link at this time with the academic study of music, offered the chance to fill a varied role in the musical life of the university and city. The three successive Professors of Music who served in that role during the second half of the eighteenth century were also prominent in the establishing of Oxford concerts on a new basis.

---

[37] MCA, Paget, Diary, 1789.

[38] This must have been the father of William Cross (b. 1777), who later succeeded Crotch in his organistships at Christ Church and St John's and is described by Watkins Shaw as organist of St Martin's Church 'from an early age . . . as was his father before him' (*Succession of Organists*, 214).

[39] Heighes, 'Hayes', i. 69. In July 1780 the 'Oxford Choirs' under Dr Hayes visited Abingdon to 'open' the new organ (built by Byfield) at St Helen's Church (*JOJ*, 13 July 1780).

[40] Ob, MS Top. Oxon. d. 247, p. 185 (1 July 1793).

[41] Cf. Heighes, 'Hayes', i. 111 ff. on Philip Hayes's charity performances and festal anthems generally.

4

Concert Life
in Eighteenth-Century Oxford

Oxford's concert life received its greatest impetus from the establishing of the Holywell Music Room (opened 1748).[1] The opening of the Music Room marked not so much a new beginning, as a significant stage in a process of development that can be traced back to the seventeenth century. It was in the eighteenth century that a remarkably rich flowering occurred of a tradition based on various performing elements and contexts, including regular music meetings (documented from the time of the Civil War), special and commemorative ceremonial music, and the periodic injection of distinguished visiting talent into the local musical scene.

In the seventeenth century, Oxford concert life (in the sense of musicians meeting to play together) had 'a special function in helping to maintain a seriously threatened musical culture'.[2] From 1642 to 1646, when Charles I was in residence at Oxford, the musical life of the court continued, in spite of the preoccupations of war: the establishment at the King's Oxford court included the lutenist John Wilson (later holder of the Heather Professorship, 1656–61) and the organist George Jeffreys.[3] During

---

[1] The chief source of published information on the Music Room is still Mee, *Music Room*. See also the discussion in Wollenberg, 'Music in 18th-Century Oxford', *PRMA* 108 (1981–2), 83–9.

[2] Ibid. 83. On the 'major cultural upheaval' of the mid-17th cent., see further M. Chan, 'A Mid-Seventeenth-Century Music Meeting and Playford's Publishing', in Caldwell, Olleson, and Wollenberg, eds., *The Well Enchanting Skill*, 231–44.

[3] The King made Oxford his military headquarters and set up his court at Christ Church, remaining

the period of the Civil War and Interregnum, although the choral tradition was disrupted and organs were destroyed or displaced, Oxford flourished as a centre of musical activity.[4] Many musicians dismissed from posts elsewhere had fled to Oxford, joining local musicians in similar circumstances, and earning a living by alternative means such as giving private musical instruction. Various musical societies were formed along the lines of the music meetings of William Ellis (the organist ejected from his post at St John's College) at which both professional musicians and university graduates gathered regularly to play chamber music.[5]

Although Ellis's meetings lapsed after the Restoration, a new focus for weekly music meetings was created by Narcissus Marsh at Exeter College (where he was a Fellow from 1658) and St Alban Hall (as Principal from 1673). At Christ Church Henry Aldrich (Dean from 1689 to 1710) held a further series of weekly music meetings, perhaps primarily in his decanal capacity (in connection with choir rehearsals for the cathedral services) but possibly also to promote the wider repertoire of instrumental, as well as vocal, music in which he cultivated an interest. Aldrich's influence was later acknowledged as encouraging high standards of performance: 'He not only had concerts and rehearsals at his apartments weekly, but established a music-school in his college, where he both tried and rewarded genius and assiduity'.[6] In 1700 Dr Wallis, Savilian Professor of Astronomy, wrote of the 'consorts of musick (vocal and organical) to which persons of *quality* and *skill* are freely admitted . . .' at various colleges, including Christ Church and New College, 'and some other places according to the *genius* of gentlemen'.[7]

in Oxford until the city eventually surrendered to the Parliamentary forces in June 1646. See P. Gouk in *HUO* iv, and Wainwright, *Musical Patronage*.

[4] As documented particularly by Anthony à Wood: see Wood, *Athenae Oxonienses*, ed. Bliss; *Life and Times*, ed. Clark.

[5] These gatherings can be traced back further to the statutory weekly practices under the direction of the Choragus, as laid down in Heather's original plan (1627) and later maintained under the professorship of Edward Lowe and his successors in connection with the refurbishment of the Music School. See Crum, 'Early Lists of the Oxford Music School Collection', *ML* 48 (1967); and Ford, 'The Oxford Music School in the late 17th Century', *JAMS* 17 (1964).

[6] Quoted in Bergsagel, 'Music in Oxford in Holberg's Time', in *Hvad Fatter gjør . . . Boghistoriske, litterære og musikalske essays tilegnet Erik Dal* (Herning, 1982), 43, from Burney, *History*, ed. Mercer, ii. 479.

[7] Quoted in Bergsagel, 'Music in Oxford', 42, from *Collectanea* (first series), ed. C. R. L. Fletcher (Oxford, 1885), 317. Wallis added that 'there want not those who may instruct them . . .'. Further on the market for musical instruction in Oxford see Bergsagel, 'Music in Oxford', 38. Both Bergsagel and Chan ('A Mid-Seventeenth-Century Music Meeting') develop theories of a commercial connection with the

As Hawkins later depicted the situation, after the Restoration 'meetings of such as delighted in the practice of music began now to multiply, and that at Oxford, which had subsisted at a time when it was almost the only entertainment of the kind in the kingdom, flourished at this time more than ever'.[8] Among the surviving evidence for late seventeenth- and early eighteenth-century Oxford musical societies are the 'Orders to be observ'd at the Musick Meeting' dating from around 1690,[9] an elegantly presented set of rules showing that (in theory, at least) a strong sense of formal organization shaped the character of these meetings, with not only a fixed venue and pre-appointed times:

> I. THAT IT be kept every last Thursday in the Month at Mr. HALL's Tavern at five of the Clock precisely in the Evening, and continue till Ten.[10]

but also regular subscriptions, a rota of stewards, and some severely worded disciplinary clauses:

> II.   THE Club One Shilling each . . .
> III. EVERY ONE to stand to his Club, whether he is in Town or not . . .
> VI.   THE Stewards to serve in Order, as they are entred of the Club.
> VII. WHOEVER does not come before Seven a Clock is to forfeit Six Pence, besides his Club . . .
> XII. THE Steward is obliged to sconce any that makes a noise in time of performance, or to be sconced himself.[11]

Subscriptions were paid a month in advance, and if the steward 'be absent, and doth not send the Money' he was to be fined five shillings (Rule IV) as well as being liable to pay the 'Overplus' when expenditure was inadvertently allowed to exceed club income. The membership was fixed (presumably partly for reasons of space) at a maximum number of forty-

---

phenomenon of music meetings in their respective periods of enquiry, especially concerning the publishing activities of the Playford family, which was itself connected with Oxford.

   [8] Hawkins, *History*, iv. 374.

   [9] Ob, MS Top. Oxon a. 76, from which these quotations are derived. See also Crum, 'An Oxford Music Club, 1690–1719', *BLR* (1974), 83–99.

   [10] The Oxford Hall's Brewery existed only from 1795 (see *EO*, 164). 'Mr Hall's Tavern' has been identified as the Mermaid Tavern kept by Anthony Hall near Carfax (further on Hall, see Crum, 'An Oxford Music Club', 83).

   [11] 'Sconcing' required the victim to drink a tankard of ale without pause. Problems of audience decorum recurred during the subsequent history and expansion of the Oxford music meetings. An account of the music meetings held in Aberdeen refers to the 'playing members' complaining of disturbance by 'Peoples' talking' during the performance (Farmer, *Music-Making in the Olden Days*, 52).

one. Among the forty members listed with these Orders, and including college Fellows, Chaplains, and organists, are some well-known names: Daniel Purcell (brother of Henry, and organist of Magdalen College from *c*.1689); John Shadwell (son of the Poet Laureate); and James Brydges (later first Duke of Chandos and patron of Handel). Several of Oxford's leading musical figures were associated with the club, either at the height of their careers, as with Richard Goodson senior (Heather Professor from 1682), or at an earlier stage, as with Simon Child (subsequently organist of New College from 1702, if the same person). Many of the club members led distinguished careers in the University and beyond.

Goodson's name recurs in a list of club members dating from the early eighteenth century,[12] although it has been suggested that 'this may have been just a formality since he never attended'.[13] The documentation extant for this period of the club's meetings and summarized by Crum gives a lively impression of its activities.[14] Significant features were the regular weekly meetings on Monday evenings, which were well attended, and the rota of stewards (elected from among the performing members to serve for a month each) who were responsible for the society's accounts and administration. Non-performers included the Duke of Queensberry; after he joined in 1715 (aged 16), the non-performing members were listed, as Crum notes, 'in order of social precedence'. Much of the detail recorded by the stewards is of a mundane, although revealing, nature: the recurrent expenses of the club featured ale, candles and fire, and other domestic services lending a convivial atmosphere to the proceedings. As Crum observes, generally in this kind of documentation the information we would most wish to have is not recorded, and so it is all the more valuable to find indications of the musical repertoire that was performed. According to the stewards' notes, Corelli's chamber sonatas (especially those of his Op. 4) were regularly featured in the club's programmes, together with other Italian sonatas. Vocal items included works by both Italian and English composers, such as Carissimi, Bononcini, and Purcell, the latter particularly from *Orpheus Britannicus* (1698), which was evidently a

---

[12] Records survive for the years 1712–19 in a book preserved in Merton College Archives, 4.33. See Crum, 'An Oxford Music Club', 91 ff., for a detailed account.

[13] Bergsagel, 'Music in Oxford', 44; cf. Crum, 'An Oxford Music Club', 91. Richard Goodson junior was an active member of the club during the year he became Heather Professor (succeeding his father in January 1718).   [14] Ibid. 91–9.

favourite source. Concertos and cantatas appeared in the club's holdings of music books: the general impression is of an up-to-date Italianate repertoire.

At this period, as during the previous phase of the club's history, several members were distinguished as singers (there was a strong association with Christ Church and Dean Aldrich's group). Boy choristers were also engaged on an occasional basis to sing, for a fee. The club owned musical instruments, including a harpsichord, and ran a loan system for its music books (together with administering fines). Payments were noted for tuning and repairs to the instruments, as well as for the copying, binding, and hiring of music. The numbers of members enjoying the club's facilities virtually doubled between 1712 and 1716, reaching a total of fifty-five; non-performers began substantially to outnumber performers, so that there were attempts to regulate the ratio. Venues mentioned include two taverns, the King's Head and the Wheatsheaf.

By the mid-eighteenth century the activities and resources of the music club could no longer adequately be contained in its customary tavern or college accommodation. The Heather Professor, William Hayes, described in his 'History of the Music Room' the problems encountered with weekly concerts at the King's Head Tavern, and benefit concerts in college halls. In particular he discussed the difficulty of fitting instruments and performers at the King's Head Tavern among the audience in a low-ceilinged, crowded room:

It had been customary for the Harpsichord to stand on one Side of the Room & at a Table near it sat the Performers on Violins & c, which being on a Level with the Auditory Members, was inconvenient. It was therefore agreed to have portable Floors to raise the Performers which with proper Desks had a grand Effect, The Harpsichord being placed in the Front the Violins on each Side so that all was seen & heard to as much advantage as the scanty Height of the Room would admit of.[15]

Hayes gave the unsatisfactory nature of these premises as the main reason for the launching of an appeal in the 1740s for a new music room, together with the awkward need to borrow college facilities for larger ventures:

[15] Ob, MS Top. Oxon d. 337 fo. 2ᵛ. A printed version of Hayes's account appeared in Peshall's edn. of Wood's *Antient and Present State of the City of Oxford* (London, 1773), 247; repr. in Wood, *History and Antiquities*, ed. Clark, i. 390–2.

At this Time all public Concerts such as Benefits were had in some College Hall: for the Kings Head Room would not contain the number assembled on those Occasions. & the meeting in College Halls was attended with inconvenience to the Society where it happened to be.[16]

One of the singing members of the musical club in the stewards' lists for the early eighteenth century was a Mr Powell, very possibly Walter Powell, chorister of Magdalen College until 1714 and then a singing Clerk—remaining so until his death in 1741. (Before Powell's entry to the club in 1717, he had occasionally earned a shilling or two for taking singing parts; later he was to achieve a lasting fame as principal countertenor taking the part of Joad in Handel's *Athalia*, on its first performance at the Sheldonian Theatre in July 1733.[17]) Walter Powell, by this time one of the Esquire Beadles,[18] was credited by Hayes with both a fine voice 'of great compass' and also a central role in promoting the subscription scheme that was launched successfully in 1741 to raise funds for the new music room.[19]

Some of the circumstances outlined by Hayes reflect the kinds of problems endemic in such ventures. After a false start with one site (the Racket Court) the organizers then 'purchased of Wadham College' for £100, as Hayes later related, 'the Ground whereon the present Music Room stands'—and indeed still stands today.[20] But 'by the Time the Walls were raised' the subscription money (a total of over £490) had been 'swallowed up', and the project came to a halt for some years. It was decided that the club would put on monthly 'Choral Music' to raise the amount needed to finish the building. The work then proceeded 'with Chearfulness' and in July 1748 the Holywell Music Room—reputed to be the first purpose-built concert hall in Europe—was opened.

The design—attributed to Thomas Camplin, Vice-Principal of St Edmund Hall—combined simplicity with elegance and functionality. The room was renowned for its ideal acoustical properties: as one observer noted, 'there is not one pillar to deaden the sound'.[21] The performing area was carefully arranged to house orchestra and singers, while the benches

---

[16] Ob, MS Top. Oxon d. 337 fo. 2ᵛ.   [17] See Ch. 2 above.

[18] The several 'Bedels' represented the ancient ceremonial office of the University which has survived into the present, although the title 'Esquire Bedel' was abolished in 1856.

[19] Ob, MS Top. Oxon d. 337 fo. 3ʳ.

[20] Ibid., from which all quotations in this paragraph are derived.

[21] Mee, *Music Room*, 34. See Ob, Gough prints, vol. 27 (fo. 95) for an architectural sketch.

for the audience were reportedly 'calculated for 400 persons commodiously'.[22] (In its present form it seats about 250.) From the mid-century, the Musical Society (as it was now officially named), with its own premises and the nucleus of a resident orchestra and chorus, together with the option of enlisting the services of the local choristers, and with an established audience, set up an impressive series of weekly subscription concerts and occasional special events.[23] It also possessed, in *Jackson's Oxford Journal* (founded in 1753) an outlet for publicity. The Holywell concerts served to unite 'town and gown', while their organization on a democratic basis chimed with the progressive growth of concert life away from the courts in the eighteenth century, presenting a challenge to the tradition of aristocratic establishments with resident musicians subject to the whims and tastes of their patrons and performing for a socially exclusive audience in often highly artificial conditions.

The resident performers engaged to play at the Holywell Music Room were governed by a set of regulations drawn up for the Musical Society and periodically revised. Members of the band were required to reside in Oxford as a condition of their appointment, and to abide by the Society's rules: 'All Performers who receive Pay are expected to attend all Rehearsals' (rule XXXII, 1757).[24] The 1757 Articles suggest a lineage from earlier such documents, with stewards elected to serve in rotation, committee members fined for non-attendance at meetings, and borrowers similarly penalized for failing to return books and instruments. But a greater sense of formality emerges than in the Society's previous existence. Membership of the committee was regulated to ensure a consistent level of representation and seniority, 'the Person to be chosen' (one from each college) to be 'a Fellow, Scholar, Exhibitioner, or Chaplain of some College, a Vice-Principal of an Hall, or one who bears some public Office in the University' with 'at least four full Years standing' as a graduate.

Among the members of the Holywell Band were performers distinguished both on the local scene and in the wider musical world. Several

---

[22] Hayes, Ob, MS Top. Oxon d. 337 fo. 3ʳ.

[23] The taverns (and coffee-houses) remained important as outlets for the sale of concert tickets in Oxford. In addition, the concert advertisements frequently mention music shops such as 'Mr. Cross's' and 'Mr. Mathew's' as well as performers' private addresses, where tickets could be purchased for Benefit concerts.

[24] For the 1757 *Articles of the Musical Society in Oxford* see Ouf, rare books; reprinted in Mee, *Music Room*, 45–53.

were associated with well-known musical families such as the Mahons. Some members illustrate the contemporary tendency to specialize in more than one instrument, or to combine a variety of musical functions within the city and university. The band benefited from the wave of emigration during the years of turbulence in France, which brought performers to England; some émigrés joined the band at an earlier stage. Thus the violinist John Baptist Malchair (1730–1812), son of a Cologne watchmaker, and trained as a chorister at Cologne Cathedral, was reputed to have arrived in London in his youth; by 1759 he was a (successful) candidate for leadership of the Holywell Band. Besides his duties as leader of the orchestra (1760–92) and his involvement in such diverse activities as cataloguing the music at Christ Church Library and collecting folk tunes locally, Malchair was active as an artist. Crotch included in his memoirs of Malchair an account of the latter's audition for the Holywell Band:

When the present B[isho]p of Durham was Steward of ye Music Room, Hellandael (afterwards leader at Cambridge) and Malchair were Candidates to be leader of ye Band, Malchair played Geminiani's Concerto in D. Hellandael played a solo Concerto of his own. Mr Barrington persuaded the Stewards to Elect Malchair as more useful than a Solo player. Hellendael was handsome and renowned for his beauty—poor Malchair tho' a fine figure was ugly . . . both excellent musicians.[25]

Among later arrivals from the continent was Paul Alday (*c.*1763–1835), Malchair's successor as leader of the band (from 1793 to 1796). Alday, billed in Oxford as a 'celebrated Performer on the Violin in Paris',[26] was a pupil of Viotti and had played at the Concert Spirituel (1783–90) before coming to England in 1791.[27] His wife joined the Holywell Band as a harpist shortly after his appointment. Such appointments brought new musical perspectives to the Oxford scene.

[25] Ob, MS Mus. d. 32, p. 51. Malchair served as President of the Great School of Art in Oxford; see Harrison, *Malchair*. As a collector of folk songs and dances he provided Crotch with material for his *Specimens of various styles of music* (see Ch. 3 above; and, further on Crotch and Malchair, Ch. 6 below). Ob, MS Mus. d. 32 contains Crotch's arrangements of 'Malchair's tunes'. Biographical and source information given here on members of the Holywell Band is derived in the first instance from Mee, *Music Room*, supplemented by reference works (such as *Grove*, various edns.) and documentary collections in archives and libraries.

[26] *JOJ*, 25 May 1793.

[27] Pierre, *Histoire du concert spirituel*, 209–10 *et seq.*

On investigation, the background of many of the musicians whose names occur in the local newspaper advertisements, concert programmes, and other sources, presents particular points of interest for a variety of reasons. For example the violinist James Lates (*c.*1740–77), son of the Hebrew scholar David Francisco Lates, has been described as 'the first Oxford Jewish composer'.[28] (On the title-pages of his publications of string music he is referred to as 'James Lates Junior of Oxford'.[29]) His duets for violins or flutes (Op. 1 and Op. 2) were dedicated to 'Richard Kaye Esquire of Brazen-Nose College in the UNIVERSITY OF OXFORD' as a 'little Tribute of Gratitude and Esteem . . . Humbly Offered' (they presumably embody the abilities of Lates and perhaps the somewhat lesser aspirations of Kaye: see Ex. 4. 1) while the sonatas for violin, cello, and continuo of Op. 5 were dedicated to the Duke of Marlborough, 'for whose private amusement they were principally composed'. (As well as contributing to the Holywell concerts, where he seems to have led the second violins,[30] Lates served as violinist to the Duke at Blenheim.) Lates's publications made a considerable contribution to the development of English string music. The extent of his reputation and connections is indicated by the long and impressive list of subscribers printed in his Op. 4 (*Six Sonatas for Two Violins, or a German flute and Violin, with a Thorough Bass for the Harpsichord*).[31] His concert career may have begun in the 1750s with a childhood appearance in Abingdon at a Benefit concert and ball for Miss Lates

[28] Lewis, *The Jews of Oxford*, 5.

[29] There is some confusion over the identity of various members of the family. James Lates's son John James (b. 1769) has sometimes been confused with his father. Another son, Charles (b. 1771) was also a composer (Charles matriculated from Magdalen College in 1793, taking the B.Mus. degree). Presumably the 'Mr. James Lates of this City' recorded in *JOJ*, 5 Nov. 1768 as having been 'married to Miss Joanna Day, only daughter of Mr. Day in St. Ebb's Parish; a Lady of exceeding good Accomplishments, with a very handsome Fortune', on 29 October 1768, was the Holywell violinist: the sons' dates of birth and the entries in the register of baptisms for St Ebbe's fit with this.

[30] This suggestion originates with Mee (*Music Room*, 68) and is borne out by the wording of advertisements and programmes for the concerts, where his name is coupled with that of Malchair. Advertisements for the termly Choral Music (cf. *JOJ*, 12 Nov. 1768; 16 Nov. 1771; and 18 Mar. 1775) routinely list the instrumentalists as including 'Messrs. Malchair, Lates, &c.': since Malchair was leader of the orchestra, this billing suggests that Lates may have been principal second violin. (The performances may sometimes have featured just one string player per part.) Lates's compositions also appeared in the concert programmes: their idiomatic and stylish writing probably reflects the kind of string style that he helped to promote at Holywell in the 1760s and 1770s.

[31] Among those subscribing to the publication were various clerical and university dignitaries, including a Canon of Christ Church and a Fellow of All Souls; William Hayes (Heather Professor) and his son Philip; Mr Church (organist of Christ Church and New College); John Byfield ('Organ Builder to His Majesty'); a number of patrons from Winchester; and leading London performers such as 'Mr. Crosdill'.

Ex. 4.1. James Lates, *Six Sonatas or Duets for two Violins*, Op. 1, London, 1761,
        No. 3 third movement

(probably his sister) who sang on this occasion, while 'First Violin, and a Solo' were by 'Master Lates'.[32] During the time when he flourished particularly as a violinist and composer in Oxford, in the 1760s and 1770s, Lates played at the Holywell Music Room alongside such outstanding performers as 'the celebrated Mr. Fischer' (oboe) and Crosdill (cello), and published the solos, duos, and trios of his Opp. 1–5. His death after a long and painful illness, in November 1777, occasioned the description of Lates as an 'Eminent Musician' of the locality.[33]

Members of the Holywell Band might pursue professional activities in other spheres concurrently with their musical employment. When Monro, who succeeded Orthman as principal cellist, held a Benefit concert in November 1768, the advertisement for the occasion appeared together with an announcement that by permission of the Vice-

[32] Advertised in *JOJ*, 22 Oct. 1757; tickets were to be obtained, *inter alia*, from 'Signor Lates' in Friar's Entry. This probably refers to the father, David Francisco. The 1750s marked the beginning of his academic activity in Oxford; on his death in April 1777 he was described (*JOJ*, 3 May 1777) as a teacher of Modern Languages in the University for 'upwards of twenty years'.

[33] *JOJ*, 22 Nov. 1777.

> **CHEAP MUSIC, at HARDY's Warehouse, Oxford.**
> THE VOCAL WORKS of HANDEL, in SCORE; consisting of Acis and Galatea, Alexander's Feast, Saul, Dettingen Te Deum and Jubilate, Messiah, Judas Maccabæus, Jeptha, L'Allegro il Penseroso, Samson, Coronation and Funeral Anthems, FOR SALE, at *Ten per Cent. under the Publisher's prices*; together with the most elegant and Classical Musical Publications, Grand and Square Piano Fortes (worthy the notice of schools, being much cheaper than at any other house), Pedal and Æolian Harps, Violins, Violoncellos, Patent Flutes and Flageolets, Bugle and Hunting Horns, with every article in the musical line, warranted.
> A capital Finger Organ, sufficient for the use of a church.

FIG. 4. Advertisement for Hardy's Music Warehouse
(*Jackson's Oxford Journal*, 17 October 1812)

Chancellor 'Mr MONRO, DANCING-MASTER (appointed by the University to succeed Mr. Orthman)' had opened a 'Dancing-School' at his home in New Inn Lane, Oxford.[34] He also offered peripatetic teaching for schools within a twenty-mile radius of Oxford. Subsequent announcements referred to Monro's 'Lectures in Dancing' at his house in Holywell, 'facing the Music-Room'. The description of these as 'Lectures for the Coming Term' gives an official aura to these extra-curricular activities. They were supplemented by the offer of private tuition to gentlemen.[35] The violinist Philippe Jung (of Viennese origin) who was probably principal second violin during his membership of the Holywell Band from 1781 to 1808, also taught French and German, opened a series of music shops in Oxford, and published a tourist guide to the locality, in French.[36]

Oxford life provided plentiful opportunities for varied musical activity. Hardy, a resident violinist in the Holywell Band, also offered to teach 'Gentlemen of the University', and after taking over Matthews's music business in High Street (from 1792),[37] continued in the early years of the nineteenth century to sell second-hand musical instruments left by students of the University who had 'gone down'.[38] He may have been the H. Hardy who published *The Violoncello Preceptor with a Compleat Set of Scales for*

---

34 *JOJ*, 12 Nov. 1768.
35 *JOJ*, 31 Oct. 1772. Woodforde referred to his regular music lessons with Philip Hayes and Orthman in the 1760s and 1770s as 'Lectures' (cf. W. Hargreaves-Mawdsley, ed., *Woodforde at Oxford, passim*).
36 *Guide d'Oxford* (1789).
37 *JOJ*, 25 Feb. 1792. For Matthews see p. 56 below.
38 Presumably his was the business advertising its wares in *JOJ*, 17 Oct. 1812.

fingering in the VARIOUS KEYS . . . by which the Student will be enabled to obtain A PROFICIENCY (Oxford, *c*.1790).[39] William Woodcock, organist of New College (1799–1825) was active as a singer and as viola player in the Holywell concerts. (He had served as assistant organist to Thomas Norris at Christ Church from 1778, and as lay clerk at Christ Church, New College, Magdalen, and St John's from 1784.)[40]

Among the well-known names represented in the Holywell Band, Joseph Reinagle junior, scion of the distinguished musical family of Scottish origins, and principal cellist in Salomon's London orchestra, appeared both occasionally in Oxford (for example in the 1789 Commemoration concerts, as 'the celebrated Mr. Reinagle')[41] and then regularly (during the 1790s and after 1800), probably as leader of the cello section.[42] In several cases, musical families provided a plentiful supply of personnel for the Holywell concerts over a considerable period of time. Most numerous and notable among these musical dynasties were the Mahons.[43] During the 1770s William and John Mahon (described by Matthews as the two brothers who 'were to become the foremost British clarinettists of their day, though both played other instruments')[44] appeared at the Holywell Music Room playing oboe and clarinet. Items advertised in such terms as 'Concerto, Clarionet. Mr. Mahon' were regularly included in the Holywell programmes during this decade.[45] There were also five sisters, at least four of whom sang in the Oxford concerts and established successful reputations as singers elsewhere. The eldest Miss Mahon (Mrs Warton) performed duets with her sister Mary (Mrs Ambrose) in the 1770s;[46] in the 1780s both sang at the Handel commemorations in Westminster Abbey as well as at concerts in Oxford. The most

---

[39] Information kindly provided by Brenda Neece.

[40] For Norris see p. 56 below. On Woodcock see Shaw, *Succession of Organists*, 392.

[41] *JOJ*, 20 June 1789. Further on Commemoration concerts see pp. 64–5 below.

[42] In Jung, *Concerts* (p. xiv) he is the sole cellist listed, which could have various implications.

[43] Besides the sources already referred to (see n. 25) Matthews, 'The Musical Mahons', *MT* 120 (1979) provides further biographical information, and clears up some of the confusion in earlier sources. Particularly confusing is the identity of the two William Mahons, father and son, whose dates and careers have become entangled. What is clear is that Mrs Mahon presided over 'the musical family of that name . . . so justly celebrated throughout the whole kingdom' (ibid. 482).

[44] Ibid. 483.

[45] See e.g. *JOJ*, 31 Oct. 1772 (Benefit for Monro).

[46] See Highfill *et al.*, *Biographical Dictionary*, x. 57, for Miss [M.] Mahon (Mrs Warton) and i. 70–1 for Mrs Ambrose, née Mahon.

successful and popular was probably Sarah Mahon (Mrs Second), who also appeared at Oxford in the 1780s. She was principal singer at many of the major music festivals and events in London and the provinces in the last decade of the eighteenth century, and in the early years of the nineteenth. Another sister, Mrs Munday, was perhaps the youngest of the Misses Mahon; her first Oxford engagement was in 1792.

Two of the longest-serving and most illustrious singers in the Holywell concerts were Thomas Norris (tenor) and William Matthews (bass) who—like members of the Mahon family—often appeared in programmes together.[47] Both established outstanding reputations beyond Oxford as well as developing a characteristically diverse musical profile within the city and the university. Touching evidence of the performers' friendship comes in the entr'acte item of Matthews' Benefit concert at the Music Room on 10 March 1791, consisting of a 'Four-part GLEE, to the Memory of the late Mr. NORRIS, with Words adapted to his own Music'.[48] In general the Holywell musicians formed a close, mutually supportive community, and the structure of the concerts enabled them to work on behalf of one another and their families. They rallied for their colleagues' Benefit performances; among many examples, a poignant note is struck in the advertisement for Mr Wall's Benefit Concert of Vocal and Instrumental Music in 1791:

R. WALL begs Leave to present his humble Respects to the Publick; and as the Vice-Chancellor, from a Motive of Humanity, has been pleased to permit him to have a BENEFIT, and the Performers have been so kind to promise him their Assistance, he thankfully embraces this Opportunity, having been confined by a long Illness, and humbly hopes for generous Support.[49]

While the 'Concert of Vocal and Instrumental Music' was the usual formula on these occasions, Benefits sometimes consisted of large-scale choral works, as with the performance 'For the BENEFIT of Mr. ORTHMAN' on Friday 15 November 1754, at the Music Room, of

---

[47] For instance, among the soloists in Oxford performances of the *Messiah*; as in Lent Term 1774, advertised as: 'MUSICK-ROOM, OXFORD', for 'Monday next, the 21st Instant . . . (as the Choral Musick of the present Term) The MESSIAH; a Sacred Oratorio' with the 'principal Vocal Parts by Miss Linley, Miss Mahon, Messrs. Norris, Mathews, &c.' (*JOJ*, 19 Mar. 1774). On their careers generally see 'Norris' in Shaw, *Succession of Organists*, 212–13, and in Highfill *et al.*, *Biographical Dictionary*, xiii. 285; and 'Mathews', ibid. x. 137.

[48] Ob, Mus. 1. d. 64/1 (Oxford Concert Bills).　　　[49] *JOJ*, 6 Aug. 1791.

ALEXANDER's FEAST.

IN WHICH

Signor PASSERINI who was first Violin, and
Signora PASSERINI a principal Singer at the Opera
last Winter, will perform in each Capacity.
To begin exactly at Seven o'Clock.[50]

The regular Benefit concerts permitted to the resident principal performers at Holywell under the society's rules provided a source of extra income during their careers with the band. They were established under Malchair's predecessor as leader, Joseph Jackson:[51] in March 1759 an advertisement in the *Journal* announced a 'Concert of Vocal and Instrumental MUSICK' at the Music Room on Thursday 29 March 'for the Benefit of Mr. JACKSON', featuring particularly 'a CONCERTO and SOLO on the Violin, by Mr. JACKSON', as well as a harpist from London, 'the celebrated Mr. PARRY'.[52] The sad sequel to this came in November 1759, when the *Journal* advertised an event 'BY Permission of the Rev. Dr. BROWN, Vice-Chancellor' on Thursday 29 November, consisting of a performance of *Alexander's Feast* at the Music Room 'for the Benefit of Mrs. JACKSON (Widow of the late Mr. JACKSON, first Violin) and her Family'. (Tickets, at 'Two Shillings and Six-pence each', were to be had 'at the Coffee Houses, Mr. Cross's Music Shop, and at Mrs. Jackson's in Holiwell'.[53])

The Holywell performers also formed part of a kind of 'rent-a-crowd' of musicians, appearing at venues outside Oxford: on the lighter side these included the annual entertainment at Oakley Wood House during the Cirencester Races. For example, in August 1773 the *Journal* announced that *Acis and Galatea* would be performed there, featuring 'First Violin, with a Solo, by Mr. Malchair' and vocal parts by Norris, Matthews, and others. The performance was scheduled for 11 a.m., followed by a 'Cold Collation for the Company' at 2 p.m. and 'Tea in the Afternoon' (with tickets correspondingly more expensive at a quarter of a guinea each). The day was rounded off with a ball at the Assembly Rooms.[54] On the more serious side,

---

[50] *JOJ*, 9 Nov. 1754. The reference to the Passerinis' operatic connections raises the thought that these may have constituted a particular attraction in Oxford, where opera itself was not normally on offer. (An exceptional instance occurs in July 1759 when for the Commemoration and Installation of the Earl of Westmorland as Chancellor, Tenducci and an 'Italian Band' performed opera in the Sheldonian Theatre: cf. Thewlis, Notes, iii. 643–4 and Mee, *Music Room*, 15.)   [51] See ibid. 77–8.

[52] *JOJ*, 24 Mar. 1759.   [53] *JOJ*, 24 Nov. 1759.   [54] *JOJ*, 7 Aug. 1773.

the Oxford musicians contributed to the Three Choirs Festival (founded *c.*1713), and to the great Handel commemorations held at Westminster Abbey (from 1784): the singers Norris and Matthews were much in demand for these events. The secular concerts that developed in conjunction with the Three Choirs Festival shared many features with their Oxford counterparts (Watkins Shaw notes the influence of the fashionable London 'Concert of Ancient Music').[55] For the 1790 festival in Gloucester, among the soloists—as well as Madame Mara, Mr Parke (playing an oboe concerto), and Miss Parke (singing Handel)—the Oxford chorister Master Mutlow appeared, performing 'Pale was the Moon' (*The Ghost of Edwin*), billed as a new song by Hayes.[56] From the 1750s onwards 'the best singers and instrumentalists in the land performed at the Three Choirs Festival', while the Handel commemorations, given by hundreds of performers, reflected the idea of 'presenting Handel in the most grandiose way possible'.[57]

The Holywell musicians were part of a two-way traffic: many of the vocal soloists and instrumentalists associated with prestigious venues such as the Three Choirs and the Handel Commemorations, and with the fashionable London concerts and pleasure gardens, were booked by the stewards to appear at the Holywell Music Room alongside the resident band and vocalists. The list of visiting performers from outside Oxford involved in the Monday evening subscription concerts and Choral Nights is a star-studded one.[58] Rarely did these soloists make only a fleeting appearance in Oxford. The pattern was normally that the invited performers featured during a season and over several years: the faithfulness of the Oxford stewards and audiences to their favourite performers, and of the performers to their Oxford venues (chiefly the Holywell and the Sheldonian at this period) is evident.[59] Besides Miss Linley, Mrs Billington, and Signora

55 Shaw, *The Three Choirs Festival*, 10. The 'Ancient Concerts' ran from 1776; no music less than twenty years old was to be performed (cf. McVeigh, *Concert Life*, 22 ff.).

56 Shaw, *The Three Choirs Festival*, 11. Mutlow (chorister at Magdalen, 1788–93) sang Hayes's 'The Ghost of Edwin. (New.)' in Oxford for Malchair's Benefit on 9 December 1790: cf. Ob, Mus. 1 d. 64/1.

57 Johnstone and Fiske, *The Eighteenth Century*, 20–1 and 255.

58 Besides *JOJ*, sources of information include programme collections and recollections such as Paget, Diary (MCA).

59 Among those who returned to Oxford was Mrs Billington (née Weichsel), sometimes 'accompanied by her Spouse' (*JOJ*, 23 June 1787); she performed originally as Miss Weichsel in the early 1780s (cf. Mee, *Music Room*, 26 and 28).

Storace the list includes Miss Cantelo (Mrs Harrison), Signora Davies ('L'Inglesina'), Madame Mara, Miss Poole (Mrs Dickons), and the castrato Giusto Ferdinando Tenducci. Walker's remark that 'English music lovers could hear a great deal of admirable vocal and instrumental performance at this time' could be applied to Oxford perhaps more consistently than to anywhere else outside London.[60] Oxford audiences were enabled to compare against high standards; thus Paget opined in 1788 of the 'three very capital concerts at the Theatre': 'Principal Singer, Sigr Marchesi, who is far superior to any I ever heard not even Mara excepted. Billingtons, Fisher, &c. Old Pan's breath as good as ever.'[61]

Among the instrumentalists, the wind players included the oboists J. C. Fischer (noted by Paget), John Parke, and Gaetano Besozzi, while leading string players regularly heard in Oxford included the violinist Wilhelm Cramer and the cellist John Crosdill. These were all players of the first rank.[62] The structuring of the concert programmes was characteristically designed to offer solo slots to several visiting virtuosi within one programme rather than featuring a single solo performer exclusively (this was actually a much later development). A typical arrangement for the regular subscription concerts at the Music Room would consist of some ten items, vocal and instrumental (generally alternating), divided into two 'Acts', with often an extra item inserted between the Acts, perhaps a 'glee' (which could consist of an eighteenth-century part-song or a sixteenth-century madrigal) or an instrumental solo such as the Hummel harpsichord sonata performed by its 9-year-old author during a Monday evening programme in 1788.[63] The audience's penchant for demanding encores is evidenced by the warning at the foot of the programmes: 'By the ARTICLES OF SUBSCRIPTION no *Performance*, whether *Vocal* or *Instrumental*, is to be repeated.'[64] Besides the entr'acte slot, within the two Acts solo numbers appeared in the form of arias excerpted from operas or oratorios, as well as independently composed songs; and the inclusion of concertos typi-

[60] Walker, *Music in England*, 273.

[61] Paget, Diary, 25–7 June 1788 (MCA).

[62] Their names recur throughout reference works and memoirs, such as Burney's *History*, and W. Parke's *Musical Memoirs*.

[63] Ob, Mus. I d. 64/1, 27 Oct. 1788. Hummel undertook an extended European tour in the late 1780s and early 1790s with his father, 'arousing particular interest in England, where he met Haydn' (*NGCDM* 378).

[64] See Ob, Mus. 1 d. 64/1, *passim*.

cally enabled the instrumental soloists to be featured as both composers and performers. In addition, the solo vocalists might join in a duet, trio, or glee, while the instrumentalists similarly might co-operate in an ensemble piece. The genres ranged from Baroque-type trio sonatas to the fashionably *galant*: a 'Quartetto, flute' appeared in Act I of the concert at the Music Room on 9 March 1767, and an 'accompanied sonata' (piano trio) on 27 November 1788, billed as 'Sonata, Mr Clark—Upon the Grand Piano Forte, accompanied by flute and violoncello obbligato'.[65]

The emphasis, then, was on variety of texture and timbre. The repertoire equally offered a broad spectrum of styles and genres. At a time when English writers on music such as, most notably, Burney and Hawkins, were promoting a historical 'overview' as well as—Burney particularly—a lively interest in the contemporary and continental repertoire, the Oxford concert programmes reflected to some extent, and in miniature, this sense of a sweep of musical history and a firm grip on modernity. And in the climate of enthusiasm for 'ancient' music that developed in eighteenth-century England, the Oxford concert repertoire showed the establishment of early music in the canon.[66] Thus Corelli and Purcell were heard alongside Galuppi and Haydn; Dowland and Morley as well as Boyce and Arne; local composers—William and Philip Hayes, Thomas Norris— together with more exotic imports such as Mysliveček and Toeschi. The earlier genres of trio sonata, concerto grosso, and French overture jostled with the fashionable solo sonata, solo concerto, and symphony. The 'galant' or early Classical style in its various manifestations was represented by a considerable range of composers: among them C. F. Abel, J. C. Bach, and Ciampi (all of whom brought continental styles to London in the second half of the eighteenth century) and the Mannheim symphonists (Filtz, Richter, Stamitz, and others)[67] whose vivid orchestral writing will have tested and displayed the prowess of the Holywell Band; and also the contemporary Austrian school (Dittersdorf, Vanhal, Haydn, and his pupil Pleyel).[68]

[65] Programmes in Ob, Mus. 1 d. 64/1.

[66] Cf. Weber, *The Rise of Musical Classics*. Jung noted in his *Guide d'Oxford* (1789) that Malchair had a particular penchant for the music of the 'celebrated Handel', Geminiani, Corelli, and other 'old authors' (Mee, *Music Room*, 79).

[67] Mee speculates that the younger Stamitz (Carl) was the one represented; similarly with Toeschi.

[68] For the list of music belonging to the Society in the early period see Mee, *Music Room*, 54–62; cf.

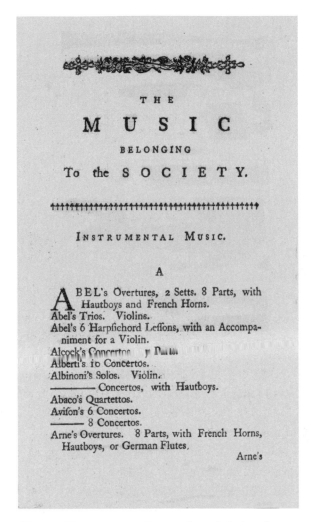

FIG. 5. First page, catalogue of music belonging to
the Musical Society at Oxford, early 1760s

The genre of symphony occupied a particularly strong position in the
Oxford concert repertoire at this period. Each half of the proceedings
might both begin and end—in programmes of the early 1770s, for
instance—with an 'Overture' or symphony, so that these might constitute

Catalogue in Ouf, Rare Books. Lists of performers are included in Jung, *Guide d'Oxford* (1789) and *Concerts* (1808); cf. Mee, *Music Room*, 31; 158–60. Copies of Handel's works survive with the Musical Society's imprint, for example the score of his opera *Julius Caesar*, inscribed 'This belongs to the Musick-club at the King's Head-Tavern, Oxon.' (Ob, Mus. 22 d. 81) and his *Berenice* (Ob, Mus. 22 c. 13).

almost half of the total number of pieces in the programme (and two-thirds of the instrumental fare on offer).[69] The centre-piece of the 'Acts' might be a chamber work such as a trio or quartet; this is apparent from the earliest programmes extant.[70] Vocal chamber music, too, was frequently programmed in Oxford during the second half of the eighteenth century: duets ranged from the 'ancient' to the modern, with on the one hand Purcell's 'When Myra sings' (performed by Norris and Matthews in 1773) and on the other William Jackson's captivating 'Time has not thinn'd my flowing hair', sung probably by Mr Woodcock and Master Miller, in 1791.[71] A constant source of items in these programmes was the choral repertoire. In this respect Handel held undisputed sway. Among the earliest surviving concert programmes—those dating from the 1760s—in the category of 'Song' might be found excerpts from Handel's oratorios and dramatic works, as in the programme for 4 August 1766, when the song following the overture (by Jommelli) that opened Act I was billed as 'Sweet as sight to the blind' from Handel's _Jephtha_.[72] A nice symmetry with this juxtaposition was created by the programming of a Handel overture to open Act II of the concert, followed by a Jommelli aria ('Prigioner che fa ritorno'). And the vocal item preceding the concluding instrumental piece in each half was in Act I a modern Italian number, Galuppi's popular 'Donne, donne', and in Act II, balancing this, Handel's 'The flocks shall leave the mountains'.[73]

From the earliest documented phase of the Holywell concerts, the 'Quarterly Choral Performances' mentioned by William Hayes were interspersed with the miscellaneous programmes.[74] For these termly choral nights complete oratorios might be offered. And in this sphere too Handel reigned supreme, with _Messiah_ holding the central place. Within Handel's lifetime _Messiah_ received—following its Oxford première in 1749 under William Hayes's direction—annual performances in the city from

[69] The title 'overture' could be, but was not necessarily, synonymous with symphony: in the Oxford programmes it covered Handel's overtures to his oratorios as well as the new concert symphonies of Norris.

[70] See e.g. the 1773–4 programmes reproduced in Mee, _Music Room_, 37–8; and Ob, Mus. 1 d. 64/1.

[71] 6 Dec. 1773 (cf. Mee, _Music Room_, 37–8); 9 Dec. 1791 (both in Ob, Mus. 1 d. 64/1).

[72] The Air 'Sweet as light to the Blind' occurs in Act III of _Jephtha_.

[73] Trio, Act II of _Acis and Galatea_.

[74] See Hayes, 'History of the Music Room'; Ob, MS Top. Oxon d. 337.

FIG. 6. Title page, Handel's *Berenice* with the Musical Society's imprint

at least 1754 onwards.[75] Occasionally a partial performance only was offered, as in 1755 when it was announced that 'The First Performance in the New Subscription, on the 31st of March', would be 'the two last Parts of The MESSIAH'; subsequently this was readvertised: 'THE Performance of the two last Parts of The MESSIAH, which was intended on the 31st Instant, is postponed till Monday the 7th of April, on account of the Absence of several of the Performers.'[76] On another occasion the work was divided into two chunks, advertised separately: the performance in February 1757 'at the MUSICK ROOM' of 'the First Act and Part of the Second of the MESSIAH, beginning at *Lift up your Heads, O ye Gates, &c.*' was followed in March of that same year by its completion:

> *Oxford, March 25.*
>
> AT the MUSIC-ROOM on *Monday* Evening the 28th Instant (being the first Night of the New Subscription) will be performed so much of the MESSIAH as was omitted in a former Performance.
>
> *N.B.* Mr. PRICE is expected from *Glocester*, and the TRUMPET from *Salisbury*.[77]

But generally, where such specific modifications are not mentioned, the advertisements can be taken to refer to unabridged and undivided performances of 'The Sacred Oratorio'.[78]

Besides its Lent Term placing (on the Monday evenings routinely used for the Holywell subscription concerts) *Messiah* was featured regularly at this period in the summer Commemoration performances. These were advertised, and reported on, in suitably more inflated terms; thus in June 1756 it was noted in the *Journal* that

> On Tuesday the 6th of July (being the Day appointed for commemorating the Benefactors to the University) will be performed in the Theatre, the Oratorio of Judas Maccabaeus; on Wednesday the 7th, Joshua; and on Thursday the 8th, the Messiah. The principal Parts to be sung by Signora Frasi, Miss Young, Mr. Beard,

---

[75] Mee, *Music Room*, 19–21, prints a list of oratorios 'performed in the Music Room between February 1754 and April 1789', from the sources available, including several revivals of *Athalia*. H. J. Marx has documented over eighty English performances of *Messiah* between 1742 and 1759 (personal communication, 1993).

[76] *JOJ*, 15 Mar. 1755 and 29 Mar. 1755.

[77] *JOJ*, 5 Feb. 1757 and 26 Mar. 1757. A similar division obtained in 1758 (cf. *JOJ*, 4 Feb. and 25 Feb. 1758).

[78] This was its usual designation in the Oxford programme books and concert advertisements: see also Mee, *Music Room*, 21.

Mr. Thomas Hayes, and Others. The Choruses will be supported by a great Number of Voices and Instruments of every Kind requisite, and no Expence will be spared to make the whole as grand as possible.[79]

And on July 10 the *Journal* carried the notice:

On Tuesday last a grand Convocation was held in the Theatre . . . On Thursday a third Convocation . . . in which the honorary Degree of Doctor of Laws was conferred . . . During these three Days the Oratorio's (conducted by Dr. Hayes) were attended with crowded Audiences, viz. on Tuesday Evening, Judas Maccabeus; on Wednesday, Joshua; on Thursday, the Messiah; all composed by Mr. Handel. 'Tis supposed there hath not been so large a Meeting of Nobility and Gentry, on any Academical Occasion, since the Public Act, in the Year 1733.[80]

In some years the 'crowded Audiences' for Handel's oratorios during Commemoration week were accommodated in the Holywell Music Room, as in 1757, when the *Journal* reported that 'On Wednesday last was celebrated the anniversary Commemoration of the Benefactors to the University . . . In the Evening the Oratorio of MESSIAH was performed, at the Music Room in Holiwell, to a very numerous Audience; as was that of ESTHER on Thursday Evening'.[81] For these performances (on 6 and 7 July) the 'considerable Number of Voices and Instruments, from *London* and other Places' particularly included 'Mr. *Savage*'s celebrated Boy, who supplied the Place of Signora *Frasi* in the last Performance of MESSIAH at the *Foundling Hospital* . . . and several others'.[82]

The Lent Term and other choral performances at Holywell also featured Handel's 'secular' music: Mee draws from his list the statistics that ' "Acis" appears fifteen times, "L'Allegro" thirteen times, and "Alexander's Feast" thirteen times' during the period 1754 to 1789.[83] The Coronation Anthems were popular as concert pieces, with *Zadok the Priest* leading in numbers of performances (as it did elsewhere).[84] The 'astonishing indifference with which sacred and profane music was intermingled' in the

---

[79] *JOJ*, 19 June 1756.   [80] *JOJ*, 10 July 1756.   [81] *JOJ*, 9 July 1757.
[82] *JOJ*, 2 July 1757.
[83] Mee, *Music Room*, 21. As Johnstone notes (Burrows, *Cambridge Companion to Handel*, 71), the Musical Society at Oxford 'subscribed to all of Handel's later publications'.
[84] Johnstone and Fiske, *The Eighteenth Century*, 40. *Zadok the Priest* appeared in a secular context in the early seasons of the London Pleasure Gardens (ibid. 71).

early nineteenth-century programmes as noted by Mee (from his early twentieth-century viewpoint) had been established in the earlier history of the Holywell concerts. Its cultural roots may have included associative elements such as the expression of royalist sentiments,[85] and the style of listening (and listeners' expectations) at the time. Among the earliest programmes is a wordsheet for the comic song 'Well! Sirs, then I'll tell you' performed by Miss Linley at the Music Room on 29 April 1771, 'BY DESIRE', evidently between the Acts of Handel's *Esther*.[86] In the three concerts of the 'GRAND MUSICAL FESTIVAL' that marked Haydn's honorary degree in July 1791, the composer heard his own music alongside that of Handel (as well as Purcell) in a characteristic mixture of the 'ancients' and 'moderns'; and overtures and vocal numbers from Handel's 'sacred oratorios' appeared next to secular works in the current instrumental genres (Haydn's 'Oxford' symphony among them). The first concert opened with the Overture and chorus 'O the pleasure of the plains!' from *Acis and Galatea*; the third and final concert ended with Handel's *Zadok the Priest*.[87]

While Oxford performers and audiences retained their attachment to Handel's music throughout the remainder of the eighteenth century, following his earlier appearance in the city, a place was found in the Holywell programmes for the new music of Haydn long before his visit to Oxford in 1791. Haydn had connections in Oxford: Andreas Lidl, a baryton player from the Eszterháza establishment directed by Haydn, appeared in Oxford in 1776.[88] And Philippe Jung (the Holywell violinist, originally of Vienna), as Mee notes 'appears to have been a friend of Haydn, whom he induced to assist at the benefit concert of . . . Hayward, a member of the Music Room Orchestra'.[89] The first sighting of Haydn's music among the Holywell repertoire is, slightly unexpectedly, a string quartet (Op. 9 No. 5) performed in a concert of 1773.[90] Haydn's name 'appears for the second time in the programme for November 16, 1775, when an [unnamed] overture of his composition opened the concert'.[91] Thereafter Haydn's

---

[85] Cf. Temperley's evaluation of the Coronation Anthems' nationalist meaning in ibid. 366.
[86] Ob, Mus. 1 d. 64/1 (cf. *JOJ*, 27 Apr. 1771).
[87] Programmes in Ob, Mus. 1 d. 64/1.
[88] Mee, *Music Room*, 24.
[89] Ibid. 133. See also Ch. 2 above.
[90] Mee, *Music Room*, 36–7. Oxford kept up with London in this regard; McVeigh (*Concert Life*, 94) documents the first known performance of a Haydn symphony in London in 1773.
[91] Mee, *Music Room*, 39.

[xiv.]

INSTRUMENTAL.

Madame FERRARI, on the Piano Forte,

Dr. CROTCH, on the Organ,

Mr. LEO, on the Violin,

AND

Mr. WEIPPERT, on the Harp.

First Violins, . Messrs. MARSHALL, JACKSON, and TEBBIT.

Second Violins, Messrs. JUNG, HESTER, and HEMMING.

Viola, ... W. WOODCOCK, M. B.

Violoncello, . . Mr. REINAGLE.

Flute, ... Mr. JACKSON.

Clarionets, . . Messrs. J. and C. HALDON.

Horns, ... Messrs. P. and J. HATTON.

Trumpet, . . . Mr. DROVER.

Double Bass, . Mr. H. HALDON.

Bassoons, . . . Messrs. FELDON, JOY, and WILKINS.

Drums, ... Mr. JOY.

FIG. 7. List of orchestral personnel,
Holywell Band (1807–8)

symphonies (billed often as 'overtures') became an established item. In 1781 'A Favourite Symphony of Giuseppe Haydn' (Symphony No. 67 in F major) was published in an arrangement by 'Dr Phil. Hayes', 'adapted to the Harpsichord or Piano-Forte'.[92] Other Oxford favourites among the symphonies included No. 63, 'La Roxelane', and No. 53, the 'Festino'. By the late 1780s, in terms of the number of his works included in concerts at the Holywell and the Sheldonian, Haydn came second only to Handel.

In the period after 1791, Haydn's music was secured in the Holywell repertoire, with a clear monopoly amongst the symphonists. Taking the

[92] Printed by 'W. Mathews in the High Street, Oxford'. The symphony had been composed by 1779.

documentation by Jung for the concert season from October 1807 to October 1808, we find that twenty-three of the twenty-seven concerts feature a Haydn symphony.[93] To the earlier works heard in Oxford were now added the 'London' symphonies produced during Haydn's two English visits of 1791–2 and 1794–5: in particular the 'Military' symphony (No. 100 in G major) became a favourite and was represented on at least two occasions within the 1807–8 Oxford season.[94] Haydn's vocal music began to appear: the joint Benefit concert for Marshall and Reinagle in March 1808, which was spread over two nights, included in Act II on the first night the Haydn 'song: "Ombra del caro bene" ', as well as ending Act I of the second night's programme with a 'Grand Overture' by Haydn (most probably one of the 'London' symphonies).[95] And among Haydn's 'London' works adopted in the Holywell programmes were his vocal canzonets: for the concert on Wednesday, 25 June 1800 at the Music Room Act I of the programme included Haydn's canzonet 'Now the dancing sunbeams play' (*The mermaid*) sung by Master [G.V.] Cox, 'BY DESIRE' (while Act II had a Haydn 'Quartetto'), and on Monday, 30 April 1804 Master Walker sang *The Mermaid* in a programme that also included a Haydn symphony (alongside music by J. C. Bach, Handel, Avison, and Pleyel).[96]

Besides documenting the repertoire and performers associated with the Music Room, the programmes that have been preserved, and the newspaper advertisements, give numerous indications of the context surrounding the concerts, ranging from domestic matters—lighting, heating, ventilation—to personnel difficulties. Traffic problems surface in the notice of 'the MESSIAH, a sacred Oratorio' as the 'Choral Music for the present Term' on Monday, 17 March 1775 ('principal Vocal Parts, by Miss Linley, Miss Mahon, Messrs. Norris, Mathews, &c. The Instrumental by Messrs. Malchair, Lates &c.') which concludes with the plea: 'N.B. The Gentlemen and Ladies are requested to order their Carriages to take them up at

93 Jung, *Concerts*, 1–146. This reflected the trend generally around the turn of the century. In the year 1803, for example, of over twenty Monday evening concerts, every one contained a Haydn symphony (as well as these being programmed in extra concerts such as Benefits).

94 Programmes of 12 May 1808 and 28 June 1808; cf. Jung, *Concerts*, 115–22; 141–6.

95 Ibid. 93–104.

96 Programmes in Ob, Mus. 1 d. 64/1. See also Ch. 9 below on *The Creation* in Oxford.

the great Gate only.'[97] The audience was encouraged to voice any dissatisfaction through the official channels, as a note at the foot of a 1779
programme (for a Monday evening subscription concert) shows: 'The
Committee will readily hearken to Complaints against any of the Performers; and will be careful, on all Occasions, to give due Redress'.[98]

The 'ARTICLES of SUBSCRIPTION for the Support of the MUSICAL SOCIETY'
dating from this period set out both what was offered to the audience and
what was hoped of them, for example 'that for the future, Gentlemen will
not suffer Dogs to follow them to the Room, which are a great Annoyance
to the Company'.[99] (This plea was made 'in Compliance with the earnest
Request of a very considerable Number of Subscribers'.) While these and
other documents refer to the holding of rehearsals, it was made clear that
these were not intended to provide free concerts: 'N.B. No Person, who is
not a Member of the Committee, will for the Future be admitted to the
Rehearsals, but upon the . . . Terms of Admission to the Choral Concert.'

At this time—the mid-1770s—the proportion of choral to miscellaneous concerts changed in favour of the latter. The 1775–6 Articles of Subscription promised that

I. THERE will be a Concert of Vocal and Instrumental Music every Monday
Evening, except in the Month of September, and in Passion-Week.

II. The Oratorio of the Messiah will be performed as usual in Lent Term, and
some other Oratorio, or Piece of Choral Music, in Act Term; and in Easter and
Michaelmas Terms, instead of the Oratorios as usual, will be substituted two
grand Miscellaneous Concerts; in which will be engaged at least one capital
Vocal Performer, and one capital Instrumental Performer. This Alteration is
made at the Request of a large number of Subscribers, and it is hoped will prove
agreeable to the Subscribers in general.

The terms of subscription offered, on payment of one guinea 'at the Time
of subscribing', two tickets, one gentleman's and one 'for the Admission of
a Lady'.[100] But in addition, it was stated that 'several Ladies having

---

[97] *JOJ*, 18 Mar. 1775.

[98] 20 Dec. 1779: Ob, MS Top. Oxon d. 281 (165).

[99] Cf. *JOJ*, 1775–6 (*passim*), e.g. 16 Mar. 1776.

[100] Examples of Ladies' and Gentlemen's Tickets survive in Ob, Mus. 1 d. 64/1 and Ouf. The ladies
were admitted under this scheme gratis to the regular subscription concerts and to Choral Nights and
Grand Miscellaneous Concerts on payment of 2s. 6d. 'either at the Door, or at Mr. Hawting's, where
Tickets are to be had; unless the Music be performed in the Theatre, when, to avoid the Inconvenience of
receiving Money at the Door, proper Tickets will be provided'.

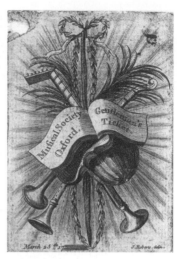

Fig. 8. Lady's and gentleman's ticket (25 March 1785)
for the Musical Society at Oxford

expressed their Desire of contributing annually to the Musical Society,
their Subscriptions will be thankfully received' on very favourable terms:
Article V provided that 'Every subscribing Gentleman shall pay One Shilling for each Concert, but a subscribing Lady shall pay nothing'. (The
prices for non-subscribers were 2s. 6d. for the 'ordinary' concerts, 4s. for
the special ('Choral, or grand Miscellaneous') concerts and 5s. 'when the
Choral Concert is performed at the Theatre'.)

From the late 1770s until 1793, during which time the concerts were
under the direction of Philip Hayes (as Professor of Music), the musical
scene was troubled by tensions partly arising from personality clashes and
a measure of professional pique. The quarrels among members of the
band incited by Hayes were brought to the attention of the university.
Thus Monro described in an open letter of 27 November 1780, concerning his dispute with Hayes over permission to engage the singer Miss
George for a Benefit, how he

waited . . . 'till it becoming proper for me to draw out the Plan of my Concert, I
called upon Mr. George to know if Dr. Hayes's PERMISSION had been obtained,
and received for Answer, that *it was not agreeable* that she should sing. Now it having
been generally expected that Miss George would sing at my Benefit, I thought it
prudent to mention in my Bills why she did not.

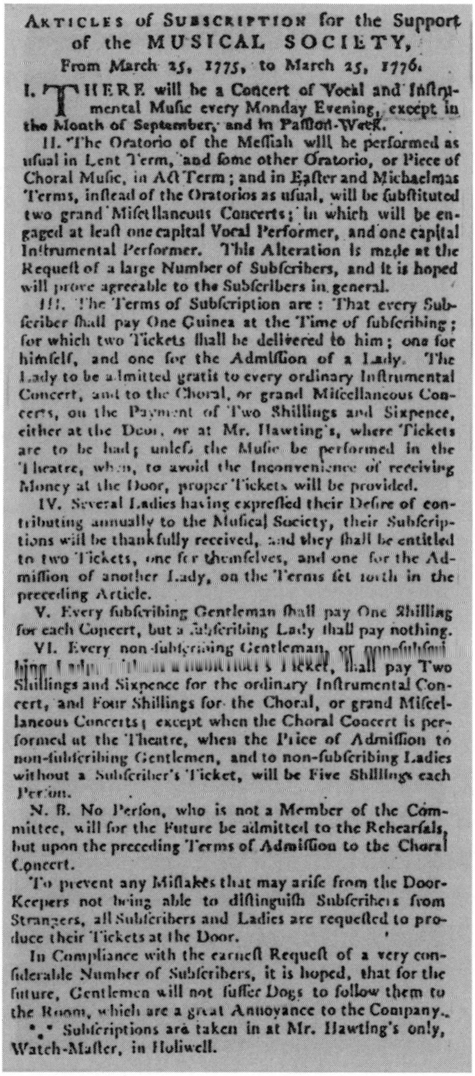

ARTICLES of SUBSCRIPTION for the Support
of the MUSICAL SOCIETY,
From March 25, 1775, to March 25, 1776.

I. THERE will be a Concert of Vocal and Instrumental Music every Monday Evening, except in the Month of September, and in Passion-Week.

II. The Oratorio of the Messiah will be performed as usual in Lent Term, and some other Oratorio, or Piece of Choral Music, in Act Term; and in Easter and Michaelmas Terms, instead of the Oratorios as usual, will be substituted two grand Miscellaneous Concerts; in which will be engaged at least one capital Vocal Performer, and one capital Instrumental Performer. This Alteration is made at the Request of a large Number of Subscribers, and it is hoped will prove agreeable to the Subscribers in general.

III. The Terms of Subscription are: That every Subscriber shall pay One Guinea at the Time of subscribing; for which two Tickets shall be delivered to him; one for himself, and one for the Admission of a Lady. The Lady to be admitted gratis to every ordinary Instrumental Concert, and to the Choral, or grand Miscellaneous Concerts, on the Payment of Two Shillings and Sixpence, either at the Door, or at Mr. Hawting's, where Tickets are to be had; unless the Music be performed in the Theatre, when, to avoid the Inconvenience of receiving Money at the Door, proper Tickets will be provided.

IV. Several Ladies having expressed their Desire of contributing annually to the Musical Society, their Subscriptions will be thankfully received, and they shall be entitled to two Tickets, one for themselves, and one for the Admission of another Lady, on the Terms set forth in the preceding Article.

V. Every subscribing Gentleman shall pay One Shilling for each Concert, but a subscribing Lady shall pay nothing.

VI. Every non-subscribing Gentleman, or non-subscribing him[...] upon [...] a [...] Ticket, shall pay Two Shillings and Sixpence for the ordinary Instrumental Concert, and Four Shillings for the Choral, or grand Miscellaneous Concerts; except when the Choral Concert is performed at the Theatre, when the Price of Admission to non-subscribing Gentlemen, and to non-subscribing Ladies without a Subscriber's Ticket, will be Five Shillings each Person.

N. B. No Person, who is not a Member of the Committee, will for the Future be admitted to the Rehearsals, but upon the preceding Terms of Admission to the Choral Concert.

To prevent any Mistakes that may arise from the Door-Keepers not being able to distinguish Subscribers from Strangers, all Subscribers and Ladies are requested to produce their Tickets at the Door.

In Compliance with the earnest Request of a very considerable Number of Subscribers, it is hoped, that for the future, Gentlemen will not suffer Dogs to follow them to the Room, which are a great Annoyance to the Company.

. Subscriptions are taken in at Mr. Hawting's only, Watch-Master, in Holiwell.

FIG. 9. Articles of subscription, Musical Society (1775–6)
(*Jackson's Oxford Journal*, 16 March 1776)

and added:

I am well aware that Disputes between TWEEDLEDUM and TWEEDLEDEE are beneath the Notice of the Gentlemen of the University, but I thought it incumbent on me to clear my Character from the Imputation of having published a Falshood at the *Bottom of my Music Bill.*[101]

[101] Quoted in Mee, *Music Room*, 91; cf. Ob, MS Top. Oxon e. 48, fo. 14ᵛ—15.

At this period lack of audience decorum was a recurrent problem. Riots broke out, as in the case of Madame Mara in 1785; and in 'about ye year 1792', in Crotch's words, the 'fine Cremona violin' on which Malchair played as leader of the Holywell band was 'broken by an Orange thrown ... during a tumult of ye young men', after which 'he never lead'.[102] (The objection seems to have been to the Society's Articles rather than to Malchair.) At the same time the Holywell organization was beset with financial problems. In a phase where the concerts continued to offer the chance to hear music and musicians of fine quality, the stewards became increasingly concerned about the viability of the enterprise: as Mee put it, 'the times were bad' and, 'whatever were the causes, the subscription list did not fill'.[103] Among their periodic appeals for support from 'the Public, and particularly ... those Families who are desirous that the only Amusement of the Place be not lost'[104] were some stirring declarations: in 1800 the stewards begged their subscribers, and 'the University and City at large', to consider whether

after a commodious Room has been built and furnished at a great expence, and the Orchestra has been provided with a complete set of Instruments and Books; and after a Band of Instrumental Performers, of acknowledged Abilities in their Profession has been collected; they will suffer the Room and its Furniture to be rendered useless, and the Performers to be dispersed, by withdrawing their support from an Institution which has been established upwards of 50 years, and which provides so much rational and elegant Amusement at an Expence comparatively inconsiderable.[105]

Among aspects of the stewards' efforts stressed by Mee were their alertness to new talent and capacity to spot prospective stars: 'time after time they are to be found recognising the merits of singers and of players before the world at large had perceived them.' For example Mee mentions Crosdill, engaged at Holywell at the age of 18, and Miss Linley at 16, and suggests that 'the merits of Signora Sestini seem to have been recognised in Oxford ... before they were perceived in London'.[106] The fact that Lidl, and later Salomon, were brought to Oxford not long after their arrival in

---

[102] Ob, MS Mus. d. 32, title-page, verso.
[103] Mee, *Music Room*, 113. See ibid. 109–30 for an outline of the efforts to keep the concerts afloat.
[104] *JOJ*, 16 Apr. 1796.
[105] *JOJ*, 8 Febr. 1800; cf. Ob, Mus. 1 d. 64/1.   [106] Mee, *Music Room*, 27.

England is a tribute to the stewards' entrepreneurial acumen. No doubt the networking among musicians which certainly operated in the nineteenth century also obtained at the earlier period, and helped secure some prestigious bookings. The English fashion for child prodigies (represented by Mozart on his visit to London in the 1760s) was followed at Holywell most notably in the case of the 3-year-old Crotch, as well as Hummel at the age of 9, and Miss Poole at a Benefit in 1785, 'not eleven years of age'.[107] The stewards' appeals for support also elicited some impressive subscribers. In the 'LIST OF SUBSCRIBERS TO THE MUSIC ROOM, Oxford, From October 14, 1799, to October 14, 1800', the Chancellor ('HIS GRACE THE DUKE OF PORTLAND') and Vice-Chancellor (Reverend Michael Marlow of St John's) received top billing, whereafter the twenty-three colleges listed (ranging from All Souls to Worcester College) produced over 250 subscribers, including from Christ Church, the Revd the Dean and the Lord Bishop of Oxford; and a further thirty or so names represented subscribers from the City, among them Miss Lates, Miss Matthews, Mrs Parsons (of the Bank), and Sir Digby Mackworth.[108]

In that year, as—in spite of the difficulties—the stewards steered the Society safely through towards a period of 'tranquil prosperity',[109] a snapshot of the concerts known to have been on offer during one month of the Lent Term (March 1800) shows a variety of events and a not entirely conservative outlook on repertoire. For Monday, 3 March *Messiah* was put on, while the Grand Miscellaneous Concert following this on the Tuesday was to include the music to *Macbeth* attributed to Locke. The subscription concert planned for Monday, 10 March at the Music Room featured in the two Acts of the programme a Haydn 'Overture' (to open the second Act), and a generous-sized portion of Handel from *Athalia*: 'Gentle airs, melodious strains' (accompanied on the cello by Mr [Francis] Attwood), and the chorus 'Cheer her, O Baal with a soft serene'; the Air 'Tyrants would in impious throngs' and the chorus 'Tyrants, ye in vain conspire!' Mr Attwood then held a Benefit on Friday, 14 March; one item (a song) on the surviving programme has been crossed through and was probably deleted.[110] (The remaining items included a 'Concerto. *Grand Piano Forte*, Dr. Crotch', and a string Trio attributed to the Marquis of Blandford.) For the Monday

[107] Mee, *Music Room*, 27.   [108] Ob, Mus. 1 d. 64/1.   [109] Mee, *Music Room*, 146.
[110] Ob, Mus. 1 d. 64/1.

evening subscription concerts held on 24 and 31 March, the repertoire on offer encompassed Purcell (music from *King Arthur*) and Handel as well as symphonies by Pleyel and Haydn. There was then an Easter break until Monday, 28 April.[111]

The maintaining of concert life in eighteenth-century Oxford following the setting up of the Holywell Music Room gained its character and inspiration from a variety of local, repertorial, and performing elements. Although it so markedly served the University (as well as the city) it did not depend primarily on the university ceremonial which generated high points in the concert calendar such as Handel's and Haydn's visits. Its style related to the needs and tastes of the resident music-loving population throughout the year, as well as reflecting the individual abilities of the Professors of Music and their colleagues. The Holywell concerts also created their own circle of musicians; and if this was not an invariably serene community of artists, still perhaps as Mee suggests the disturbances that surfaced will have caused a 'buzz ... of excitement' that served in a perverse way to enhance the sense of communal interest.[112] And with all this, the concert culture survived in a sufficiently healthy state to allow several more decades of music-making at Holywell after 1800.

[111] Ob, Mus. 1 d. 64/1.   [112] Mee, *Music Room*, 90.

5

The Colleges, I

Organized musical societies within the individual colleges of the University were more a feature of the later nineteenth century;[1] in the eighteenth century informal musical gatherings regularly took place in the domestic setting provided by collegiate life. Members of the Holywell Band appeared in this context too:

> Then Crotch and two musicians more
> And amateurs near half a score
>   To play in concert meet . . .
>
> Crotch, as director of the band,
> On harpsichord with rapid hand
>   Sweeps the full chord . . .
>
> The next performer, Mr. Jonge . . .
>   Loud on the fiddle scrapes . . .
> After Parisian mode of speech
> French he professes us to teach,
>   Italian, as at Rome . . .
>
> So much for Jonge:- Inchbald the last
> (Of those I thus now sketch in haste)
>   With fingers large and fat

[1] Curthoys in *HUO* vi. 284 notes that as late as 1850 Queen's was unusual in having a music society. Compared with the documentation on the 19th cent., there is a relative paucity of detailed information on the colleges in the 18th cent.

On his bass viol strums away
And little more can think or say
  Beyond a sharp or flat.

Whilst pause the flute's and viol's sound
The tea and toast are handed round . . .[2]

But the most systematically recorded aspects of college musical life at this period are those concerning chapel music. Throughout the eighteenth century the choral foundations continued to devote part of their financial resources to the upkeep of their choirs and choir schools. At a time when cathedral choirs suffered a 'slow decline due to inflation, which the deans and chapters... made no attempt to remedy', the college chapels (together with the Chapel Royal) played a vital role in maintaining the choral tradition. Being 'somewhat more generously treated', by the end of this period these 'were the largest and most efficient choral foundations in the country'.[3] The sixteen boy choristers attached to Magdalen, New College, and Christ Church represented a provision at the higher end of the range among the English cathedrals and comparable establishments. Money was also regularly spent on college organs, organists, singing-clerks, chaplains, and chapel music. The production of music for chapel use was a flourishing industry in eighteenth-century Oxford.

During this period a sense of continuity was ensured partly by the long service given by a number of the organists to the college chapels. At New College, for example, Simon Child served as organist for thirty years from 1702, apparently dying in office. (He was probably the same Simon Child who was listed as a chorister at Christ Church in the late seventeenth century.[4]) Child's successor at New College, Richard Church, remained in post for forty-four years. The pattern in Oxford was to combine several organistships: Richard Church was also organist at Christ Church from 1741 until 1776, the year of his death, and at the city church of St Peter's-in-the-East. And as Philip Hayes's great-nephew recorded, communicat-

---

[2] Description of a day at Trinity College, quoted (from Ob, MS Top. Oxon c. 41; 1790–4) in Quiller-Couch, *Reminiscences of Oxford*, 195–7. On earlier college 'consorts of musick' see Ch. 4, p. 45 above. Further on music in the homelier setting of the college, see W. Hargreaves-Mawdsley, ed., *Woodforde at Oxford*, *passim*; Woodforde documents Oxford musical and college life generally, with much detail on the cost of various purchases and services including 'Hire of a Spinett & Harps[ichord]' (paid to Cross, 29 Oct. 1760).

[3] Johnstone and Fiske, *The Eighteenth Century*, 358–9.   [4] Shaw, *Succession of Organists*, 390.

ing to Bloxam the reminiscences of Hayes's nephews: 'Dr Philip Hayes
was organist of New College (his favourite College), also of St John's College, and S.M. Magdalen College; was elected Organist of Christ Church
and ousted by a man named Norris. Often went to London and purchased
pictures, and presented them to the College.'[5] Watkins Shaw deduces that
Hayes may have been acting organist of Christ Church 'shortly before the
appointment of Thomas Norris in 1776', although there are no official
records of this.[6] But the other appointments mentioned are documented:
at New College from 1776 to 1797 (the year he died); at Magdalen from 1777
(succeeding his father in this post, as also in the Heather Professorship);
and at St John's from 1790. In addition, and in accordance with tradition,
as Heather Professor Philip Hayes also served as organist of the University
Church, at St Mary's.

   The career of Thomas Norris shows a not unusual combination of
posts by Oxford standards: he succeeded Richard Church at Christ
Church from 1776 (having become organist of St John's College in 1766)
but additionally pursued his activities as a leading professional singer. As
Watkins Shaw notes, 'Bloxam . . . identifies him with the Thomas Norris
who was a clerk of Magdalen College, 1771–90'; an insight into one way in
which the various combined appointments might be feasible is given by
Bloxam's further observation that 'he only attended the College to draw
his pay, going there accompanied by his servant carrying his surplice and
hood'.[7] But Norris certainly sang frequently—and to much acclaim —
elsewhere, as well as apparently at Christ Church.[8] Even after his appointment as organist in 1776 he continued to be listed among the eight
'singingmen', signing for his quarterly pay in both categories.[9] Norris's
successor as organist at Christ Church from 1790, William Crotch,
followed Philip Hayes in 1797 as organist of St John's as well as Heather

   [5] Quoted in Shaw, *Succession of Organists*, 391.

   [6] Ibid.; Philip Hayes's name does not appear in the Christ Church Disbursements Book for 1776
(CCA, MS xii. c. 219). Perhaps the nephews' reference to the Christ Church appointment implies that
Hayes was an unsuccessful candidate, possibly after some awkwardness over the appointing procedure.

   [7] See Shaw, *Succession of Organists*, 212. Shaw (p. 213) sifts the somewhat conflicting evidence for
Norris's career and wonders if 'two men with the same name . . . have been confused'. The combining of
organistships with clerkships was not unprecedented; Richard Church was also lay clerk at Magdalen,
1732–6 (ibid. 211).

   [8] On Norris's singing career generally see ibid.; on his concert performances in Oxford see Ch. 4
above.

   [9] CCA, Disbursements Books for 1776 ff.

Professor and, like Hayes, with this latter post was concurrently organist of the University Church. Whatever the exact circumstances of these multiple appointments, the succession of organists in the college chapels was enabled to influence musical standards in Oxford from a strong base.

Considerable information is available concerning career patterns of the choristers and singing clerks, especially from Bloxam's documentation of Magdalen. Thomas Hayes, a clerk at Magdalen 1750–9, later graduated BA and MA, became Precentor of Durham Cathedral and also perpetual curate of St Oswald's, Durham from 1759.[10] Richard Wallond [Walond], son of the organist William Walond, and clerk at Magdalen 1775–6 as well as singingman at Christ Church, having matriculated at Christ Church in 1770 aged 16, later became Vicar Choral of Hereford Cathedral.[11] Many of the clerks and choirboys came, like the Hayeses and Walonds, from local professional musicians' families; a series of boys from one family might be appointed to the choir over a period of time. Musical careers or service to the church (or a combination of these) were the usual paths taken subsequently; university appointments might be held in conjunction with aspects of these, as with William Matthews (d. 1791), clerk at Magdalen 1759–91 (as well as at Christ Church), who was elected Yeoman Bedel in Law 1782 and Esquire Bedel in divinity.[12]

The archival documents record primarily the financial side of the chapel arrangements. The Christ Church Disbursements Books, in totalling the payments for personnel, refer to 'the Several Allowances for the Students [Fellows] Chaplains Choiristers Singingmen … of Christ Church in Oxford'; the total amount paid to personnel was typically about £1,000 per quarter. Of this, which also included various college servants, some £400 covered the monies for the Dean, subdean, and canons, while the musical appointments totalled a standard amount of £28.13s.4d. The eight chaplains were paid £1 each per quarter, the eight clerks received £2.10s.0d. each, and the allowance for the eight choristers was 1s.8d. each. (As eight choristers are regularly listed it would seem that the system of appointing eight probationers—thus making up the statutory sixteen— and moving them up into places in the choir probably obtained at this

[10] Bloxam, *Register*, ii. 94–5.
[11] Ibid. ii. 110. Cf. CCA, Disbursements Books 1775–6 (MS xii. c. 218–19).
[12] Bloxam, *Register*, ii. 103.

period, as it certainly did later.) The organist was paid by the college under two headings, as 'Informator Musicae' (drawing £1.10s.0d. for this function per quarter) as well as 'Organistae' (£2.10s.0d. per quarter). Clearly for the adult musicians the possibility of holding several posts simultaneously, and of earning extra money for singing on special occasions, and for teaching, and copying music, offered a necessary complement to the basic pay.

Besides the regular quarterly payments to musicians for singing and playing in the chapel services, incidental expenditure under the relevant heading in the college account books covered such items as repairs to the organ, music copying, extra singing, and teaching the choristers.[13] At Christ Church, for example, numerous entries under the category of 'Expences in the Church' refer to musical matters, among the miscellaneous items such as payment for candles, ringing the bells, and sweeping the cloisters. Regularly throughout this period the Disbursements Books record the annual settling of Mr Byfield's bill 'for the care of the Organ' (at £8.0s.0d.). 'Mr Byfield' featured in the New College accounts too. A series of alterations and additions was made to the New College organ during the course of the eighteenth century, by a succession of leading organ builders: first Renatus Harris, followed by his son John, then by John Harris's partner John Byfield and his son (John Byfield, junior), and finally by Samuel Green, who followed Byfield in 1776. These works included lowering the pitch (for which Renatus Harris was paid £35 in 1714), a new bellows (£10 in 1726), an 'Eccho and Swelling Organ' in 1735 (a new manual department for the instrument, at a cost of £50), 'a new stop and altering the organ' in 1716 (this last was evidently a relatively major overhaul, at £160) and, with Green's eventual rebuilding of the instrument, a radical reconstruction at a cost of £844.8s.0d.[14] The current organist would doubtless have been involved in these decisions. The most major of the works formed part of an extended programme of restoration work on the chapel towards the end of the century, and resulted in an organ of 'sumptuous appearance'.[15]

The financial records also give indication of the provision of musical

---

[13] As at New College, recorded in the Long Books (held in NCA).

[14] See Hale in Buxton and Williams, *New College, Oxford*, 272–3.

[15] Ibid. 275–6. On a tour of the college chapels in 1796 (including New College) see *The John Marsh Journals*, 630–1.

repertoire. At Christ Church the 'Expences in the Church' included various occasional payments for items of a general nature such as 'Binding Books for the Choir',[16] 'writing in the Choir Books'[17] and 'M^r. Vicary for writing Music'.[18] More specific references occur in connection with the purchase of printed music. In 1774 Mr Church received £8.2s.0d. for five books of the '3d & last Vol' of Boyce's *Cathedral Music*,[19] while in 1775 'Mr Cross's bill for ten Books of Dr Hayes's psalms' was recorded as paid, at £1.10s.0d.[20] Sometimes such payments were entered as a 'subscription' (to printed editions). Regular additions were thus acquired to the repertoire of the choir. The service books from New College and Christ Church surviving from this period show a mixture of 'ancients' and 'moderns', ranging from sixteenth-century composers (Byrd, Tallis) through seventeenth (Aldrich, Gibbons, Purcell) to eighteenth-century (Alcock, Crotch, Dupuis, William and Philip Hayes).[21]

To some extent the sacred music produced for college use at this time reflected specific local needs and customs. When Philip Hayes added a Benedictus to an early Te Deum setting by William Hayes, this may indicate that it was destined for New College, 'where the Benedictus replaced the Jubilate at Founder's Commemorations'.[22] However, William Hayes's 'Sixteen Psalms . . . Set to Music for the use of Magd: Coll: Chapel in Oxford' was issued 'for general use in 1773' and thereafter reprinted and anthologized: in 1810 *Jackson's Oxford Journal* advertised

DR. WILLIAM HAYES'S PSALMS.

THESE favourite and much-admired PSALMS, which are used in the University Church and the several Choirs in Oxford, are re-printed, as the plates were extinct . . .[23]

And William Hayes's anthems were widely disseminated and well represented in a collection 'Used in His Majesty's Chapel Royal': Heighes found that many of Hayes's anthems were, 'well before their eventual

---

[16] Cf. CCA, MS xii. c. 184 (1741), Term 4: 11s.   [17] Ibid., Term 2: £5.4s.0d.
[18] CCA, MS xii. c. 234, Term 1.   [19] CCA, MS xii. c. 217, Term 3.
[20] CCA, MS xii. c. 218, Term 4.
[21] The books may bear witness to their intended use: see e.g. from New College, Ob, MS Mus. d. 169 ('Chants/Basso/Fellows' copy'). Contemporary catalogues survive, such as Heathcote's at New College ('Church Music proper for New Coll: Chapel', 1794).
[22] Heighes, 'Hayes', i. 96.
[23] *JOJ*, 30 June 1810.

publication at the end of the century', already 'firmly established in the repertory'.[24]

Writing for the choirs at their disposal afforded the college organists the chance to experiment with aspects of structure and idiom, trying out new styles on the choir as well as fitting the music to the particular occasions and performers. As organist of Christ Church, William Crotch produced his *Ten Anthems* (Cambridge, 1798) 'respectfully Dedicated (by Permission) To the Reverend The Dean & Chapter of Christ Church and Composed for the Use of that Cathedral'. Besides displaying his sense of 'the best traditions of cathedral music', the collection shows Crotch venturing into new territory with the anthem *How dear are thy counsels*, which 'belongs to a new type of one-movement full anthem, predominantly lyrical in character'.[25] Its attractive melodic simplicity and the restrained decoration of its finely judged harmonic structure suggest a well-disciplined choir. And within the context of this style, the occasionally more declamatory setting of the text and the inclusion of expressive chromaticism make all the more memorable effect (see Ex. 5.1).

Although the status of the chapel musicians within the college hierarchy at this period was generally anomalous (the organist, for example, was not a Fellow of a college) their role could enable them to wield considerable influence through teaching, and directing the performances. The college organists were in a position to groom the choirboys for solo performance; at a time when the selection of the choristers was not as systematic as later, Philip Hayes at New College personally picked his young singers. Prior to this, the Place Book of Warden Purnell (begun in 1759, and covering a variety of college appointments over some twenty years)[26] shows a system of requests and recommendations: when Walond asked for a place for his son it was noted that 'the man had many children, but there is added at the end of the note "a very bad boy"'. The Keeper of the Coffee House at the corner of the Turl Street asked on behalf of a nephew,

[24] Heighes, 'Hayes', i. 98. See ibid. i. 99 for a table of anthems by Philip and William Hayes.

[25] Johnstone and Fiske, *The Eighteenth Century*, 376. The subscribers to Crotch's publication included academic and clerical dignitaries, among them Revd Heathcote, Revd Osborne Wight, and Revd the Warden, and Fellows of New College (nine copies altogether); Sir Digby Mackworth, Bart; numerous organists and musical societies; Uvedale Price of Foxley, Herefordshire; Dr Burney, his friend Thomas Twining of Colchester, and the cathedral organist William Jackson of Exeter; and several ladies.

[26] NCA, 976: quoted in Edmunds, *New College Brats*, 32.

Ex. 5.1. William Crotch, anthem, *How dear are thy counsels*, from *Ten Anthems*, 1798, pp. 39–41, bars 16–36

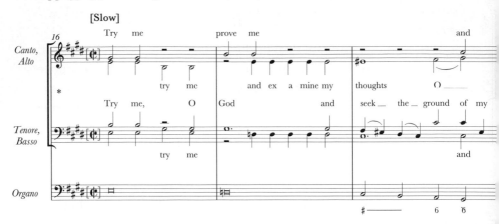

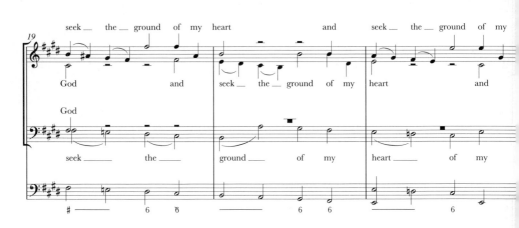

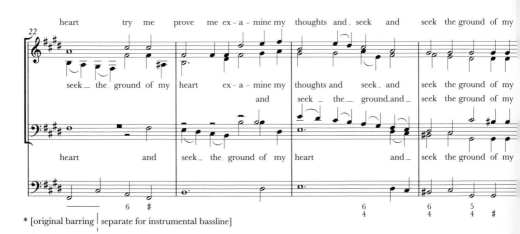

* [original barring | separate for instrumental bassline]

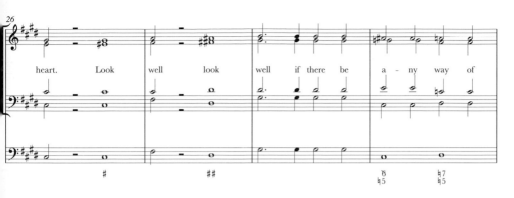

heart. Look well well look well if there be a – ny way of

wick-ed-ness a – ny way of wick-ed-ness in me: and lead me in the

loud

loud

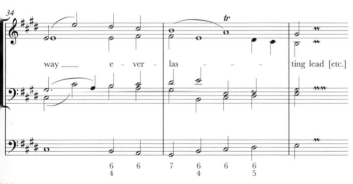

way ____ e – ver – las – – – ting lead [etc.]

tr

[♯♯ signifies ✕ (double sharp)]

described as well behaved, with a 'pretty voice'. It was only in 1769 that more specific suitability was mentioned: the Warden declared himself amenable to the request from Mr Brewer for a place for a boy from Wantage, 'provided it can be well certified to me he is likely to be useful in the Choir—and no future promises to be made without this condition'.[27]

The advent of Philip Hayes brings explicit reference to the holding of voice trials for the choir. George Valentine Cox—later Master of New College School (1807–57)—recalled being taken to Hayes's house 'in my very early days *to have my voice tried*; he had been for many years remarkable for his state of obesity, and I have not forgotten the awe I felt at the huge *projection* over the keys of his harpsichord, contrasted with his delicate, small hands, and accompanied with a soft, velvety voice'.[28] (Cox became one of Hayes's solo 'stars', singing for him in the Holywell concerts.) A further glimpse of the experience of life as a choirboy at this period is provided by the piece of paper 'stuffed in a statue in the chapel by a chorister the year before Hayes's death', and quoted by Hale and Edmunds:[29]

[Apparently written during Evensong] Yeates just gone out of chapel, making as if he was ill, to go to Botleigh with Miss Watson. Mr. Prickett reads prayers. Mr. Lardner is now reading the second lesson . . . Slatter shams a bad eye because he did not know the English of the theme and could not do it. A whole holiday yesterday being St. Mark. Only the Subwarden of the Seniors at Prayers.

Hayes was instrumental in improving the accommodation for practices in the college, succeeding in taking over the chaplains' common room, which was then refitted 'for the use of the Organist, in order that he may therein instruct the Choristers in the Art of Singing'.[30]

Among the older singers in the college choirs, some fine voices were heard during the eighteenth century—indeed some of the finest in the country. At Christ Church in the first half of the century, when the Goodsons (both father and son) held the post of organist and choirmaster (Richard Goodson, senior from 1692 to 1718, and Richard Goodson, junior from 1718 to 1741), the leading countertenor Walter Powell is listed among the singingmen at the Cathedral throughout the period from 1714

[27] NCA, 976: quoted in Edmunds, *New College Brats*, 32.
[28] Cox, *Recollections*, 148 (quoted by Hale in Buxton and Williams, *New College, Oxford*, 274).
[29] Hale, ibid. 275; Edmunds, *New College Brats*, 34.
[30] Cf. Hale, in Buxton and Williams, *New College, Oxford*, 273.

to 1741.[31] An obituary printed in the *Gentleman's Magazine* in 1744 described
Powell's as the best voice in England, and included the lines 'written *extempore* by an Oxford scholar, on hearing of his death':

> Is Powell dead?—Then all the earth
> Prepare to meet its fate;
> To sing the everlasting birth;
> The choir of heav'n's compleat.[32]

During the second half of the century, together with Thomas Norris,
William Matthews is listed as a singingman at Christ Church. Such singers
as these were sought after as soloists for performances at venues outside
Oxford; in addition, the choir as a whole might be booked to sing, as with
the New College choir under Philip Hayes at the Handel Commemoration in 1787.[33]

In some ways the early eighteenth century represented a 'golden age' in
the choral tradition, especially at Christ Church where 'Aldrich's management of the cathedral choir was excellent'.[34] The legacy of Aldrich's training remained visible (or audible) through the succeeding decades. William
Hayes, writing in his *Remarks on Mr. Avison's Essay on Musical Expression* (1753)
of the efficacy of Aldrich's methods, cited the case of Estwick as a
'remarkable Instance of the Effect of such an Education: He was not only
an excellent and zealous Performer in the Choral-Duty, until extreme
Old-Age rendered him incapable of it, but a remarkable fine Reader
also'.[35] Estwick was appointed as a chaplain of Christ Church in 1678,
serving alongside Edward Lowe, Richard Goodson, and Henry Aldrich.
He remained on the list of chaplains until 1711 and continued to sign in
person for the quarterly payments of £1.0s.0d. until 1700, thus for a considerable period of time after his appointment as a minor canon of St
Paul's in 1691.[36] The minor canons in the eighteenth century 'were
expected to say and sing the daily offices in the chapel and choir, to celebrate Holy Communion, and to preach as required'.[37] Perhaps partly

---

[31] See CCA, Disbursements Books, *passim*.
[32] Quoted in Lysons, *Three Choirs*, 17–18.   [33] Cf. Heighes, 'Hayes', i. 65.
[34] *DNB*, 'Estwick', 877.   [35] Quoted ibid.   [36] CCA, Disbursements Books, *passim*.
[37] W. R. Matthews, ed., *A History of St Paul's Cathedral and the Men associated with it* (London, 1957), 240.

thanks to the excellence of his early training, Estwick continued to fulfil his choral duties at St Paul's until 'near the time of his decease'.[38]

The Christ Church Library also benefited from Aldrich's efforts; as T. B. Strong observed, although his involvement in music-making would account for some of the works owned by Aldrich, 'it is also plain that he was a real student of music, and collected not only for purposes of performance but also as a connoisseur'.[39] In bequeathing his musical collection to Christ Church, Aldrich specified:

I make it my request to the Dean and Chapter of the said Church that they will be pleased to take care of my Prints and books of Musick that they may not be exposed to common usage nor to any man without their leave and appoint-ment, because they are things of value in themselves and to be found in very few Libraries.[40]

Richard Goodson, senior, Aldrich's colleague at Christ Church, made the only substantial addition to the collection. And, like Aldrich, he composed liturgical music which survives in Christ Church Library.

Surveying the aftermath of the Aldrich era, Strong suggested that 'the interest in music prevailing in England shortly after the Restoration lasted throughout the eighteenth century . . . then passed away altogether, and for a long period of years music was regarded in high academic circles as an eccentric if not a mischievous pursuit'.[41] Eventually, indeed in Strong's own time and the period leading up to it, the colleges as well as the Univer-sity participated in a revival of music's importance, and a regeneration of musical activity and study.

[38] *DNB*, 'Estwick' (going on to quote Hawkins's vivid description of the almost 90-year-old Estwick bending beneath the weight of years but 'preserving his faculties, and even his voice, which was a deep bass, till the last').

[39] Preface to Arkwright, *Catalogue of Music in the Library of Christ Church*, p. iv.

[40] Ibid. pp. iv–v. Further on the Christ Church holdings see Wainwright, *Musical Patronage*.

[41] Ibid. p. v.

6

Personalities: The Goodsons, William and Philip Hayes, Crotch, and Malchair

In the line of holders of the Heather Chair of Music during the eighteenth century, the Goodsons (father and son) have only a shadowy effect compared with what is known of their successors in the post, William and Philip Hayes, and William Crotch. Their musical activity as composers seems to have been closely bound up with university ceremonial.[1] Again, a lack of clarity exists over the attribution of works to the older and younger Goodsons. Neither appears to have been widely known as either composer or performer outside Oxford.[2] In Oxford they contributed as organists to college chapel music.[3] And in an interesting parallel to the early performance history of Purcell's *Dido and Aeneas*, Goodson senior provided music for the production of a dramatic version of the Orpheus legend at an Oxfordshire school, in Besselsleigh, in 1697.[4]

William and Philip Hayes, between them holding office as Professor for a total of over fifty-five years, continued the traditional association of the Heather Professorship with an involvement in composing: both contrib-

---

[1] See Ch. 2 above.
[2] Cf. *NG2* x. 148–9, 'Richard Goodson' (i), (ii).
[3] For further discussion of their work at Christ Church, see Ch. 5 above.
[4] See Zaslaw, 'An English "Orpheus" ', *MT* 118 (1977).

uted, in works that were known and performed beyond as well as within Oxford, to the development of eighteenth-century English musical idiom in a variety of genres. But they were active on many other fronts musically, again both on the local Oxford scene and in the wider musical world. William Hayes's contribution to Oxford music-making was characterized particularly by his championship of Handel; he played a very significant part in the cultivation of Handel's music in the provinces, as Heighes remarks:

for a period of about forty years between the mid-1730s and early 1770s, William Hayes was probably the single most active conductor of Handel's oratorios and other major choral works outside London, and was thus responsible for the widespread dissemination of some of Handel's greatest music.[5]

Indeed, William Hayes's first documented connection with Oxford seems to have involved a Handelian occasion, when he travelled to the city in 1733 to hear Handel's performances at the Oxford Act. The impressions left by this experience may have included not only the sound of Handel's vocal music but also the composer's brilliant organ-playing during his oratorios. As Burney later recorded,

It was in the summer of 1733, that [Handel] went to the university of Oxford, on occasion of a public act . . . at this solemnity he had the Oratorio of *Athalia* performed in the public theatre, where he opened the organ in such a manner as astonished every hearer. The late Mr. Michael Christian Festing, and Dr. Arne, who were present, both assured me, that neither themselves, nor any one else of their acquaintance, had ever before heard such extempore, or such premeditated playing, on that or any other instrument.[6]

These recollections followed on, in Burney's account, from a discussion of Handel's organ concertos in terms of their novelty: it was, he noted, during 'these early performances of Oratorios' (in 1732–3) that Handel 'first gratified the public by the performance of CONCERTOS ON THE ORGAN, a species of Music wholly of his own invention'.[7] An Oxford tradition along these lines was perpetuated by William and Philip Hayes in their practice of performing Handel's organ concertos during oratorios.[8] (William

---

[5] Heighes, 'Hayes', i. 28.

[6] Burney, *Handel*, 23; although Burney's (and Hawkins's) claim is not now supported by any 'multi-movement organ concerto that we can date as early as 1733' (Burrows, *Cambridge Companion to Handel*, 203), this does not necessarily invalidate it.   [7] Ibid.   [8] Heighes, 'Hayes', i. 174–6.

Hayes was himself by the time he came to Oxford an experienced organist with a considerable understanding of the instrument.) After taking up the privileges of the university in 1735, shortly after his appointment as organist at Magdalen College, William Hayes graduated B.Mus. (8 July 1735).[9] Subsequent to his election to the Heather Professorship in January 1741, he 'proceeded D.Mus. on 14 April 1749, following the official opening of the Radcliffe Camera'.[10] This latter occasion, too, was of special Handelian significance. It was during this event that William Hayes conducted the *Messiah* in its first performance in the provinces, securing its leading place in Oxford's choral tradition thereafter.[11] Among Hayes's own choral compositions was his *Ode to the Memory of Mr. Handel* (to words by William Collins, 1759) which was performed in various venues outside Oxford during the 1760s and was clearly 'popular with the public'.[12]

A regular setting for the public performance of Hayes's works from 1748 onwards was provided by the Holywell Music Room. The early years of Hayes's tenure of the Professorship were characterized by his enthusiastic support of the project to establish the new Music Room, and his account of the process leading up to its opening forms a vivid and valuable source of information on its history.[13] The autograph manuscript and printed sources of Hayes's compositions contain many references to the Holywell Music Room and other local performing contexts.[14] These include instrumental (chamber and orchestral) pieces with typically Handelian and Corellian connotations, such as the concerto for organ and strings in D major (score dated 5 March 1755, and inscribed 'Music Room Feb 15 1774') and the trio sonata in E minor, marked in the composer's hand as performed in 'the Music Room Feb. 6 1775'.[15] And Hayes's *Supplement To the Catches, Glees, and Canons . . .* (1765) was 'dedicated . . . to the

[9] On the privileges see *HUO* v. 206 and *EO* 338 ('Privileged Persons'). This status (granted to non-students) was frequently sought by musicians.

[10] Shaw, *Succession of Organists*, 383. This authoritative account of Hayes's career is supplemented by Shaw, 'Oxford University Chair'.

[11] Further on the 1749 occasion see Ch. 2 above. Heighes, 'Hayes', ii. 8, n. 83 observes that the word-book for the Oxford *Messiah* indicates Hayes's changes at a few points. See also Donald Burrows, ed., *Messiah*, Source G, pp. 246–50 (noted in Heighes, 'Hayes', i. 23–7, esp. n. 81). Further on W. Hayes's copy of *Messiah* (the 'Goldschmidt' MS) see Burrows and Shaw, 'Handel's "Messiah": Supplementary Notes on Sources', *ML* 96 (1995), 359.

[12] Trowles, 'Musical Ode', i. 68.

[13] Used by, among others, Mee (*Music Room*, 3–9; 39). See also Ch. 4 above.

[14] Documented in Heighes, 'Hayes', iii. 7–88, *passim*.

[15] Ob, MS Mus. d. 82, fos. 15–23^v; Ob, MS Mus. c. 21, fos. 80–84^v.

worthy members of the Catch-Club, or Phil-harmonic Society, at the King's-Head Tavern in Oxford, for whose Amusement they were intended, by their very affectionate Friend, W. H.'. In a more solemn context, William Hayes's *Sixteen Psalms Selected from the Revd. Mr. Merrick's new Version* (1773) were described on the title page as 'for the use of Magd: Coll: Chapel in Oxford, and ... humbly Inscribed to the Revd. the President and Fellows of that Society'.[16]

Hayes's publications included writings on music conceived in response to (indeed provoked by) the work of others, and published anonymously.[17] His *Remarks on Mr. Avison's Essay on Musical Expression* (1753), which constitutes an extensive review of Avison, also shows the breadth of his own knowledge. Apart from considering Avison's aesthetic and critical propositions, Hayes assesses the merit of Avison's compositions, finding, in professorial manner, many technical solecisms therein, and even correcting his harmony. The discussion further ranges over the present state of church music, a matter of concern to Hayes in which he declares himself partly in agreement with Avison. Here some of the most practical points in the *Remarks* occur. Hayes has very precise views on the 'chusing of Organists', wishing that those responsible would 'give the Preference to such as come recommended on account of their Sobriety and discreet Behaviour; provided the Candidates be nearly equal in point of Abilities'. And he justifies deftly his own priorities in such an appointment: 'Were I concerned in the Election of an Organist, I should certainly vote for the Man who seemed best to understand his Business; with a moderate Share of *Execution*, preferable to one with *great Execution*, and *moderate Understanding*'.[18] Hayes's shrewd musicianship earned him a reputation of some importance beyond Oxford through his conductorship, for example at the Three Choirs Festival.[19]

[16] As Heighes notes ('Hayes', iii. 7), Merrick was a Fellow of Trinity College, Oxford. Further on Hayes's involvement with the genre of catch, see Robinson and Hall, eds., *The Aldrich Book of Catches* (Introduction, pp. 13–14).

[17] See Deutsch, 'Ink-Pot and Squirt-Gun', *MT* 93 (1952); and Heighes, 'Hayes', ii. 37–9.

[18] *Remarks*, 76–7. Later in this part of the discussion comes the description of Aldrich's methods at Christ Church (see Ch. 5 above).

[19] William Hayes's identification with Handel performances is documented as far afield as Chester, where he conducted 'Three of Mr. HANDEL's most celebrated "ORATORIOS"' (*Messiah*, *Samson*, and *Judas Maccabaeus*) at the three-day festival in the Cathedral in 1772, with Norris, Price, Matthews, and others associated with his Oxford performances; see Bridge, *A Short Sketch of the Chester Festivals*, [3].

Philip Hayes, too, besides making a varied and substantial contribution on the local scene, pursued his musical career outside Oxford in various respects. He was admitted as a 'Gentleman of the Chapel Royal' in 1767 and was later mentioned as the possible successor to John Stanley as Master of the King's Musick.[20] For many years he conducted the performances at the annual Festival of the Sons of the Clergy (held in St Paul's Cathedral). As a composer he showed a keen awareness of new currents in style and medium; his six keyboard concertos 'for Organ, Harpsichord or Forte-Piano' of 1769 may have been the first in Britain to specify the piano in their title (thus forestalling J. C. Bach, regarded as the pioneer in this field).[21] Among their up-to-date features is the use of crescendo during solo passages in No. 2, which belongs in the three of the set designed as organ concertos: the swell-box was then a rarity in the English organ and Hayes was 'among the first to count on one'.[22] He also composed in the new genre of accompanied sonata popular in England from around 1760: his sonatas of Op. 2 have been described as 'well written, often attractive and certainly among the leading English examples of the genre'.[23] In general, Hayes's style is influenced less by his father's idol, Handel, and more by the current *galant* trends: his writing, in both his vocal and instrumental works, is more akin to that of his own contemporary, Haydn.

Philip Hayes commented in his 'Life of W. Hayes' on his father's 'sweetness of Temper';[24] he himself was renowned for his irascibility, and a fund of anecdotes became attached to his reputation, often featuring his enormous girth (the nickname 'Fill-chaise' and the story of its origins recur throughout the sources). He became notoriously involved in quarrels with his Oxford colleagues, but his potentially disruptive effect on Oxford's musical life was amply counterbalanced by his efforts on behalf of music in the colleges, the Music Room, the Music School, and other fund-raising projects. He was also involved with charitable events for the New Musical Fund (founded in 1786), a parallel organization to the Society of Musicians but geared more towards provincial members of the profession. Hayes collaborated with Dr Edward Miller, one of the founders, in London concerts.[25] For both William and Philip Hayes, their tenure of the

---

[20] Heighes, 'Hayes', i. 71.
[21] See Johnstone and Fiske, *The Eighteenth Century*, 224–5.   [22] Ibid. 225.   [23] Ibid. 340.
[24] Preface to W. Hayes, *Cathedral Music* (1795).
[25] On Hayes's conducting for charitable purposes see Heighes, 'Hayes', i. 65–8; on the New Musical

Heather Professorship offered a favourable environment for the development of their careers: as Philip Hayes commented of his father, in respect of his earlier appointments as organist, 'his genius was not designed for so narrow a sphere: Oxford was the place . . . he wished to settle in'.[26] In taking up the opportunities offered by Oxford, both Hayeses contributed greatly to its musical growth.

Philip Hayes's successor as Heather Professor, William Crotch, was probably the only Oxford professor ever to have made his first public appearance in the city as 'a Child in a Frock on his Mother's Knee', performing 'on the organ in the Music Room, to the great astonishment of a large Audience': Crotch was then aged 3.[27] Mrs Crotch has been criticized for her exploitation of her son's infant talents, but her instincts were correct, and the exceptional performing feats exhibited by 'Master Crotch, the self-taught musical child' on his concert tours and in his audience with the King at Buckingham House were the prelude to a sustained degree of success and influence in his adult career as a musician.[28] At the age of 15— having served an apprenticeship to the Professor of Music at Cambridge, John Randall—Crotch succeeded Thomas Norris as organist of Christ Church. He was elected to the Heather Professorship at the age of 21.

The friendship with Malchair (leader of the Holywell Band) was crucial for Crotch's intellectual and artistic development, as well as bringing elements of warmth and support into the last decades of Malchair's life. Although evidence of this close friendship (and of their shared interests) is documented only for the later period, from the 1790s onwards, Crotch's earlier association with Oxford would have provided him with plentiful opportunities to encounter Malchair, especially in the Holywell Music Room context. His first appearances in Oxford, on tour as a child prodigy in 1778–9, offered the occasion to meet Malchair as leader of the band, as well as the Heather Professor. After a visit to Oxford in 1783, when Crotch

Fund see Ehrlich, *Music Profession*, 29. Further on Hayes's conducting outside Oxford see Fawcett, *Music in Eighteenth-Century Norwich and Norfolk*, 15; as Fawcett notes, Philip Hayes's connection with the Norwich organist Edward Beckwith ('a convinced Handelian') extended to Beckwith's son John. John Beckwith served under William Hayes at Magdalen College from 1775, and later worked for Philip Hayes at New College (cf. Shaw, *Succession of Organists*, 204–5).   [26] Preface to W. Hayes, *Cathedral Music*.

[27] Ob, MS Top. Oxon d. 247, p. 147. As Rennert (*Crotch*, 18) points out, Crotch met the Professor of Music (Philip Hayes) in Oxford on this occasion, who doubtless had no inkling that he was talking to his successor.

[28] For details of his early career as a prodigy see ibid. 15–17 ff.

met his future patron, the Reverend Alexander Schomberg (tutor at Magdalen College), Crotch returned in 1788 to reside in Oxford, lodging with the singer William Matthews (a close associate of Malchair). At this point he became increasingly involved in the Oxford musical scene, including regular engagements as soloist at the Holywell Music Room.

Besides collaborating with the progressively blind Malchair during the 1790s on various musical projects ('he brought a music book under his arm for me to play to him, and sometimes brought a new tune for me to write down, as his eyes became too dim to see even his large notes any longer'[29]) Crotch discussed artistic matters with his friend. He succeeded Malchair as President of the Oxford association of artists, the 'Great School of Art'. The discussions and demonstrations of matters relating to folk music and to aesthetics, in particular, which Crotch and Malchair cultivated, will have shaped Crotch's outlook and (as he acknowledged) influenced his published writings.[30]

Of all the eighteenth-century Oxford professors, Crotch was the most 'highly influential as a lecturer and writer on musical subjects';[31] and 'the extraordinary range and depth of Crotch's mental activity can be judged from his voluminous writings on many subjects besides music'.[32] During his Oxford tenure of the post (before he left the city, giving up his Oxford organistships, in 1806–7) Crotch's career reflected the versatility characteristic of the eighteenth-century professors: lecturing, writing, editing and arranging, collecting musical 'specimens', composing, performing, directing the Musical Society concerts and university ceremonial music as well as continuing the tradition of combining the Heather Professorship with the various organistships.

In his intellectual activity, as well as developing the historical study of music generally—in which he was a pioneer within the university context—Crotch cultivated a particularly strong interest in early music: Temperley credits him with being 'an important force in the revival of early English church music'.[33] Following his publication of psalm tunes together with Tallis's Litany and *Veni creator* in 1803, 'several churches and colleges at Oxford began to revive these tunes and some of the Eliza-

---

[29] Ob, MS Mus. d. 32, p. 21.

[30] On their artistic endeavours, see Rennert, *Crotch*, 93–6; and Harrison, *Malchair*. On their friendship and its musical aspects cf. particularly Wollenberg, 'Malchair', ibid. 33–43.

[31] *NG2* vi. 730, 'William Crotch'.   [32] Ibid. 730–1.   [33] Ibid. 730.

bethan and Jacobean cathedral music' (well before 'the more general revival' of the 1830s).[34] He concerned himself in close study of such diverse matters as the keyboard music of J. S. Bach and early English musical theory; his annotations to Bach's '48' and to Morley's *Plaine and Easie Introduction* survive ('Fie Mr Morley, do not be so cross!').[35] As a composer Crotch developed a distinctive, learned, and fastidious style encompassing not only the influence of 'ancient' music (especially that of Handel) but also contemporary modes of expression, and some original and experimental effects.[36]

Of the eighteenth-century musicians appointed to the Heather Professorship, Crotch was the best known outside Oxford (he was invited to be first Principal of the Royal Academy of Music, founded in 1822) and the most influential on British musical thought. As well as fulfilling the multiple functions traditionally associated with the Oxford Chair, as a specialist scholar he took the study of music to a new level. His active involvement in musical education beyond as well as within Oxford earned him the respect, for his scholarship and his musicality, of his pupils and contemporaries: 'Sterndale Bennett, arguably Crotch's most successful pupil, so admired his master's erudition that, when Mendelssohn was planning to visit England to do research on Handel, Bennett referred him to Crotch, saying that he was the only man in the country who truly knew and understood Handel's music.'[37] Crotch's connection with Oxford lasted through sixty-eight years; he held the Heather Professorship for fifty of those years, linking the nineteenth century, with its new focus on musical education, to the eighteenth with its dedication to 'ancient music'.

[34] *NG2* vi. 730, 'William Crotch'.

[35] Crotch's copy of Morley (inscribed 'kind gift of the Hon[ora]ble B. Bertie') is in University of Birmingham, Music Special Collections, MT6 (1771 edn.).

[36] On his contribution to various genres see Chs. 5 and 8.

[37] Rennert, *Crotch*, 89. Caldwell, *OHEM* ii. 110–11, provides an appreciative assessment of Crotch.

PART II

The Nineteenth Century

7

Music in an
Academic Context, II

For music in Oxford, as for many other spheres of activity, the period from 1800 to 1914 was very much an age of documentation.[1] In the university context, the official records of the time contain some quite intense arguments relating to music that emerged during the processes of reform.[2] Evidently these matters aroused considerable feeling among participants and observers. As one (himself clearly much agitated) writer put it: 'Music is now the great question that agitates the whole nation.'[3] This was probably to some extent true. Many major changes, upheavals and experiments were taking place in the musical world of later nineteenth-century Britain.[4]

The reports of the University's Hebdomadal Council, and later (from 1911) those of the Music Board, afford numerous insights into the workings of university committees and their business during this period.[5] The aca-

[1] See e.g. Buck, Mee, and Woods, *Ten Years*, chronicling the activities of the Oxford University Musical Union, and the sequel *Ten More Years* (ed. Kemp and Mee). But this urge to document musical life can be traced back at least as far as Jung in 1808.

[2] Outlined below, and in Wollenberg, 'Music in Nineteenth-Century Oxford' (1999), and *HUO* vii (*Nineteenth-Century Oxford*, pt. 2), ch. 18 ('Music').

[3] Maurice, *What shall we do with Music?*, 23. Peter Maurice, DD, 'Chaplain of New and All Souls' Colleges in Oxford', was remembered by Bishop Mitchinson of Pembroke as 'a Militant Evangelical, and had taken his DD. Degree that he might stand on the same level in controversy with Dr Pusey' (Mitchinson, 'Oxford Memories' (unpublished memoirs), PCA, MS 60/15/83, p. 19).

[4] See especially Ehrlich, *Music Profession*; and Temperley, *The Romantic Age*.

[5] Held in the UA. There is much documentation on the college side also, including, for instance,

demic status of music in Oxford naturally takes on a special interest for the historian at the point where the structure of the music degrees became a matter of pressing concern to members of the University. Although 1862 has usually been pinpointed as the crucial year of change,[6] in fact this was not the starting-point, but came some years after the launch of the long and complicated process towards the new style of degree.

Writing shortly after graduating as B.Mus. in 1889, Abdy Williams drew a striking contrast between musical degrees formerly and currently: 'At one time, to be a Mus. Bac. or Mus. Doc. meant little . . . now it means that the holder has passed several very severe examinations.'[7] While his assessment of the B.Mus. and D.Mus. degrees in former times was slanted for the purpose of his argument, it is nevertheless true that standards had not been noticeably high.[8] Whereas at the turn of the century the degrees were still awarded solely on the basis of an exercise in composition submitted by the candidate for the Professor's approval, the requirements by the end of the nineteenth century present quite a different impression, including not only the traditional (and still important) exercises in composition, but also a series of written papers together with a viva voce, covering harmony and counterpoint, history of music, and a critical knowledge of prescribed scores. (The set works for 1873 were: Beethoven's 'Pastoral' Symphony, Weber's overture to *Der Freischütz*, Handel's *Alexander's Feast*, and Mendelssohn's *St Paul*.) What follows here is an outline of the stages in the development of musical studies at Oxford which led through the changes of the nineteenth century to the establishment of the Music Board in the early twentieth century.

A revealing insight into the possible social connotations of the old B.Mus. comes in the anecdote quoted by Fellowes: 'Gaisford, Dean of Christ Church, told Ouseley, when he proposed to take the Mus. Bac. degree, that it was unbecoming for a man in his position to present himself for examination in music in the University'.[9] Notwithstanding this difficulty, he duly took the degree: the minutes of the Hebdomadal Board

financial and Governing Body records touching on musical matters; Choir Committee minutes; and proceedings of college musical societies. And it was at this time that a scholarly interest in chronicling the history of the University and colleges was increasingly manifesting itself, as in the work of Bloxam, at Magdalen, or the publications of the Oxford Historical Society.

[6] As for example by Westrup in *NG* xiv. 38 ('Until 1862, when a regular examination was instituted . . .') and Wollenberg in 'Music in 18th-Century Oxford', *PRMA* 108 (1981–2), 92.

[7] *Degrees in Music*, 42.   [8] See Ch. 2, p. 15 above.   [9] Fellowes, *English Cathedral Music*, 214.

(11 June 1849) record that leave was given to Sir Frederick Gore Ouseley, Bart., MA of Ch. Ch., to proceed to the B.Mus. 'in the regular way'.[10] (The degree was conferred on 24 January 1850.) It is to Ouseley that the subsequent impetus for the reform of the music degrees is generally, and rightly, attributed.[11] The year 1856 seems to have marked the point when Ouseley (by then Professor of Music) began to agitate for changes of the statutes relating to his subject.[12]

While the significance of 1862 has been taken in some sources to be that it saw the introduction of Ouseley's initial scheme, under which candidates must 'pass an examination held by the Professor of Music, the Choragus, and some other graduate, and . . . compose a piece of music in four parts with organ and string accompaniment [*recte*: of four parts at least, with organ accompaniment; or if stringed instruments, not more than five], which was to be performed in public. A Bachelor wishing to proceed to the Doctorate had to pass an examination and compose a piece in eight vocal parts with full orchestra', the new examination can be traced back further.[13] The statutory exercise and its performance remained a constant feature; the novel elements here were the written examination and— importantly—the introduction of a panel of examiners, replacing the Professor's previous role as sole adjudicator. The team of three, including the Professor and Choragus, was standard, with some variations, for the remainder of the period.[14]

[10] HCM, vol. 6, p. 169. Reference to the 'regular way' seems to have no specific implications here. Candidates were sometimes given dispensation to have their exercises performed elsewhere than in the Music School (see e.g. HCM, vol. 5, p. 212: 'Leave was given for Mr. Elvey Mus. Bac. [George Job Elvey] to apply to Convocation for a dispensation to enable him to have his [D.Mus.] Exercise . . . performed in the Music Room instead of in the Music School': 18 May 1840. (The performance took place there on 27 June 1840; see Ob, MS Mus. Sch. Ex. d. 45). Ouseley's B.Mus. exercise is inscribed 'performed in New Coll. Hall in June 1849' (MS Mus. Sch. Ex. c. 40). When Ouseley's D.Mus. exercise, the oratorio *The Martyrdom of St. Polycarp*, was performed in 1854 with a band including friends of the composer (among them Miss Dolby, Mr Weiss, W. H. Cummings, and John Hampton), Dean Gaisford attended at the Sheldonian: see Joyce, *Life of Ouseley*, 85.

[11] Abdy Williams (*Degrees in Music*, 42) mentions in addition that the Oxford reforms were inspired by the ideas of Sir Robert Stewart at Dublin. On the views of Ouseley's predecessor, see Ch. 8 below, and Wollenberg, 'Bishop and Music', *MT* 127 (1986), 609–10.

[12] See HCM, vol. 7, p. 101 (21 Jan. 1856) *et seq.* Hadow later indicated the decisive date of change: 'The system of granting musical degrees on examination dates from 1856, when it was established by the University at the proposal of Sir Frederick Ouseley. Before that time . . . candidates . . . were not required to pass any examination, musical or otherwise' (HCP 1898, p. 42).

[13] Abdy Williams, *Degrees in Music*, 41; cf. *OU Calendar*, 1858 ff. (on degrees and exercises), and *JOJ*, 9 Feb. 1856 on changes of statute for Music.

[14] The post of Choragus (originally part of Heather's foundation) was re-established in 1848. By

While it was certainly with this new scheme that the decisive move towards a music degree with greater academic implications was made, there were many stages to be negotiated, not always entirely smoothly, before the academic standing of the subject was satisfactorily established within the University. Rather than simply viewing 1856 as a dramatic turning-point (which in a sense it was) it is necessary to take a longer view of the period of Ouseley's reforms, from 1856 to 1889, in order to see their repercussions in the later nineteenth- and early twentieth-century developments. During that period certain trends are clearly in evidence: first, a desire to increase the content of the B.Mus. examination, and secondly, a definite though irregular rise in the numbers of candidates. Throughout the second half of the nineteenth century the Professors of Music and their associates, and the various university committees, were frequently occupied in discussing possible improvements to the system of examining for the B.Mus. Periodically there were reports of special committees, leading to the promulgation of new statutes; in all there was a progressive redesigning and refining of the syllabus, with each change tending to generate the need for further change.[15]

What is perhaps most striking is the extent to which these changes were actually realized, rather than remaining plans on paper. Evidently the arguments put by Ouseley and his colleagues, and their successors, were often persuasive, their efforts thorough and dedicated, and the results sufficiently convincing to promote the acceptance of further suggestions for steps along the road to reform. (The process must have seemed to some Oxford observers unduly restless: Warden Sewell of New College noted Ouseley's wish to alter the Music Statutes, 'although it is not very long since the Statute was amended'.)[16] It is also possible that the wider climate acted favourably in the interests of the musical reforms. Other university disciplines such as medicine were moving in similar directions, while within the musical world an increased emphasis on education and educational standards was becoming noticeable: the Prince of Wales 'at a

about 1900 Hadow (G.A. Oxon b. 41 (7): 'FACULTY OF ARTS: Degrees in Music') described the panel of examiners as including the Professor of Music *ex officio* or (as his delegate) the Choragus, with two others nominated by the Vice-Chancellor and Proctors.

[15] See *HUO*, vi and vii (*Nineteenth-Century Oxford*, pts. 1 and 2) for general accounts of the changes in the University.

[16] Sewell to Ouseley, 12 Feb. 1875 (NCA 8666, p. 100).

meeting held in 1882 to float the scheme for a Royal College of Music' imagined such an institution taking on 'the more extended function of a University'.[17] In connection with the four 'major schools of music in the metropolis, as well as the Royal College of Organists (1864)', Mackerness suggests that 'the provision of disciplined musical study in a professional situation which had changed radically since the early nineteenth century did help to create an appropriate "atmosphere"....'.[18]

For various reasons, then, this must have seemed the right time for reform. Another factor in the gathering of support within the university may have been the perceived possibility of links between music and theology. This emerges from an early stage in the proceedings. Among the problems that exercised Maurice in 1856 was his perception that Oxford sent an 'academic population' out into the world as pastors without sufficient musical training.[19] It has been suggested that the critical call for the formation of a satisfactory musical school within the university was informed by an 'explicit ecclesiastical impulse': Cuddesdon theological college had been founded in 1854, and Professor Hussey and others were probably concerned to prove 'that the university could supply all the training that was necessary for clergymen'.[20] Before Ouseley's appointment to the Professorship, a report of the seventh annual meeting of the University Motett and Madrigal Society in 1853 stressed that the course of instruction thereby offered by Dr Corfe enabled members to acquire useful skills in reading and singing at sight, for their future involvement, as clergymen, in parish church choirs. (There was some feeling at that time that in a university where music should be viewed as essential to undergraduates intending to become clergymen, it was inappropriate to have a Professor appointed who was not a church musician.[21])

[17] Quoted (via Frank Howes, *The English Musical Renaissance*) by E. D. Mackerness, in 'George Bernard Shaw and the English Musical Renaissance', *Durham University Journal* (June 1987), 303.

[18] Ibid.

[19] Maurice, *What shall we do with Music?*, 9. The idea was still resonating in the 1880s: following the death of Ouseley in 1889, T. L. Southgate in the *Musical Standard*, commenting on Music at Oxford, echoed Maurice's call of some thirty years previously; and indeed still in 1990 a series of letters printed in *The Times* reflected considerable anguish over the status of music in the contemporary church, leading one writer to aver that 'It is a sad reflection on our theological colleges that little if any time is given to prospective ordinands in the study of church music and its place in the context of the liturgy'.

[20] Personal communication from Mark Curthoys (1990), concerning the history of the university. Hussey (Professor of Ecclesiastical History) had supported the new statute of 1856.

[21] On all these matters see particularly the *Oxford University Herald*, 10 Dec. 1853, 8–13, *passim*.

The energy directed by Hussey, Ouseley, and others in the 1850s towards revision of the statutes governing the music school did not dissipate when that immediate goal had been achieved. At this point it is worth mentioning that the matters under discussion here affected hundreds of candidates. Examination records survive for approximately 369 successful B.Mus. candidates in the period 1854–1914. Numbers naturally fluctuated in accordance with the state of change in the examinations. For example when the *Gazette* in 1878 published the figures for matriculations and degrees over the previous ten years it was noted that the 'large increase in the numbers of matriculations in 1877 is due to the number of candidates for the degree of Bachelor of Music'.[22] In 1876 a new statute had been approved, to take effect from after Hilary Term 1878, requiring more rigorous entrance conditions for music degrees;[23] evidently there was a rush to enter before the new requirement came into force. In the early 1890s there was a similar increase in the numbers taking music degrees when it became known that the University was considering the imposition of residence requirements.

After Ouseley's new examination scheme of the late 1850s, the next significant stage came in 1871, when the B.Mus. examination was expanded to encompass two parts, the first (in harmony and counterpoint, in not more than four parts) held in Michaelmas Term and acting as a preliminary to the second, in Easter or Act Term, which tested not only more advanced harmony and counterpoint (in up to five parts) but also music history, form, and set works. In the same year (1871) the requirements for the B.Mus. exercise were increased from a four-part to a five-part composition; the examiners' approval of the exercise was needed before the candidate could present himself for the second written examination.[24]

---

[22] *OU Gazette*, 25 Jan. 1878, 195.

[23] *OU Gazette*, 29 Feb. 1876, 231 and 20 June 1876, 44. The 1876 statute is discussed in more detail below.

[24] The statutory public performance of the B.Mus.exercise seems to have been abolished in 1870 (see *Addenda ad Corpus Statutorum 1870*, 806), not 1878 as stated in *NG* (xiv. 38). Earlier, Maurice (p. 5) had ridiculed the public performance of the exercise: 'Is not the performance in the Music School a burlesque, an academic sham?' and evidently felt it to be undesirable on humanitarian grounds: 'Can any human being with a heart, to say nothing of his nerves, witness the performance of any exercise in the Music School without thinking of the distracting purgatory through which the author of the same is doomed to pass?' The public performance of the exercise was also a source of extra expense for the candidates. But it could still be an enjoyable and effective occasion in the right hands, as with Samuel Sebastian Wesley's accumulated B.Mus. and D.Mus. (1839) when Wesley afterwards 'delighted his audience by a voluntary on the

Already by this stage, for a process that was designed to test essentially external candidates, the University's new requirements were quite demanding. The changes must have affected the way that the degree was perceived both within and beyond the University.

If the mention of music history, harmony and counterpoint, and set works seems close to the standard academic syllabuses familiar from our own time, the style of questions and the focus of emphasis in these various papers were very different from modern expectations. A reading of the examination papers is revealing in relation to the development of the subject in the nineteenth century; it is important to bear in mind that before 1858 there had been no written examination questions set, so that there was no tradition in this respect. It was now created, in a series of papers showing both a broad scope and considerable depth in certain ways, as well as some distinctive 'period' flavour.[25] Prior to 1871 the single B.Mus. examination contained two papers, one in harmony, one in counterpoint; the questions covered harmonic and contrapuntal theory (for example requiring definition of such terminology as 'false relation' or 'per arsin et thesin', or answering 'Why are Consecutive Octaves and Fifths forbidden?') and practical exercises (mainly in the form of adding parts to a given part). Among elements evidently of special importance to the examiners were the deciphering of figured harmony and the manufacturing of species counterpoint.[26]

These elements persisted after 1871, though perhaps with less theory and more practical writing and analysis. A noticeable feature of all technical papers from the period under review is that given material is almost always unattributed to any specific composer or style. The emphasis is on particular techniques of counterpoint (adding parts in various 'species' to a given cantus firmus, supplying 'correct' tonal answers to some very complex fugue subjects, and constructing double counterpoint and canon) or

organ', and the *Journal*'s critic, in a generally rapturous review, congratulated Vicary, organist of Magdalen College (where the performance took place), on 'the very excellent way in which his choristers, assisted by some members of the Oxford Choral Society, sustained the very difficult and elaborate chorusses' (*JOJ*, 22 June 1839).

[25] Sets of papers are preserved in Ob, Per. 2626 b. 8 (1867–90) and Per. 2626 e. 319 (1891–1902). A record of the 'first public examination for Musical Degrees that has ever taken place in Oxford', held at the Music School, is in *JOJ*, 2 May 1858, under 'University and Clerical Intelligence'.

[26] To the historian of theory it is interesting to observe that these two techniques have enjoyed a considerable revival in contemporary pedagogy.

on what might be called the grammatical aspects of harmony. In the harmony questions generally a 'Romantic' free chromaticism and modulatory adventurousness pervade the largely anonymous extracts given for comment or completion, especially in the more searching D.Mus. examination.[27] The examiners sometimes specify some stern prescriptions, as in 'Write a melody and harmony on the above ground-bass six times, and never twice using the same harmony', and 'Harmonise the above [figured bass] in five parts, *with strictness*'.[28]

For the D.Mus., questions in which (on the harmony paper) seven parts were to be added to a given figured bass, or five parts, using specified devices, were to be added to an unfigured bass, while to the cantus firmus (on the counterpoint paper) a total of seven added parts was required to be put, seem to be placing an emphasis on the sheer numbers of parts with which a candidate could cope. The increase in parts for the D.Mus. goes back to the old distinction between the rules for the B.Mus. and D.Mus. exercises, as noted a century earlier by Hawkins, consisting of a five-part composition for the former, and one in six or eight parts for the latter.[29] The statutory testimonials mentioned by Hawkins ('under the hands of credible witnesses') remained a requisite; thus the *University Calendar* for 1869 stated that 'A candidate for the Degree of Bachelor of Music must produce a certificate signed by two or more trustworthy persons that he has been studying music, whether at Oxford or elsewhere, for seven years'. (This was subsequently reduced to five years: see the 1872 edition of the *Calendar*.) And the statutory gap between B.Mus. and D.Mus. remained, in the later nineteenth century, the same five-year period as noted by Hawkins in his description of the eighteenth-century regulations.

In the later nineteenth century the technical papers created a new 'Oxford harmony and counterpoint' based on the testing of both detailed textbook knowledge and practical compositional ability. They could therefore be regarded as backing up the submitted exercise in composition which still formed a central element. The new musical history papers were apparently less directly relevant to the compositional exercise, but much of what appeared under the guise of history was designed to link up with harmony and counterpoint studies, as well as with the church music

---

[27] See e.g. 28 Oct. 1891 (D.Mus. harmony paper).
[28] 6 April 1875 (Second B.Mus. harmony paper).   [29] Quoted in Ch. 2, p. 13, above.

context to which most candidates still tended to belong. In the second B.Mus. examination of 23 April 1872 it was thought appropriate to ask under 'Musical History' the question 'Who first introduced unprepared dominant sevenths?', although a more genuinely historical slant was sometimes applied to points of technical interest: 'At what date, and in whose works chiefly, can we trace the germ of modern tonality?' English church composers featured often, among an impressively wide range of subjects including continental and Catholic traditions, and with considerable emphasis on the earlier (Renaissance and Baroque) periods of musical history.

The feature that 'dates' these historical papers is not, as might be expected, a preoccupation with nineteenth-century music (though there are some challenging questions on Berlioz, Liszt, and Wagner) but a kind of gossipy approach (two of the other questions in 1872 were 'Can you mention any musical anecdote in connexion with King Louis XII of France, and a celebrated composer?' and 'Have any English sovereigns been musical? If so, which? . . .' and a penchant for possible scandal: 'Relate the story of Stradella and his misfortunes' (second B.Mus., 14 October 1884). But the appearance of questions on organum, on early and exotic instruments (the crwth, the 'rebeck'), the music of Dufay, Josquin, Frescobaldi, Monteverdi, Couperin, the sons of Bach and their influence, and some historiographical issues, among what seem to be the standard questions on Palestrina, the madrigal, J. S. Bach, Gluck's reform of opera (and the Gluck–Piccinni 'quarrel', which the examiners recurrently mentioned); the clarinet, violin, Beethoven's symphonies, and various English composers (Crotch, Balfe—Irish, but London-based; Bennett), suggests a broad view, and some informed reading. There are some quite surprising glimpses of past and present interests: one D.Mus. question (8 November 1893) required candidates to compare the operas of Lully and Scarlatti, and a question in the second B.Mus. examination (13 October 1886) asked: 'Give the names of some of Handel's successful operas . . . What hinders their being performed in entirety in modern times?'

These papers reflect a sense of systematic study of the subject and the establishment of a corpus of historical data, secondary literature, and repertoire–elements that tend to be associated more with the century that followed, or with the emergence of systematic musicology on the continent in the late nineteenth century. Papers of this sort could hardly have been offered to earlier eighteenth-century candidates for Oxford degrees. By the nineteenth century, Burney and Hawkins had left their mark (already visible in Crotch's syllabus of lectures),[30] and by 1879 the first volumes of Grove's *Dictionary* had begun to appear (with contributions by various Oxford, or Oxford-related, authors). An Oxford historical tradition in music had pre-dated *Grove*. The involvement of the Heather Professors in scholarly research activities as well as practical composition and performance was re-established by Ouseley after a hiatus in the mid-nineteenth century. The later nineteenth-century examination papers presuppose a foundation of scholarly reading. What then were the 'textbooks' and 'authorities' with which candidates were expected to be familiar?

The concept of an Oxford academic tradition in music at this period is reinforced by the fact that many of the authoritative texts then current were written by senior members and musical graduates of the University.[31] Stainer's 1891 booklet providing notes for candidates in music listed as recommended texts for the First B.Mus. examination: Ouseley, *Treatise on Harmony*; Macfarren, *Harmony*; Stainer, *Treatise on Harmony*; Bridge, *Counterpoint*; Cherubini, *Counterpoint*; and Ouseley, *Counterpoint*. Additional texts for the Second B.Mus. included Bridge, *Double Counterpoint*; Prout (as well as Berlioz) on *Instrumentation*; Ouseley, *Treatise on Form*; and Parry's article on form in *Grove*. (Ouseley's works, incidentally, were published by the Clarendon Press at Oxford.) Historical texts included Burney's and Hawkins's Histories, and some more recent authors: Hullah (*History of Modern Music* and *Transition Period of Musical History*) and Naumann (*History of Music*) . For the D.Mus. examination, with regard to the study of acoustics the recommended authorities were Helmholtz, Pole, Stone, and Sedley Taylor.[32] Without promoting a narrow adherence to local scholarship, these lists give due prominence to 'Oxford' productions, especially on the technical side of the subject.

Of course what is asked, and recommended, by examiners does not necessarily indicate what is done and delivered by candidates. And

[30] Music School, Oxford, 1800–4 (Ob, MS Top. Oxon d. 22/II and G.A. Oxon b. 19 (265)).

[31] For detail on the various literature, see Wollenberg, 'Music in Nineteenth-Century Oxford' (1999), 203–4.

[32] Ob, G.A. Oxon 8° 620 (35), J. Stainer, *Directions for Candidates for Degrees in Music*.

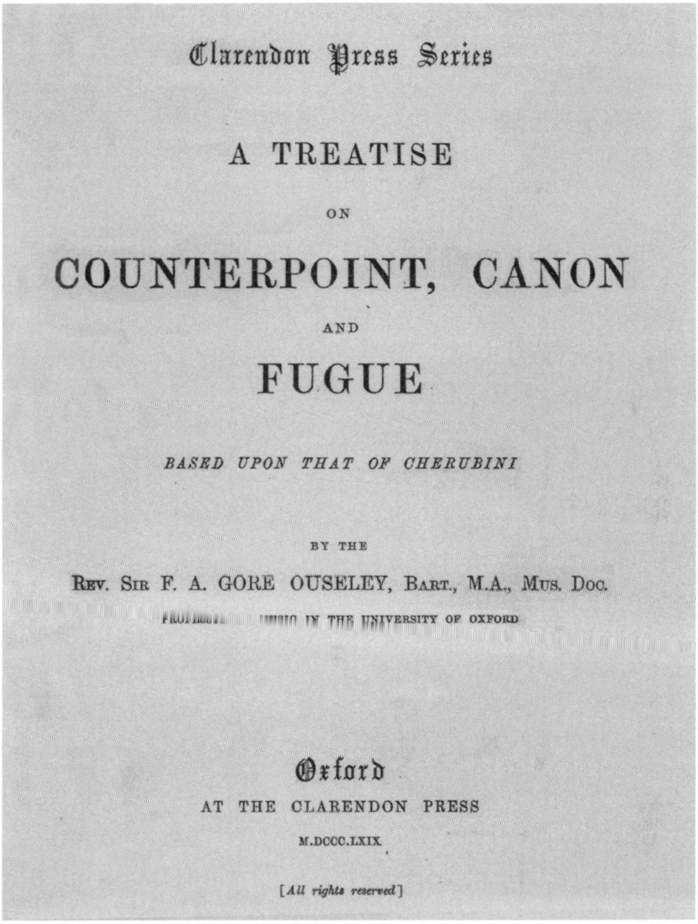

Clarendon Press Series

A TREATISE

ON

COUNTERPOINT, CANON

AND

FUGUE

BASED UPON THAT OF CHERUBINI

BY THE

REV. SIR F. A. GORE OUSELEY, BART., M.A., MUS. DOC.

[illegible] IN THE UNIVERSITY OF OXFORD

Oxford

AT THE CLARENDON PRESS

M.DCCC.LXIX

[*All rights reserved*]

FIG. 10. Title page, Ouseley, *Counterpoint* (1869)

Hadow, in one of a series of important writings on the state of the Oxford musical degrees around the turn of the century, characterized the B.Mus. and D.Mus. as 'still certificates of technical proficiency, not marks of university citizenship'.[33] The changes discussed, and partly implemented, during the late nineteenth century were primarily concerned with achieving greater control over candidates' general, as well as musical, education. A particularly telling expression of concern for the academic standing of the degree comes in the evidence submitted by Ouseley and Corfe (in their

33 Ob, G.A. Oxon b. 41 (7): cf. n. 14 above.

capacity as Professor and Choragus respectively) to the Selborne commission in 1877:

Those who study music, as well as those who teach it, have felt it as a continual discouragement of late years that the degrees in this subject, whatever be the amount of acquirement that they testify to, do not carry the weight that other degrees do. This arises, no doubt, from the fact that the education testified to by the examinations is one of a narrow type, and does not involve those elements of a liberal education which are requisite before the degree can be placed on a level with . . . a general course of study at this University . . . A small beginning has already been made in this matter by the requirement of passing an elementary examination in subjects other than technical music.[34]

The 'small beginning' was made in 1876, and introduced one of the most important additions to the regulations so far. For the first time a knowledge of subjects other than music was prescribed: the statute passed in 1876 required B.Mus. candidates who were not members of the University to show (before being permitted to enter for the B.Mus. examination) 'evidence of having received a liberal education' either by certifying that they had passed Responsions (pre-degree tests) or an equivalent, or by taking tests administered by the Masters of the Schools (University examiners) in English and Mathematics, Latin, and either Greek or a modern language. Again the developments in the music degrees reflected broader educational concerns of the time. And when (presumably in response to difficulties experienced by candidates) the scheme was modified, the relaxation of these requirements was viewed with disapprobation by its close observers, as in Ernest Walker's comment on 'the regrettably backward step' taken by the University in 1890 'in instituting a special "Preliminary Examination for Students in Music" as a "soft option" . . .' enabling candidates to enter without a knowledge of Classical languages.[35]

Discussing the new requirement of 1876, another commentator referred to the danger of its serving only 'to sever the connection between the University and the musical world'.[36] In one sense, the element which most jeopardized Ouseley's original aim of bringing 'the ordinary [i.e.

---

[34] UOC, supplementary evidence, 374–5.

[35] *Grove* 2 (1904–10), vol. i, article 'Degrees in Music', 679. For the change in regulations see HCM/3/12 (1890). *EO*, 357, refers to a debate over compulsory Greek in Responsions.

[36] C. A. Fyffe, article 'Oxford', in *Grove* (1880), ii. 624. Fyffe (1845–92) took a First in Classics and was a Fellow of University College, Oxford: he is described in *DNB* (suppl. vol. xxii) as a strong radical in politics.

non-honorary] musical graduate into closer relation with the University'
as a whole was the traditional absence of any residence requirement.[37]
Although music candidates were required to matriculate nominally at the
University, thus to 'enter [their names] . . . on the books of a College or
Hall, or become a Non-Collegiate Student'[38] and pay a specially adjusted
fee (which varied from college to college, hence probably the popularity
among musicians of certain, presumably cheaper, colleges) this gave outside candidates only a tenuous connection with their colleges. The *Oxford
Magazine* in 1896 summed up the situation in its report of a would-be
D.Mus. candidate formally attached to New College who was discovered–
after he had been admitted to the B.Mus. degree–asking directions:

Last Friday a small harvest of new Doctors and Bachelors of Music was
announced . . . There is one true story of the new recipients which should not be
passed over. Last Thursday we discovered a pathetic figure wandering vaguely in
the vicinity of Broad Street . . . He explained that he was a Mus. Bac. of New
College, and was anxious, before ascending to the Doctor's degree, to see the
College to which he was a credit, but that he could not find it any more, as he had
never yet entered its precincts.[39]

Reflecting on the 'general condition' of music in Oxford on the occasion
of Ouseley's death in 1889, T. L. Southgate was eloquent in his identification of two main problems remaining after Ouseley's improvements: one
was the lack of 'any methodical and systematised higher instruction in the
art from the Professor himself' and the other was the absence of any official University influence on music. Not entirely fairly, he judged that what
he noted as music's 'condition of healthy activity in the University city'
was achieved independently of its academic status.[40] An answer to
Southgate's two problems was to require residential status for music candidates. In fact this idea had surfaced in the University well before
Southgate's article appeared, and was to resurface: it seems to have been a
topic particularly fraught with disagreement, and its development was a
correspondingly convoluted process. Nor was it completely resolved in the

---

[37] HCM/3/16 (1898), p. 42. Mark Curthoys has noted (in a personal communication) that in the
1870s and 1890s, for which samples were taken in connection with the 19th-cent. volumes of *HUO*, 'the
men matriculating for the B.Mus. were from less obviously prosperous backgrounds than the run of
undergraduates'. This was undoubtedly a factor in the persistence of non-resident musical degrees.

[38] Stainer, *Directions for Candidates* (see n. 32), 2.   [39] *Oxford Magazine*, 15 (11 Nov. 1896), 57.
[40] 'Music in Oxford', *Musical Standard*, 11 May 1889, 382; 384.

period under consideration. Feelings on the subject continued to run high well into the new century: arguing in favour of the proposed new Musical Statute of 1911, T. B. Strong declared: 'This is the only degree in regard to which the University of Oxford appears as a mere examining-machine; in all the others it aims at influencing the educational standard of its candidates.' Strong noted that 'the Musical Degrees occupy a wholly anomalous position in the University' and that candidates were 'in no real sense members of the University'.[41] As Maurice had put it in his reflections of 1856: 'Of all the progeny of Alma Mater, she [music] alone is allowed to grow up without training and education.'[42]

An early attempt to bring music more into line with other disciplines examined by the University came in the proposed amendments to the Musical Degree Statute of 1870 (which was designed to raise the standards required for the degree). *The Times* carried a report of Congregation at Oxford with details of Mr Hatch's amendment 'requiring the same amount of residence and the same general culture from candidates for musical as from candidates for medical degrees' and proposing that music candidates should be required to take the BA first.[43] While the statute itself was duly promulgated *nem. con.*, Mr Hatch's amendment was defeated 4–42.[44] The proposal to require B.Mus. students first to take the BA became a kind of leitmotiv, next emerging most strongly during the discussions in 1898, when Hadow's eloquently phrased arguments echoed the substance of earlier criticisms:

Under the present system the connexion between musical graduates and the University is restricted to matriculation, the work of the examination-room, and the ceremony of the degree. Successful candidates bear an Oxford distinction without having . . . contributed anything to Oxford life or gained anything from its experience . . . it leaves the successful candidate in a position always anomalous and often misunderstood.[45]

---

[41] Ob, G.A. Oxon c. 310 (65): 'The proposed statute for Degrees in Music', 8 May 1911, p. 1. Strong (a member of the Music Board) was then Dean of Christ Church; he later became Bishop of Oxford (1925–37). *EO* (p. 81) refers to Dean Strong as 'the first Dean to take an active interest in the cathedral choir' (since Aldrich, perhaps).

[42] *What shall we do with Music?*, 5.

[43] *The Times*, 16 Nov. 1870 and 23 Nov. 1870. It was noted that Dr Stainer of Magdalen opposed this.

[44] *OU Gazette*, 8 Nov. 1870 and 15 Nov. 1870 (the statute was approved by Congregation on 6 December and by Convocation on 22 December). For the amendment moved by Mr Hatch (of St Mary's Hall) and Mr Thorley (of Wadham) see *OU Gazette*, 22 Nov. 1870.   [45] HCM/3/16, p. 38.

Hadow's arguments in favour of the proposal 'to require the degree in Arts as preliminary to the musical degree' and to restrict music graduates to those who were 'members of the University by residence' are particularly well developed, evidently in response to the objections that had been raised against the proposed change.[46] His ideas illuminate, briefly but incisively, the entire educational aspect of music in England at the time. It was in this general context that—with great clarity of vision—Hadow placed the Oxford degrees.

The nub of his reasoning was based partly on an Oxford perspective, expressed in his concern for 'that essential part of Oxford education —the education gained from the daily life', and partly on a more general view: the proposed enhancement of the 'educational value of the degree' was perceived as a possible corrective to what Hadow frankly described as the 'comparatively low standard of education ... hitherto ... accepted among musicians in this country'. To this, rather than to any inherent weakness in the nature of the subject itself, Hadow attributed the parlous situation of English musical education as he saw it. 'the musical profession in England is still, as a rule, somewhat behind other arts and other professions in point of general culture.' He added: 'that this [educational] standard should be raised is the desire of almost all who are interested in the future of English music.' The arguments which these statements were designed to support seem to contain a genuinely felt, rather than a falsely assumed, view of Oxford's potential role. A further argument advanced by Hadow was concerned more with the ways in which Oxford's actual role might be misconstrued under the prevailing regulations. The anomalous position of the musical graduate is here trenchantly put: 'a graduate of Oxford, and yet not a graduate of Oxford', and it was felt that this situation might misrepresent the University to the outside world:

Mr J. S. Curwen, who speaks in this matter with special knowledge, writes, 'I hardly think that the resident members of the University can be aware to what an extent the musical graduates assume the status of University men', and adds that the present system is seriously detrimental to the University, and that it would be advisable to bring it to an end.[47]

---

[46] HCM/3/16, 35–6, 39.   [47] See ibid. 38–9.

Worthy of comment here is the fact that by the 1890s, women were beginning to be represented among Oxford's aspiring musical graduates.[48]

In support of his case, Hadow had gathered an impressive list of signa-
tories including Sir C. H. H. Parry, C. V. Stanford, Sir H. S. Oakeley, C. H.
Lloyd, B. Harwood, P. C. Buck, and Sir Walter Parratt. These were all dis-
tinguished figures in the musical profession: Parry was then Choragus of
Oxford and Principal of the RCM, Stanford was Professor of Music at
Cambridge, Oakeley Emeritus Professor at Edinburgh, Lloyd Organist of
Eton College, and Parratt Organist of St George's, Windsor and Master
of the Queen's Music. Other support came from the Revd J. Troutbeck,
DD, Precentor of Westminster Abbey, the Revd E. H. Fellowes, MA,
B.Mus., Precentor of Bristol (the two Precentors on the Church Music
Committee at the Royal College) and J. A. Fuller-Maitland, MA, as well as
J. S. Curwen, President of the Tonic Sol-fa College. The matter had gener-
ated considerable concern, thanks to Hadow's efforts. Hadow noted that
all those in his principal list of supporters were 'graduates who hold the
superior degrees in Arts and Music'. He mentioned further examples of
University-educated musicians, including Sir John Stainer, Dr Mee, and
Mr Arthur Somervell, 'and many other distinguished musicians, [who]
are at the present time graduates in Arts at Oxford or Cambridge'.
(Among the objections raised against Hadow's proposal was 'that it will
lead to an increased traffic in inferior or fraudulent degrees'.[49])

Although Hadow's proposal was rejected in 1898, his intentions were
partially realized when in 1910 a motion was passed by the University's
Hebdomadal Council suggesting that some conditions of residence
should be introduced for the B.Mus., and a committee was appointed to
consider the implications of the proposed change.[50] Its brief was to confer

[48] Following the introduction of the statute in 1885 permitting the 'admission of women to the first
examination for the degree of Mus. Bac. at Oxford University' (of sufficient general interest to be
reported in *MT* 26 (1885), 224) in 1892 the 'first two ladies' to supplicate for the B.Mus. were congratulated
on this distinction in a report in the local press (*JOJ*, 5 Nov. 1892).

[49] For supporters see HCM/3/16, pp. 36–7; objections are treated on pp. 42–6. Although Stainer was
one of those cited by Hadow, he was an objector (as was Frederick Bridge), chiefly on the grounds that the
proposal would limit the musical degrees to 'amateurs of wealth and leisure'. (This was a recurrent point.)
The question of fraudulent claims had been sufficiently worrying to occasion the publication of an official list of music graduates 1830–1876 'with a view of exposing all sham degrees of Mus. Doc. and Mus.
Bac.' (Ob, 174 e. 42: 'A List of Graduates in the Faculty of Music, from 1830 to 1876' (Faculty here is used
in a generic sense), Oxford, n.d.).

[50] The preliminary stages are outlined in HCM/3/26, 1910: as Acts, p. lxxix (14 Feb. 1910) records,

with the Professor of Music, the Choragus, and others, and to report on 'the constitution of the Faculty of Music' (then not in organized existence) as well as on conditions to be required for the degree. The committee's considerable energies were expended partly on interpreting their brief to consult others by sending out a circular to music graduates; a large number of replies was received and analysed. It was thus on the basis of a variety of evidence submitted to them that the members of the committee (the Vice-Chancellor, the Master of University College, Mr Gerrans, the President of Corpus, and Professor Gotch, with the Dean of Christ Church and Mr Cronshaw attending) arrived at their conclusions. These presaged some far-reaching changes.[51]

With regard to the crucial question of residential status, the 1910 committee concluded that it would be undesirable 'to require residence as a necessary condition for a Degree in Music', but introduced an important corollary to this, whereby the University would exercise greater control over the academic standing of external candidates: 'if the student does not reside, he should have pursued a course of study at an approved place of Musical Instruction'. Echoing a perennial preoccupation, it was also felt desirable 'to require a higher standard of general education than at present'. To encourage undergraduates to consider the study of music more seriously, the committee recommended certain statutory enhancements of the First and Second B.Mus. examinations, while for the Third examination a candidate 'should have been a member of the University for three years' before entering; this was clearly designed to discourage an unduly compressed path to the degree from the time of matriculation. In accordance with the committee's recommendations, the new statutes passed in 1911 provided for the establishment of a Board of Studies in Music (necessary to exercise the required supervision of academic standards and degrees) and stipulated the various conditions the committee had formulated as prerequisites for the degree. In particular, they stated that 'No one who has not been admitted to the degree of B.A. shall be permitted to supplicate for the degree of Bachelor of Music unless he has (a)

the Master of University College's motion that 'some conditions of residence should be required for the degree of B.Mus.' was passed on a division 15–6. The investigating committee was then set up. See HCM/3/28, p. 221 ('Report of Committee on Degrees in Music').

[51] The summary that follows is based on HCM/3/28, pp. 221–3, *passim*.

passed in a Group of the Final Pass School, and (b) pursued a course of study approved by the Board of Studies.'[52] With the enactment of the 1911 Statutes (on a vote 68–26), the B.Mus. came closer than ever before to achieving the integration within the University that Hadow hoped for.[53] The 1911 changes marked not so much the beginning of a new phase as a culmination of Ouseley's original efforts.

As to the degree candidates themselves, among individual documentation are some remarkable glimpses of early achievement. Sir Hubert Parry (b. 1848) had taken the B.Mus. examination in 1866, while still in his teens at Eton, before coming up to Exeter College, Oxford, where he took the BA in 1870 (he was later awarded an honorary D.Mus.). Sir John Stainer (b. 1840) had been awarded his B.Mus. in 1859, four years before he took the BA (1863); he proceeded to the D.Mus. in 1865. Under the unreformed statute, Leighton G. Hayne (b. 1836) of Queen's College had taken the B.Mus. in 1856; *Jackson's Oxford Journal* carried a full report of the proceedings, noting that this was believed to be 'the first instance of an Undergraduate of either University graduating in music before his degree in arts, and it reflects great credit on a gentleman so young to have shown such proficiency in the science of music as to have been able to produce an exercise worthy of a degree, for it is a well-known fact that music degrees are not obtained now so easily as in days gone by . . .'[54]

As in the eighteenth, so also in the nineteenth century many candidates were active as organists and church composers (a substantial number had taken religious orders). This activity might be centred on parish churches and cathedrals of diverse location (witness the career of Samuel Sebastian Wesley, b. 1810, B.Mus. and D.Mus. 1839, cathedral organist variously of Hereford, Exeter, Winchester, and Gloucester and 'considered the first organist and church composer in England' during the 1830s)[55] or include

---

[52] *OU Gazette*, 8 Feb. 1911, p. 445; given considerable support (see ibid. 577, 713).

[53] HCM/3/16 (1898), p. 43. Ironically, in view of Hadow's aspirations towards a better-educated musical profession, while on the one hand the Master of University College argued in 1911 that the 'enhanced literary requirements of the new statute would greatly add to the new musical degree', Dr Bussell on the other hand remarked that 'the statute would prevent organists in practice from taking the degree, and that it was wrong to put restrictions on specialists of this kind. Let the University raise the musical part of the examination, but not insist on more culture for the candidates' (reported in the *Oxford Chronicle*, 12 May 1911, p. 12).

[54] *JOJ*, 17 May 1856. For official documentation of degree candidates see UA, UR/L/9 vols. 1–3 (B.Mus. certificates) and UR/L/35 vols. 1–2 (Schola musicae).

[55] Abdy Williams, *Degrees in Music*, 103.

important spells as organists in Oxford, as in the case of Stainer (organist of Magdalen College, 1859–72) and Parratt (b. 1841, who took the B.Mus. in 1873 and succeeded Stainer as organist at Magdalen, 1872–82) before moving on to hold appointments of distinction elsewhere (Stainer to St Paul's, Parratt to St George's, Windsor). From these appointments, in turn, there might then be a return to Oxford to higher office, as with both Stainer (Heather Professor of Music from 1889) and Parratt (Heather Professor from 1908). Some candidates came from families with a tradition of musical service to the church. Charles Corfe (b. 1814, B.Mus. 1847, D.Mus. 1852) was the son of the organist of Salisbury Cathedral, and brother of Joseph Corfe, organist of Bristol Cathedral. (He himself was organist of Christ Church, 1846–82.)

Not all candidates followed primarily musical careers. William Pole FRS (b. 1814, B.Mus. 1860, D.Mus. 1867) was Professor of Civil Engineering at University College, London (and also organist of St Mark's, North Audley Street). Among those who took the B.Mus. in addition to the ordinary BA was J. Barclay Thompson (Christ Church; B.Mus. 1868), who became University Reader in Anatomy. The clearest pattern (as far as any general patterns can be extracted from the hundreds of individual academic records for the period 1854–1914) shows a tendency especially among external candidates to matriculate very shortly before taking the first B.Mus. examination. Thus Charles Kitson matriculated 5 November 1894 at St Edmund Hall (having passed the Cambridge University Previous Examination in 1893) and took the first B.Mus. on 6 November 1894. He was then not quite 20 years old. After gaining approval of his exercise in September 1895 he proceeded to take the second B.Mus. in May 1897 (in which year his exercise was deposited, in accordance with the standard procedure). For some candidates the process might be not only very lengthy—perhaps encompassing examination failure—but in fact never completed. Frank Muspratt of Queen's passed his Prelim. in 1895, matriculated and took the first B.Mus. in 1897, but after his exercise was approved in 1901 he appears to have lapsed. George Butterworth (matriculated 1904 at Trinity College) passed the first B.Mus. in 1910 but apparently proceeded no further. He was killed 5 August 1916. The cause of non-completion might in general be personal or financial constraints as well as the more drastic reasons of illness and early death.

To sum up some aspects of the varied process: from matriculation and first stage to third stage of the B.Mus. examination at this period might take as little as one or two years (A. Eaglefield Hull, 1896–8; Adrian Cedric Boult, 1911–12) or less (Ivor Atkins, matriculated 16 March 1892, B.Mus. degree October 1892; George Dyson, matriculated 4 May 1909, B.Mus. degree December 1909); or as long as eighteen years (Percy George Vincent Henniker [New College], matriculated January 1887, first B.Mus. May 1898, degree completed 1905).[56] The number of years elapsing between B.Mus. and D.Mus. might be well over the statutory minimum (although sometimes below, as in the case of Dyson: D.Mus. 1910); Septimus Ernest Luke Spooner Lillingston (BA 1886, having matriculated at Charsley's Hall 1881 and 'migrated to Hertford 1884') took his B.Mus. in 1888, and his D.Mus. (started 1910) was finally taken in 1913. Again, various reasons could underlie this pattern, including the demands of a professional post as well as the heavier academic burden imposed by the doctoral examination. The 1914–18 war interrupted the process (if not indeed terminating it under tragic circumstances) for several candidates; Ivor Atkins proceeded to the D.Mus. in 1920 (completing it within that year) after an elongated gap of twenty-eight years since his B.Mus., while Adrian Boult took his first D.Mus. examination in November 1914 and completed the remainder of the degree in 1921.

Clearly there are some distinguished names among the examined B.Mus. candidates. While some of these went on to take the D.Mus. by examination, others were awarded it honorarily at a later stage in their

---

[56] In charting individual paths to the degree it should be noted that the preliminary stages (passing the Music Prelim., Responsions or an equivalent) might pre-date the first B.Mus. considerably; matriculation, especially in the case of 'internal' candidates, might also occur much earlier than the first B.Mus.; and, for reasons discussed later, the records show some terminological confusion, particularly with regard to the second and third examination; there is also a distinction to be made between passing the third stage (i.e. having successfully completed both written examinations and the exercise for the B.Mus.) and being admitted formally to the degree (this latter ceremony might follow shortly or be postponed for several months or years). Edmund Fellowes embarked on the path to the B.Mus. after matriculating at Oriel College in 1889 and taking the BA in 1892, with his first B.Mus. in November 1893 and his second B.Mus. in May 1896 (in which month he formally took the degree). Nelson Victor Edwards (see *HUO* vii. 434, for his letter to the Professor, May 1913, on the disturbance during his recent exam, which he failed) passed the Preliminary examination in September 1910, matriculated November 1910, passed the first B.Mus. the following day, and the second (i.e. the second written examination, though third stage chronologically) in Nov. 1913, but had passed the 'third' B.Mus. (i.e. the exercise) in August 1911 (he was admitted to the degree in Nov. 1913): the terminology used in the records here reflected the new system (on which see p. 127 below).

careers (Parry, for example, in 1884, Parratt in 1894, and Edmund Fellowes in 1939). Before the mid-nineteenth century the examined D.Mus. was comparatively rare; the honorary D.Mus. seems to have been even more so.[57] With the stiffening of the academic requirements for the examined degree in the later nineteenth century, there came the establishment of the honorary D.Mus. as a regular and distinctive award. From 1879 a series of composers, including many of acknowledged international standing, received the honorary D.Mus. from Oxford. (Some of these were similarly honoured by Cambridge also.) One of the earliest was Arthur Sullivan (1879). Among the names of later honorands were Elgar (1905), Grieg (1906), Glazunov and Saint-Saëns (1907). Distinguished university musicians were also among those honoured, such as Sir Herbert Oakeley (Christ Church; Professor of Music at Edinburgh, 1865–91: Hon. D.Mus. Oxon 1879) and Charles Villiers Stanford (1883), later Professor of Music at Cambridge. The tradition of awarding the honorary degree primarily to composers (rather than performers) continued subsequently: Egon Wellesz (in the Haydn bicentenary year of 1932) was thus honoured, apparently as the first Austrian composer to receive the honorary D.Mus. since Haydn.[58]

While, traditionally, particular compositions might be associated with the award of honorary degrees in music, it was in connection with the examined degrees that a corpus of academic-related compositions can most clearly be seen to have been assembled.[59] For the nineteenth century, these present a unique view of the compositional styles and influences prevalent among those qualifying professionally. In particular, they link up with the apparent growth in popularity of works on sacred subjects in the larger choral genres (oratorio and cantata), for 'concert' or paraliturgical performance. Although some degree exercises are still described as anthems, the term 'Cantata' or 'Sacred cantata' is widespread, and 'Oratorio' appears occasionally.[60] Whatever their title, the majority of works

---

[57] See Ch. 2 above on Handel and Haydn.

[58] Wellesz later became University Reader in Byzantine Music at Oxford. Honorary Degrees in Music at Cambridge followed a similar pattern: see Knight, *Cambridge Music*, 80.

[59] Copies of B.Mus. and D.Mus. exercises were preserved, following their original deposit, in Ob, MSS Mus. Sch. (see *Summary Catalogue*, vol. v, p. 262 ff.). References to individual items below relate to this manuscript collection.

[60] See e.g. S. Elvey's extended anthem setting, 'Great is the Lord' ('Exercise for Doctor's Degree in

display extended cantata forms, with the almost ubiquitous psalm texts divided up into a series of solo, ensemble, and choral numbers.[61] C. G. Verrinder's cantata 'Israel in adversity and in deliverance' is in two parts, with Part 1 introduced by a post-Handelian overture (complete with fugato second section) and Part 2 ('Israel's happy deliverance') again having its own orchestral introduction, each consisting of about half-a-dozen items.[62]

Individual ingredients of the musical settings include besides the various introductory instrumental pieces, recitative sections, predominantly lyrical arias (or 'Airs')—sometimes expressly featuring boys' (treble) voices—and the popular 'Quartett' settings (in one instance an 'Otetto', for two each of trebles, altos, tenors, and basses: no. [2] in Philip Armes's Sacred Cantata, 'Behold, the Lord maketh the earth empty!'),[63] as well as a substantial amount of chorus. Verrinder's 'Israel in adversity and in deliverance', for example, is studded with choral numbers showing (in the Handelian tradition) considerable variety of treatment: among them, the 'Chorus of Israelites' ('Jehovah's people') is set in vocal declamation in unison and octaves (although with string harmonies), possibly in an attempt at Israelite authenticity; the 'Chorus of Prophets and People' ('Let the Harp of Judah ring') is set for SATTB with an accompaniment featuring two harps; and the final number is for double choir.[64] Five-part choruses (often for two trebles, ATB), and eight-part (S [or Treble] ATB × 2), are frequently used, reflecting the statutory requirements; other

Music . . . performed in New College Chapel'): MS Mus. Sch. Ex. c. 24. Armes (1858; and 1864) and Hayne (1856; 1860) used the term 'Cantata' for both their B.Mus. and their D.Mus. exercises, based on texts from the prophets and psalms; Ouseley's B.Mus. Exercise, a setting of Jeremiah 10: 10 was described as a 'Sacred Cantata': Ex. c. 40. G. J. Elvey produced 'The Resurrection and Ascension, an Oratorio composed as an Exercise for the Degree of Bachelor of Music . . . Performed in New College Chapel Oxford, June 1st 1838' (Ex. d. 44), which extends to about 150 pages of music in score. In the secular poetic context, the traditional 18th-cent. term 'Ode' still appears, as in E. G. Monk's B.Mus., Ex. b. 17, 'Ode on the Nativity' ('a selection from Milton . . . Performed . . . In the Hall of Exeter Coll. Oxon., Dec. 2nd, 1848'); E. G. Monk's D.Mus. (Ex. c. 39) was 'The Bard', a selection from Gray's Ode, performed in the Sheldonian Theatre, 5 March 1856, 'Before the Vice Chancellor, & Proctors, By an Orchestra & Chorus of 120 Performers' (some of them possibly from Radley, where Monk was Fellow and Precentor of St Peter's College).

[61] Apart from the psalms, other textual sources include the Prophets and, more rarely, the English poetic tradition: Milton, Pope, and Gray.

[62] Ex. c. 64 ('in 2 parts with Overture + Intermezzo. Composed for the degree of Bachelor of Music and performed before the University of Oxford, June 25th, 1862'). Verrinder's career encompassed an appointment as organist at the Reformed (West London) Synagogue.

[63] D.Mus. (Ex. d. 5).   [64] B.Mus. (Ex. c. 64).

choral effects include unaccompanied chorus, and the combination of soli and chorus (Armes's 'Behold, the Lord maketh the earth empty!' has an unaccompanied chorus à 8, contrasting and uniting a solo quartet with the vocal tutti);[65] choral fugue is generally understood to be a *sine qua non* (and produces not only some accurate technical efforts but also some vivid evocations, such as the cumulatively despairing tread of Parry's fugal chorus, 'O Lord thou hast cast us out', to which the overture acts as an introduction: Ex. 7.1).[66]

Much of the technical and stylistic basis of these works (such as the carefully studied fugue—often displaying correct 'tonal' answers, stretti, and other 'learned' features—and the conspicuous references to Handelian idiom, as in Verrinder's work) can be seen as continuing from the tradition of the preceding century.[67] But the nineteenth-century exercises also reflect contemporary preoccupations. On the one hand, they form an index of more 'modern' (post-Baroque) influences on English music: the symphonic style of Beethoven, and echoes of Haydn and Mendelssohn, together with a general awareness of operatic trends. On the other hand, a new element remarkable in these exercises is the preoccupation with certain archaic forms of expression. For example, George Dixon's setting of Pope's 'Messiah' (D.Mus. exercise, 1858) contains, as its No. 10, a 'Canto Fermo (arranged from a "Gregorian Tune")' for the popular double choir and orchestra.[68] In Stainer's B.Mus. exercise ('Praise the Lord, O my soul') an antique style, making reference to species counterpoint, is apparent.[69] The hymn-like settings favoured for choral and ensemble numbers are often subtitled 'Chorale', as in G. J. Elvey's 'Chorale Quartett: Alla Capella' (No. 12 of his B.Mus. exercise).[70]

William Pole's 'Corale: All people that on earth do dwell' (No. 2 of his B.Mus. exercise, a Cantata on the Hundredth Psalm) builds up imitative figures in motoric rhythm over a pedal-point before introducing the psalm tune in long notes into this texture.[71] The Mendelssohnian duetto that

---

[65] Reference as n. 63 above.

[66] Parry's exercise (B.Mus. Ex. d. 100) was published as a Cantata from the Holy Scriptures by Lamborn Cock in 1876.

[67] Evidently either the candidates or the examiners, or both, continued to set great value on Handelian style. Manifestations of this include paraphrase to the point of near-quotation from Handel (often in 19th-cent. stylistic surroundings).

[68] Ex. d. 41.   [69] Ex. c. 57.   [70] Reference as n. 60.

[71] Ex. d. 105: dated 13 June 1860. 'Cantata for Eight Voices, Orchestra [strings only], and Organ' to

Ex. 7.1. Hubert Parry, anthem, *O Lord thou hast cast us out*, B.Mus. exercise, 1866,
No. [1], Overture, bars 1–3, 11–28; No. 2, Chorus, bars 1–13
(Ob, MS Mus. Sch. Ex. d. 100, pp. 1–2; 4–5)

follows (No. 3: 'The Lord ye know is God indeed') 'with accompaniment of Canto Fermo', incorporates the tune in long-note phrases. The archaic title 'Motett' used by another candidate, Joseph Tiley, for a whole work is

be performed 'in the Music School, Oxford' on Wednesday, 13 June 1860, at 2.30 p.m. Pole annotates the work to indicate constructional points, not only providing explanatory subtitles (No. 4: Corale 'Formed from the Psalm Tune by Retrograde Motion') but also indicating at the start that passages 'marked thus*, are formed from portions of the Psalm Tune'. With due scientific precision he gives besides the customary metronome markings individual timings, totalling 20' to allow for 'Pauses + Stops'. (Pole's D.Mus. exercise shows similar constructional and 'scientific' qualities.)

applied by Pole here to a number for voices alone (No. 6: 'Motett with Canon and Accompanying Canto Fermo').[72] Several of the procedures used in Pole's work seem to show a strong Bach influence, new in such a context.[73]

The nineteenth-century exercises in general display considerable skill in structuring, scoring, and setting their texts. The growing interest in techniques of instrumentation manifested in the examination syllabus is reflected in the orchestral style of the degree exercises. The use of the orchestra 'tutti' varies from symphonic independence to a doubling function in some of the choral writing (perhaps with independent orchestral interludes); this may go together with 'a capella' style, following the traditional method. Solo vocal numbers may feature attractive obbligato effects: examples are the effective use of woodwind and horns solo in the treble aria (No. 3) of Philip Armes's doctoral cantata, 'Behold the Lord maketh the earth empty!' and of clarinets and bassoons against horn pedals in the [bass] solo 'A day of darkness' [No. 2] of the same composer's B.Mus. exercise, 'Blow ye the trumpet in Zion'.[74] In general, a tendency to large-scale scoring is apparent (often matching massive choral effects), in which double woodwind (flutes, oboes, possibly clarinets, bassoons), horns, trumpets, trombones, timpani, and strings with organ represent the standard forces, with occasional added colour such as the ophicleide.[75] In a number of exercises the organ part is notated as a figured bass.[76] Care is generally taken over the details of dynamic markings and articulation; many exercises give metronome (MM) markings for individual numbers, as well as indicating tempo and mood. It should perhaps be pointed out here that the emphasis is not on mere 'paper effects', but on a work's effectiveness in performance, and as an evocation of its text.

---

[72] Tiley's B.Mus. exercise: 'Motett, "O Lord our Lord" Psalm 8 + Psalm 9 ver 1 & 2', Ex. c. 62, shows 'stile antico' and 'alla cappella' style; rather like Pole, Tiley is preoccupied with technical points, for example constructing an 'Amen' fugue incorporating diminution and inversion of the subject, with a special notation drawing attention to these technical features.

[73] On the English Bach revival generally, see Temperley, *The Romantic Age*, 498–9.

[74] Ex. d. 5; Ex. d. 4.

[75] Used by Ouseley, together with a full 'symphonic' orchestra including clarinets, in his B.Mus. exercise (Ex. c. 40).

[76] This is found in exercises both from before the mid-19th cent. (G. J. Elvey), and after (L. G. Hayne), and provides further evidence for the well-documented persistence of this Baroque notational practice beyond the 18th cent. Concern for detail is also shown over organ registration and performance instructions.

Indeed a feature which distinguishes these exercises from the majority of their eighteenth-century counterparts is the stronger emphasis on mood- and word-painting. A number of candidates set texts incorporating words about music (following a long and varied English musico-poetic tradition). Examples are Monk's 'The Bard'; and his 'Ode on the Nativity' where the 'Divinely warbled voice | Answering the stringed noise' evokes an apt echo effect in the music.[77] (Milton's Ode, used here, is a particularly rewarding text to set, characteristically full of musical imagery.) Scriptural sources offered traditional opportunities for musical depiction that received a vivid response. In G. J. Elvey's B.Mus., No. 4 (recit.), the bass soloist sings the words 'but he is risen' to an appropriately leaping phrase, with trumpet calls and D major harmony; in the same composer's D.Mus., the lines from 'At his sight the mountains are shaken' onwards, with their description of the storm, thunder, whirlwind, and the earth trembling, obviously offer numerous suggestions of corresponding musical effects.[78] The Prophets provided some similarly dramatic scenes: Ouseley's setting from Jeremiah has the earth trembling in both text and music.[79] Personification of natural phenomena vividly informs the psalm-derived text of G. J. Elvey's chorus 'All thy Works' (No. 15 of his B.Mus. oratorio), with opportunities for depicting 'Let the Sea make a noise', 'Let the floods clap their hands', and 'Let the hills be joyful'.[80]

In the light of this discussion of nineteenth-century exercises, Parry's B.Mus. anthem appears as a miniature masterpiece, brilliantly creating mood and combining Bach's and Beethoven's influences with his own individuality of thought.[81] An example of his capacity to 'go his own way' is the strikingly effective use of a dominant pedal (on A) during the fourth entry of the fugal exposition in the opening number, unbound by conventional ideas of reserving the pedal-point until the later part of the fugue. It

[77] D.Mus., Ex. c. 39, No. 8 (chorus), p. 154: a curiosity of this piece is the introduction (on p. 155) of 'God Save the Queen', against which the voices enter declaiming 'What Strings symphonious tremble in the air'; B.Mus., Ex. b. 17.

[78] B.Mus., Ex. d. 44 (cf. n. 60); D.Mus., Ex. d. 45, Anthem: 'The ways of Zion do mourn'. The latter piece was not only 'cordially approved' by Crotch, but also 'universally admired' by a 'large company', including Queen Victoria and Prince Albert, on its performance at Windsor Castle in April 1840 before the conferral of the degree; see Lady Elvey, *Life of Elvey*, 53–5.

[79] Ex. c. 40 (B.Mus.): cf. n. 60.

[80] Reference n. 78.

[81] The fugal passages in D minor (p. 2 of the MS) strongly recall Bach's '48': II. 6. For a detailed account of the circumstances of composition and examination, see Dibble, *Parry*, 37–45, 48.

Andante. 76
Duett.
(with Canto Fermo.)
The passages in Red to be played on a Solo Stop.
Viola and Violoncello
Sopr.
SOLI.
Tenor
Organ
Ped
The Accompt. on the Swell, moderately brilliant.
The Pedals, soft 16 ft stops.
The Lord ye know is God in deed without our aid He did us make
SOLO

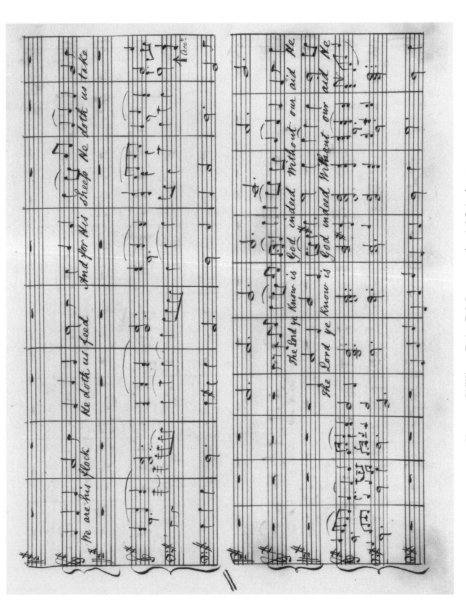

Fig. 11. William Pole, B.Mus. exercise (1860), duet

is interesting to follow through the examiner's comments on Parry's exercise: the chief examiner was Ouseley, as Professor. Where the second fugal entry in the opening number begins on e, Ouseley has suggested 'better have D to make a proper tonal answer'. In fact the fourth entry uses D (Parry may have been inspired here by his evident knowledge of J.S. Bach's fugal practice, since Bach sometimes demonstrates two different forms of answer within a four-part exposition). In the same fugue, where Parry has filled in the texture (bars 39–40) with crotchets, the examiner suggests 'better let the 2nd .V rest until it enters with the subject'. But these are minor matters, and at the close of the fugue the examiner's summing-up is 'all good' (p. 4). A point during the second number (the five-part fugal chorus 'Lord thou has cast us out') evoked the censure 'I dislike bringing in a point on a dissonance'; but the masterly weaving of imitative entries here, including some fine passages of stretto, again earned the final comment 'all good' (p. 11). Ouseley displays some flexibility where he comments on the abrupt arrival on a seventh chord (in No. 7, the five-part chorus 'Praise God from whom all blessings flow', interlude: bar 27) '*unprepared* but I will allow it here': it is in fact a highly effective progression.[82]

It was not only with the more conscientious examining style of the Ouseley era that the examiners scrutinized the exercises critically. On Stephen Elvey's doctoral anthem 'Great is the Lord', Crotch (then Professor) in his generous hand, and with generosity of spirit, has pencilled 'good' at the end of various numbers, sometimes 'very good', 'all very fine' and 'very sweet' (this last for the lovely, rather Haydnesque duet for two trebles with the accompaniment of flute and strings: 'We wait for thy loving kindness O God'). Crotch admired the expressive chromaticism (incorporating the chromatic fourth, long associated with lamenting and pain) used by Elvey in the F minor sextet 'Fear came there', for example at the words 'As upon a woman in her travail'. Again it is apparent that the degree exercises were not expected merely to be bland demonstrations of technical points, but allowed much scope for the display of skill in expressive interpretation of the text, and—in the best English tradition—fine

---

[82] Parry took in Ouseley's criticisms when the work was published. Among occasional documentation of failures, Thewlis (Notes, ii. 351) cites, from Joyce's *Life of Ouseley*, the case of the candidate who wrote unwisely to Ouseley as follows: 'Sir, — Your rejection of my exercise confirms the opinion I have long entertained of your utter incompetence for the office you hold.' For an abstract of Bishop's criticisms of Ouseley's B.Mus. exercise, see Shaw, *Ouseley and St Michael's, Tenbury*, Appendix C, p. 118.

choral writing, with often plentiful evidence of a well-founded sense of choral effect.[83]

The post-Ouseley reforms focused attention on the exercise as well as on the examination papers. While the successful exercises deposited in the Bodleian show the positive side of the process, the negative side was evoked by the examiners' description (apropos of some revealing statistics of passes and failures for 1902) of the 'exhausting experience' of dragging themselves through a quantity of exercises sent in 'year after year' by 'hopelessly bad' (but evidently tirelessly persistent) candidates. The examiners also noted that the removal of the restriction whereby candidates who had passed the B.Mus. were debarred from entering for the D.Mus. for five years, meant that 'candidates who have just scraped through with their Mus.Bac. exercise after several years of failure, begin the same tactics with their Mus.Doc. exercise, possibly in the hope of wearying [*sic*] out the examiners'. It was felt that if the exercise were 'properly recognized as part of the examination, and candidates had to enter their names and pay fees when they send it in, there might be a little check upon their venture-someness'.[84]

Eventually, in November 1911 the newly established Board of Studies for Music asked Hebdomadal Council to amend the statute 'so as to make the written examination come first in order, and the Exercise last'. Although the new regulations were expressly intended to ensure that candidates 'should show their proficiency on the theoretical side' (by examination) before submitting practical evidence of their ability in composition, this did not relegate the exercise to a merely supplementary role in relation to the written examinations: it was seen rather as 'the real climax of the examination, and should come at the end'.[85]

The work of the Music Board in its earliest stages is recorded in a series of documents revealing the range and thoroughness of its activity.[86] The

[83] As in C. H. Lloyd's B.Mus. (Ex. d . 76: inscribed 'This will do very well. F.A.G.O.'), which evinces a strong sense of choral style generally, e.g. in the impressive setting of 'What is man, that thou art mindful of him'; p. 21 (five-part chorus).

[84] HCP 1902, 21–2.

[85] HCP 1911, 221–2; and see ibid. 51. The D.Mus. was reorganized to match the new-style B.Mus. (see also FA4/12/1/1, formerly MUS M/1/1, Minutes of the Board of Studies for Music, 8 Nov. 1911, p. 5).

[86] Minutes from the first meeting onwards (13 June 1911) in FA4/12/1/1; reports of subcommittees in FA4/12/2/1, formerly MUS R/1/1.

Board had much to do: its meetings were evidently no mere rehearsal of routine matters requiring little attention, but were concerned with establishing the study and examination of the subject firmly on a new, more formalized, basis. A 'snapshot' impression of some of the issues which now came under the aegis of the Board can be gained from the handwritten minutes of the first meeting (13 June 1911).[87] Subcommittees were drawn up on this occasion from among the (small) membership of the Board, to fulfil diverse functions: the nomination of examiners in Music, the selection of scores for analysis, the organization of administrative and statutory matters, approval of termly lecture lists, library matters, and the review of courses of study at other institutions.[88]

The Board's choice of set works (in connection with the Second B.Mus. examination) presents an interesting impression of what was thought important, and what was available in convenient form, at the time. Equivalence was not consistently maintained. For the November 1912 examination, Verdi's *Stabat Mater* and Beethoven's C sharp minor Quartet were prescribed, while for the May 1913 session it was decided to require 'Weber's Freischütz Opera' and César Franck's *Les Djinns*.[89] For every pair of works set for the sessions from November 1913 to May 1915, availability in miniature scores published by Breitkopf & Härtel was specifically mentioned. Music from before 1750 (Bach's *Magnificat* in D, Palestrina's *Stabat Mater,* ed. Parratt) was scheduled for study alongside music of the past few decades (Wagner's *Tristan und Isolde*, Strauss's *Ein Heldenleben*, Rimsky-Korsakov's *Scheherezade*, Debussy's *La Damoiselle Élue*.[90] It was clearly no narrow 'English organ-loft' training that was envisaged. On the other

[87] FA4/12/1/1, pp. 1–2. Present at the meeting were Mr Gerrans in the Chair (pro tem: the Dean of Christ Church (T. B. Strong) was elected Chairman for the year), the Professor of Music (Parratt), Dr Allen (Choragus), Dr Walker, and Mr Cronshaw. Among others drawn in to serve on the Board and its committees for 1911–12 were Mr Benecke, Dr Roberts, Mr Joachim of Merton, and Sir Edward Elgar (co-opted as 'a member of the Board for three years from the first day of Hilary Term, 1912': FA4/12/1/1, 8 Nov. 1911, p. 4).

[88] This last was regarded as sensitive information: it was decided (FA4/12/1/1, 8 Nov. 1911, p. 6) that 'the list of approved institutions should be considered confidential for the present'. The minutes for 5 June 1912 (ibid. 11) recorded that an application for recognition of a course of musical study at 'Hove School of Music, 12 Grand Avenue' (Principal, Mr F. Mott Harrison) was refused. The original list drafted by the Board included Cambridge, Trinity College Dublin, London (Internal), Edinburgh, and some of the major conservatoires: see FA4/12/1/1, pp. 5–6.

[89] Ibid. 4 (8 Nov. 1911).

[90] Ibid. 12; p. 20.

hand, the admirable emphasis on the wider European and Russian musical scene apparently excluded what might have been a valuable opportunity to encourage awareness of British musical achievement. A glance at the works chosen (in January 1915) for 1915–16 shows that, with the inclusion of Byrd's Mass for four voices, Elgar's second symphony, and Parry's *Blest Pair of Sirens* (all in Novello editions), a new balance was struck: the timing is obviously significant. And it is a nice touch that Oxford music candidates were set, for study, works by two outstanding modern British composers with strong Oxford connections.[91]

By 1914, the academic status of music in Oxford was represented by a tradition of active, resident Professors and lecturers, by an increased level of intellectual aspiration, and by the existence of the administrative mechanisms necessary for the eventual formation of a true Faculty of Music in the modern sense.

[91] FA4/12/1/1, p. 26. On Parry, see Dibble, *Parry*, chs. 3, 13, and 14; on Elgar see n. 87 above (Elgar was co-opted to the Music Board for a further three years from Hilary Term 1914). An interesting sidelight comes in Peter Ward Jones's account of Elgar's acting as an amanuensis for a blind musical degree candidate at Oxford ('Elgar as Amanuensis', *BLR* 8 (1989), 180–1).

8

Music in the University
and City, II

Accounts of the Oxford Professors of Music in the first half of the nine-teenth century—from Crotch's move to London in 1806 to Ouseley's election in 1855—tend to stress the absentee character of their tenure.[1] Ouseley and Corfe in 1877 described 'the present endowment of the professorship' as 'little more than nominal'. To found a 'complete school of music' would in their opinion require 'the endowment of a first-class professorship'.[2] Bishop, in 1852, defining the Professor's duties, mentioned—apart from the examination of degree exercises—that

The Professor of Music at Oxford has also to be present at the *Annual Commemoration*, and preside at the *Organ* in the Theatre on that occasion . . . It is also the office of the Professor of Music at Oxford "to *compose for* and *conduct* all musical performances ordained by, or connected with, the Academical regulations," such as *Installation Odes*, &c.[3]

The continuing role of the Professor as a purveyor of occasional music led to the composition of several 'Installation Odes' during this period. Crotch's 1810 Ode for the installation of Lord Grenville as Chancellor is

---

[1] See Temperley, *The Romantic Age* (p. 30), quoting from Tuckwell, *Reminiscences*, the view that 'Bishop regarded his . . . appointment as a sinecure, its annual salary well earned by his appearing only at Commemoration to play the ramshackle old organ'.

[2] UOC, Supplementary evidence, p. 375.   [3] Royal Commission, Evidence, p. 265.

FIRST
GRAND MISCELLANEOUS
CONCERT.

JULY 3, 1810.

ACT I.

OVERTURE........*Samson.* . . . . HANDEL.
RECIT. Mr. Vaughan. " *This day a solemn feast.*"
CHOR. " *Awake the trumpet's lofty sound.*" . . HANDEL..
SONG, Mrs. Ashe. " *Pious orgies.*"...*Jud. Macch.* HANDEL.
SONG, Mr. Bartleman. *Tempest.* . . . . . PURCELL.
    " *Arise, ye subterranean winds.*"
QUARTETT AND CHORUS. *Te Deum.* . . . GRAUN.
    " *Te gloriosus apostolorum Chorus.*"
SONG, Mr. Braham. " *Questo è forse.*" . . ZINGARELLI.
CONCERTO, OBOE, Mr. Griesbach.
SCENA, Madame Catalani. " *Su Griselda.*" . . PAER.
THE NIGHTINGALE CHORUS. *Solomon.* . . . HANDEL.

ACT II.

GRAND OVERTURE to Henry IV. . . . . . MARTINI.
QUARTETT, Madame Catalani, Mrs. Bianchi, Mr. Braham,
   and Mr. Bellamy . . . . GUGLIELMI.
    " *Il figlio a questo seno.*"
SONG, Mr. Braham. . . . . DR. CLARK.
    " *The last words of Marmion.*"
CHOR. " *Judas Macchabæus.*" . . . . . HANDEL.
    " *O Father, whose Almighty power.*"
MOTETT. . . . . DR. CROTCH.
    " *Methinks I hear the full celestial choir.*"
OVERTURE and CHACONNE . . . . . . IOMELLI.
SONG, Mr. Bartleman. " *O Lord! have mercy.*" PERGOLESI.
SONG, Madame Catalani. " *Ah ti muova.*" . . . MAYER.
GRAND CORON. ANTHEM. " *Zadoc the Priest.*" HANDEL.

Tickets, 10s 6d each, to be had of Messrs. Lock & Son, High
   Street, and of Mr. Thorpe, Broad Street; Mr. Cooke,
   Mr. Parker, M. Bliss, and Robert Bliss, Booksellers.
†+† To avoid the great inconvenience and delay that must necessarily be occasioned by receiving MONEY at the Theatre,
   the Public are most respectfully and earnestly requested to
   purchase their Tickets as above; where also books of each
   day's Performance may be had.
*** The Doors will be opened at four, and the Performances
    begin at five, o'Clock.

Printed by N. Bliss, Oxford.

FIG. 12. Concert programme, Sheldonian Theatre, 3 July 1810

now lost; it was originally well received. His 1834 Ode for the installation
of the Duke of Wellington as Chancellor set words by John Keble. In 1853
Henry Bishop's Ode for the installation of the Earl of Derby seems to have
marked the end of the tradition.[4]

4 Trowles, 'Musical Ode', i. 74 ff. Further on the Commemorations see Ch. 9 below, where they are
discussed in the context of Oxford concerts generally.

For the 1810 occasion celebrating 'the Public Reception of the New Chancellor the Right Hon. Lord Grenville' (3–6 July) Crotch's participation encompassed not only performances of his compositions (including his 'Motett', 'Methinks I hear the full celestial choir', in Act II of the Commemoration concert on 3 July) but also the prominent role of conductor: with a dazzling row of principal vocal performers and an orchestra of over 100 players, 'the whole to be conducted by Dr. Crotch', this was a major undertaking.[5] During the first half of the century the 'Grand Musical Festival' marking Commemoration week was expanded on an ambitious scale. In 1834, for the 'Installation of his Grace the Duke of Wellington, Chancellor of the University', the new 'Sacred Oratorio' of the *Captivity of Judah* by Crotch was advertised for Tuesday, 10 June, followed by three 'Grand Miscellaneous Concerts' on Wednesday, Thursday, and Friday, featuring 'Overtures, Symphonies as performed at the Philharmonic Concerts and the Royal Academy of Music', and excerpts from 'the newest Operas', all seemingly designed to show that Oxford's music was *au courant*.[6] That the audience numbers, too, may have increased in scale is indicated by Thewlis's comment that 'Crotch's Oratorio was well received by a packed audience, many . . . almost crushed to death'.[7] Again for this event, Crotch conducted.

The Professor continued, also, at this time to contribute his expertise to the annual Radcliffe Infirmary service that formed part of Commemoration week: in 1805 the customary Te Deum and Benedictus for this service (on this occasion by Orlando Gibbons) were provided with 'instrumental accompaniments by Dr. Crotch'.[8] And in 1809 the *Journal* reported that Crotch played the organ for the Radcliffe service in June.[9] The music chosen for these charity events featured local productions and enthusiasms (Aldrich and Handel, for example) and appropriately worded texts, as with Boyce's anthem *Here shall soft Charity repair*; all these were heard in June 1814.[10] Crotch's contributions to the musical performances in Commemoration week in the years after his move to London went well beyond the dismissive descriptions perpetuated by nineteenth-century sources

---

[5] Cf. *JOJ*, 30 June 1810.   [6] *JOJ*, 7 June 1834.   [7] Thewlis, Notes, iv. 866.
[8] *JOJ*, 15 June 1805.
[9] Thewlis, Notes, iv. 782. The pattern of a June event at St Mary's for the Radcliffe Infirmary persisted through the early decades of the 19th cent.   [10] *JOJ*, 18 June 1814.

such as Cox.[11] In some years Walter Vicary (organist of Magdalen College) conducted in place of Crotch, as in 1823 (when 'selections' from Crotch's oratorio *Palestine* formed Act I of the first concert in the Grand Musical Festival; Haydn's *Seasons* and Mozart's *Requiem* also received the 'miscellaneous' treatment, and the selection was pronounced 'admirable' by the *Journal*'s critic).[12]

Whatever the nature and extent of Crotch's input, the Commemoration concerts during the early decades of the century continually achieved artistic success, often featuring soloists of the first rank: presumably the university provided financial means to secure this level of art. (Cox mentioned a subvention of £200 for such a purpose.[13]) The audiences that gathered in Oxford in June 1826 for the Commemoration heard 'Madam Pasta' (who 'fully justified the high praise bestowed upon her by the world') and Mr Sapio, as well as 'Master Thalberg' on the 'Pianoforte', having just made his début at the Philharmonic Concerts.[14] These Oxford concerts were at the Music Room (on Tuesday and Wednesday, 6 and 7 June) and as they were described as 'well attended' the Room was doubtless very crowded. Crotch conducted, and his *Palestine* was performed, in 1827 when Madame Pasta ('unrivalled now Catalani is absent') returned to sing at the Commemoration Festival in June (this time at the Theatre, to an audience of between 1,000 and over 2,000);[15] and again in 1831 Crotch was conducting, together with Neukomm, when Pasta appeared at the concerts in the Theatre (and Neukomm conducted his own compositions, among them the 'New Cantata. "Napoleon's Midnight Review" ').[16] The multiplicity of musical styles and sounds on this occasion was increased by the participation of 'the celebrated female singers from Lancashire' to sustain the choral parts, noted by Thewlis as 'the first mention of ladies taking part in the chorus'.[17]

Thewlis records also that during Commemoration week of 1831 'there were several amateur performances at different colleges, but unfortunately there are no details'.[18] This contrasting of amateur and professional events became a feature of the Commemoration, with (in the former category)

[11] Cf. Cox, *Recollections*, 150.
[12] *JOJ*, 7 June 1823; 14 June 1823.   [13] Cox, *Recollections*, 271.
[14] Thewlis, Notes, iv. 840.   [15] Mee, *Music Room*, 196.
[16] Ibid., and Thewlis, Notes, iv. 854–6.
[17] Ibid. 855.   [18] Ibid. 857.

both college and university societies putting on concerts. In the latter category, whereby the local musicians were reinforced by many visiting performers, the emphasis was on concerts 'memorable for the celebrity of the performers'.[19] A unique feature—in the perspective of musical festival culture generally—was the inclusion of academic degree exercises receiving their statutory public performance. Within the Commemoration celebrations of 1852 (when Joachim visited Oxford) Corfe's D.Mus. exercise was given at the Theatre on Thursday, 24 June.[20] The Oxford Choral Society, chapel choirs, and principal performers at the festival concerts assisted: Dr Corfe was 'loudly cheered' and Sir Henry Bishop 'shook the Composer by the hand, and congratulated him on his success'.[21]

Bishop, like Crotch, presided over the examination of the degree exercises and was heavily involved in the Commemorations generally, but otherwise not noticeably committed to Oxford music. He himself stressed that the Heather Professorship of Music did not carry the weight that other posts possessed: the table 'respecting the Professorships at Oxford' printed in the report of the Royal Commission (1852), in which Bishop's entry under the heading of 'duties as customarily performed' reads 'No Lectures', shows the Heather Professor at the lower end of the scale of pay, far below the Savile, Camden, and White's Professorships founded at the same period. Bishop in his evidence to the commission implied that for the '*whole* annual stipend of the Professor of Music, as it remains at the present time, THIRTY POUNDS', together with a fee of one guinea 'from each Candidate on their being admitted to a Degree in Music', it was unreasonable to expect any more sustained effort.[22] And he excused his failure to organize lectures in Oxford by declaring: 'that [the opportunity to offer lectures] has not hitherto occurred has been owing . . . I have no hesitation in saying, to the *absolute necessity* of my attending to those *other* sources of my

---

[19] Thewlis, Notes, iv. 870–1.

[20] *Thou O God art praised in Zion.*

[21] Thewlis, Notes, iv. 916. Bishop Mitchinson of Pembroke, in his recollections of this period, mentions the 'University Musical Exercises for Mus: Bac: and Mus Doc:' as a 'perennial attraction', distinguishing two categories of performance; for the routine occasions 'a number of old fiddlers, of whom E. [A.R.?] Reinagle was chief, unearthed from some unknown recesses in the Schools their "flutes, harps, sackbuts & c"' with the candidate himself conducting; in the case of the 'more distinguished (or more ambitious) musicians the Exercise was performed on a larger scale and in the Sheldonian Theatre'. (Mitchinson himself 'helped to swell the chorus' for two such exercises: see his 'Oxford Memories' (unpublished memoirs), PCA, MS 60/15/83, p. 21).

[22] Royal Commission, Evidence, p. 265.

professional income, by means of which I live, and have to meet the claims on me of a young family.'[23] Bishop's view of the needs of the subject was both practical and idealistic: 'Amongst other means for the advancement of the study of music, I know of none more important . . . than the establishment of a distinct *Library of Music*, which, from its completeness and classification, should comprise a perfect history of the progress of the musical art.' Noting that 'copies of all musical publications, printed in *this country*' were by Act of Parliament deposited in the Bodleian and British Museum, he felt that 'to render a library of music complete, and make it really useful to students, all superior *foreign* musical works, both theoretical and practical, of every school and of every age, should be added to the collection . . .'.[24]

Ouseley and Corfe, in their evidence to the later university commission, stated that the Choragus (the post having been divided in Bishop's time, with Stephen Elvey—organist of New College—serving as the first under the new system) received '13*l*. 10*s*. annually'. Again exercising an ideal vision, they wished to see a university school of composition that 'would form the nucleus' of their envisaged 'complete school of music', with 'the benefits of such a school in Oxford' to be made 'accessible to the far from wealthy class from which so many musicians spring' through the foundation of scholarships. 'Such provision would complete a scheme of the most advantageous character for the future of music, and for the nature of its influence on the world'.[25] While their 'development plan' (which was formulated in detail) remained largely unrealized during their time, the period of their influence on music in Oxford was marked by a number of significant educational initiatives, apart from the crucial changes to the musical degree system.

With the Motett and Madrigal Society (under Monk briefly, and then Corfe) it was felt by a commentator in the church music press that 'the members of the University of all ranks are willing, and even eager, to do their part in the great work of advancing the cause of Church Music'.[26] It was noted that 'of the Officers of the Motett Society; thirteen are in Holy Orders . . . three are Heads of Houses, among whom, as president, the

---

[23] Royal Commission, Evidence, p. 266.   [24] Ibid.
[25] UOC, Supplementary Evidence, No. 3 (pp. 374–5).
[26] *The Parish Choir*, iii. 4 (quoted in Thewlis, Notes, ii. 334). Also cf. Ch. 7, p. 101 above.

Warden of New College stands foremost', as well as the Professor of Ecclesiastical History, various graduates and undergraduates. (The editor went on: 'nothing that occurs at Oxford is of simple local interest . . . for every influence brought to bear on Oxford tells through the length and breadth of the land'.) Probably it was this same society that the Revd Hartshorne referred to in his reminiscences of Christ Church Cathedral School where he was a choirboy in 1849: 'in Term time, Dr. Corfe had a Madrigal Class at the music room, Holywell Street at 8 o'clock once a week which his boys attended. We received about 15/- each . . .'.[27]

Corfe also instigated the production of Greek plays with music, described by the *Journal*'s critic as 'an intellectual and musical treat as has rarely been enjoyed within the walls of this University'.[28] In April 1853 the *Journal* announced Sophocles' *Antigone* 'with Mendelssohn's music' on 3 May; and in May 1855 Sophocles' *Oedipus at Colonus*, similarly with Mendelssohn's music, was announced for 14 June (to take place in the Town Hall). The *Journal*'s description of the musical personnel resembles the style of the Commemoration advertisements, and Mr Blagrove, who led the orchestra (under Corfe's conductorship) had in fact fulfilled this same role at the Commemoration concert conducted by Bishop for the Installation of the Earl of Derby as Chancellor in 1853.[29] Subsequently the *Journal*'s critic praised Dr Corfe's 'energetic tuition'.[30]

The Choragus, assisting the Professor, was generally active in conducting and playing in the University. In the 1850s Stephen Elvey appeared as honorary conductor of the UAMS, for example during Commemoration week. At this time Ouseley, as Professor, played the organ in the Sheldonian Theatre for the Commemoration, and the *Journal* referred to the 'very inferior instrument on which the Professor is at present obliged to perform'.[31] This target of complaint recurred over time. There was in fact by this stage a three-tier system, with the Professor, Choragus, and the newly added post of Coryphaeus. Thewlis, while not denigrating

---

[27] *Christ Church Cathedral School register*, 7.

[28] Quoted in Thewlis, Notes, ii. 337. Cambridge developed a similar practice (see Knight, *Cambridge Music*, 78–9; 93). Cf. *JOJ*, 23 Apr. 1853, and 26 May 1855. Later, Parry was involved in composing music for the Greek plays (see esp. Dibble, *Parry*, 403–4, 467–8, and 515).

[29] Thewlis, Notes, iv. 916. Blagrove was 'adopted' by Oxford concert promoters; he was a valued principal in the Handel Festivals and concerts at the Crystal Palace and was generally a 'leading figure . . . on the continent as well as in London' (Musgrave, *Crystal Palace*, 251).

[30] *JOJ*, 16 June 1855.   [31] *JOJ*, 19 June 1858.

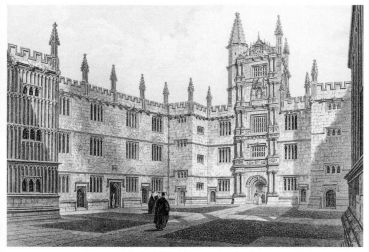

1. Bodleian quadrangle showing the doorways of the Schools

2. Sheldonian Theatre, exterior view, eighteenth century

3. Sheldonian Theatre, interior view, drawing by J. Buckler, 1815

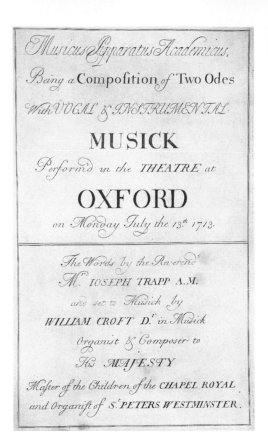

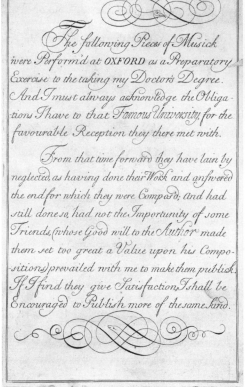

4. Preliminary pages, William
Croft, *Musicus Apparatus
Academicus*, 1715

5. University Church of St Mary
the Virgin, interior view

6. Holywell Music Room, exterior view 15 June 1822

7. Holywell Music Room, interior restored according to eighteenth-century specifications, *c*.1959–60

8. J. B. Malchair playing the violin, by his pupil W. H. Barnard, *c*.1791

9. William Hayes, Heather Professor 1741–77, in academic dress

10. Philip Hayes, Heather Professor 1777–97, in D.Mus. robes

11. William Crotch, Heather Professor 1797–1847, at the organ, Norwich, November 1778, engraving by J. Sanders after his own painting

12. Acott's music shop, 124 High Street, c.1900

13. New College chapel, interior, drawing by W. A. Delamotte, c.1821

14. Chaplains, organist, clerks, and choristers, Magdalen College, 1869

15. Choir on Magdalen College tower, May morning 1891

16. Sir Henry Bishop,
Heather Professor 1848–55

17. Sir Frederick Ouseley, Heather
Professor 1855–89

18. Sir John Stainer, Heather
Professor 1889–99, in D.Mus. robes,
by G. E. Moira, 1892

19. Sir Hubert Parry, Heather Professor
1900–8, by William Rothenstein, 1897

20. Sir Walter Parratt, Heather Professor
1908–18, in B.Mus. robes,
by G. E. Moira, 1892

21. Sir Hugh Allen, Heather Professor
1918–46, by D'Ustèle Segar

Ouseley's achievements, and while acknowledging that Elvey laboured under a physical disadvantage ('his infirmity may have been responsible in a large degree for his inactivity'), credits Corfe with establishing and maintaining high standards: 'Corfe, as Coryphaeus, took his work in wholehearted seriousness in developing and teaching the musical faculties of those students under his charge.'[32] Corfe in particular was associated with large-scale choral and orchestral performances, with Oxford remaining active in the sphere of oratorio; Corfe conducted, for instance, the 'grand performance' of Mendelssohn's *Elijah* in the Sheldonian Theatre in June 1858 (the principal vocal performers included Master R. Corfe as well as Mr Sims Reeves and Mr Weiss, the last-named being closely associated with the title role).

During the 1870s Corfe, playing the organ for Encaenia, seems to have become to some extent a 'cult figure'. At the Encaenia of 1873 the undergraduates gave three cheers 'for Dr Corfe *and* the organ blower'.[33] (The story of his 'unvarying use of a certain group of stops, wittily named the "Corfe-mixture"'—and called for by 'a wag' at Encaenia—is included in Watkins Shaw's account of Corfe).[34] By 1875 the *Journal* announced that 'The Hebdomadal Council has given its consent to the Vice-Chancellor ... appointing a place other than the Sheldonian Theatre for holding the Encaenia this year. This step has been rendered necessary by the increasingly uproarious turmoil of the last few occasions.'[35] Before this a number of references occur to the 'disgraceful behaviour' of the '*gentlemen* of the University'; in 1866 the *Oxford Undergraduate's Journal* had claimed that undergraduates were 'behaving so badly at public entertainments that no lady or gentleman from the City or County' would attend them.[36] In 1878 'at the Encaenia Ouseley gave an organ recital to keep the Undergraduates quiet, assisted by Parratt. They were cheered.' Some details of what was played by way of voluntaries and interludes are recoverable; when, at the Encaenia in 1881, Parratt 'as usual, played admirably' and was listened to 'with great attention', his programme included Bach's 'St Anne' Fugue and Handel's popular overture to *Otho*, as well as some contemporary organ works: Guilmant's *Marche Nuptiale* and Lemmens's *Marche Triomphale* (there was a distinct fashion for organ marches, chiming in with the

---

[32] Thewlis, Notes, iv. 931.   [33] Ibid. 955.   [34] Shaw, *Succession of Organists*, 214. Cf. Thewlis, Notes, iv. 951.   [35] *JOJ*, 20 Feb. 1875.   [36] Thewlis, Notes, iv. 925–6; 943.

nineteenth-century 'symphonic' writing for organ and exploiting the instrument's 'ability to imitate the orchestra').[37] The Encaenia performances, as well as belonging with the growing festival culture in Britain
(many of the invited performers were popular on the wider festival circuit,
for instance Sims Reeves) thus also contributed to the development of the
solo organ recital, as part of a generally burgeoning solo recital culture at
the time.

The long tradition of Royal visits to Oxford marked by musical performances continued. In 1883 when the Prince of Wales (an alumnus) laid
a 'Memorial Stone' for the Indian Institute he attended a concert in the
new Examination Schools (opened May 1882) in aid of the Royal College
of Music. The programme featured solos by 'members of the University
and City', and Mr Taphouse put on an exhibition of early instruments.
(The Prince of Wales spoke warmly of the event in general, including the
concert.)[38] The impression of a variety of civic and university occasions
for music-making, already apparent in the eighteenth century, becomes
ever more diversified as the nineteenth-century references accumulate. A
few instances out of the plethora available give some idea of the differing
social and cultural contexts within the local community. The City Waits
continued to accompany the traditional ceremonies. For 'Beating the
Bounds' in September 1860 the Revd J. R. Green recorded that 'we were
cheered by the merry beat of the City drum—the City fife having been
early winded and dropped behind'.[39] In connection with organ-playing,
the city churches continued to offer the chance to inaugurate new instruments; a series of these was heard during this period, with a relatively
unusual case in 1832, apropos the new organ installed at All Saints'
Church, when 'Miss Marshall' was appointed organist.[40] Guest organists
were attracted by these invitations. In 1840 the *Journal* declared: 'On Sunday the new and powerful organ, lately erected in our City Church [St
Martin's, Carfax] by Chambers (of this City) will be tried for the first time,

[37] Cf. Temperley, *The Romantic Age*, 436–7. On Parratt's 1881 programme see Thewlis, Notes, iv. 961.
[38] Cf. Thewlis, Notes, iv. 961–3; and programme of the commemorative concert at the Examination
Schools in May 1983 (private collection).
[39] Quoted in Thewlis, Notes, iii. 511.
[40] *JOJ*, 21 Apr. 1832. Other new organs 'opened' included St Paul's Church (1844), St Clement's
(1846), and St Aldate's (1859).

and the eminent organist of Westminster Abbey, (Mr Turle), will try its powers on the occasion.' Various additional elements were introduced to create a 'grand' event:

TWO SERMONS will be preached in this Church; the one in the morning by the Rev. R.D. HAMPDEN, D. D. Canon of Christ Church, and Regius Professor of Divinity; and that in the evening by the Rev. ELLIS WERE, M. A. Vicar of Chipping Norton. Collections in aid of the *funds* for the organ will be made . . . full Cathedral service both morning and evening.

The necessary flattering remarks were made about the 'liberality of the members of this University and of the inhabitants of the city' already evinced, while more was requested; a further advertisement in a nearby column referred to the subscription for the new organ.[41] The survey of Oxford churches published in 1847 (in which the correspondent seems to have been distinctly out of sorts) need not be taken at literal value, but its reference to the 'fine old organ' played by Elvey at the University Church of St Mary the Virgin, and to a 'good organist' at St Peter's in the East shows some willingness to bestow praise. Otherwise, the critic found at St Giles a barrel organ and a 'boisterous choir', and opined of Carfax Church: 'the city authorities attend this church. It contains a noisy organ, a noisy organist, and some noisy boys.'[42]

The fashion for festivals and associations brought Oxford's choirs together regularly from at least the early 1860s onwards. At the 'Festival of Parish Choirs' held in the Cathedral in 1862, twenty-two choirs and 300 voices were heard, and in 1863 the Oxford Diocesan Choral Association was founded with the Bishop of Oxford as its President, with the aim of promoting large-scale choral festivals.[43] Other musical meetings ranged from the 'University Choir' in 1867, gathering 'for the practice of Sacred Music in the Music Room on Sundays at 2 p.m.' as well as for an elementary class on Saturday evenings at the 'Conductor's Rooms', to the 'Saturday evening concerts for the working class' held at the Corn Exchange from 1862–5; at the first concert 'when, against the wish of the minority of

---

[41] *JOJ*, 20 June and 27 June 1840. On St Martin's Church, Carfax, see *EO*, 409, and Fletcher, *St. Martin's Church* (only the tower now remains of the medieval building).

[42] Quoted in Thewlis, Notes, iv. 910–11; cf. *The Parish Choir*, ii (Oct. 1847), 46–7.

[43] *JOJ*, 26 July 1862 and 17 Jan. 1863.

the committee, *Comic Songs* were allowed[,] an element of disorder was introduced which led to the discontinuance of the entertainments'.[44] Lecture series as well as individual lectures were in vogue; ironically on 20 February 1867 Mr W. A. Barrett was billed to give a lecture in the Music Room on 'the history of Comic Songs'.[45] In 1861 the *Journal* advertised the 'City of Oxford Public Lectures', with twelve Lectures and Concerts in the Town Hall. [46] At this same period Ouseley was infusing the Heather Professorship with a commitment to lecturing.[47]

From the nineteenth century, with the wider use of advertising in the local press, and the documentation provided by the census, a variety of commercial musical enterprises is recorded, ranging from music-selling to instrumental tuition. In 1810 when Hayes's *Psalms* were offered for sale by an Oxford firm, they were advertised as 'To be had at J. Wickens's Music Warehouse, near Lincoln College, where BROADWOOD'S PIANO FORTES are sold or let, warranted, and all new publications may be had as soon as possible.—Musical Instruments, Hunting and Bugle Horns, &c. at the London prices.'[48] And in 1824 the *Journal* carried an advert for the Music Circulating Library 'kept by Mr. Sharp in St. Aldate's', offering the information that 'Mr. Sharp's terms of instruction may be known at his Music and Musical Instrument Warehouse, near Christ Church'.[49] By 1829 the venture was referred to as a 'Musical Academy' set up by Mr Sharp on St Aldate's (later it was moved to Broad Street).[50] At the other end of the century there are references to individuals practising as music teachers. Research on the Jewish community of Oxford has brought to light a number of these entered in the census, such as Miriam Woolf, 19-year-old daughter of Herschell Woolf of Magdalen Street (jeweller and dealer in

---

[44] Thewlis, Notes, iv. 944; 938.

[45] Ibid. 944.

[46] Cf. *JOJ*, 13 Nov. 1861.

[47] For details see Thewlis, Notes, ii. 352–3; cf. Joyce, *Life of Ouseley*, 145, for an outline of the subjects. The scripts of Ouseley's lectures are preserved in a series of autograph notebooks (together with some musical illustrations) in Ob, MSS Tenbury 1443–63 (Professorial lectures 1861–88), which bear witness to his industry in this respect, and his range. To give a glimpse of their content: 'It will not be amiss to let you hear a composition of Seb[astia]n Bach's immediately after this one by Buxtehude, to enable you to see . . . how far Bach was influenced by the older composer's style' (MS Tenbury 1455, pp. 8–9; undated, possibly between 1879 and 1880/1 according to notes with the MS, and *pace* Thewlis, who dated it 7 Mar. 1866).

[48] *JOJ*, 30 June 1810. On Hayes's Psalms see Ch. 5, p. 80 above.

[49] *JOJ*, 1 May 1824.

[50] *JOJ*, 10 Jan. 1829; Thewlis, Notes, iv. 850.

cigars), who is described simply as 'TEACHER OF MUSIC'; and Esther A. Harris, 'TEACHER OF VIOLIN MUSIC', daughter of Henry Harris of Littlegate Street, a general stores merchant.[51] These 'snapshots' of musical activity indicate only a fraction of the enormous growth seen in Oxford during the nineteenth century in terms of provision for music. One of the strongest elements in this growth (and the one most consistently documented) was that of the public concert.

[51] Census 1871, 1891, kindly communicated by Harold Pollins.

9

Nineteenth-Century
Concert Life

Concert life in nineteenth-century Oxford reflected the unprecedented development of the colleges as centres of musical activity and resources, as Maurice in 1856 indicated, commenting on the growth of instrumental music-making:

Music has found an entrance within the walls of all our colleges, and the number of our students who can play upon some instrument, and have some knowledge of Music, is very considerable ... We can recollect that, whereas some thirty years ago there were pianofortes to be found in scarcely half a dozen colleges throughout the whole university ... now many a single college may count as many or more within its own walls, to say nothing of other instruments in great variety ...[1]

He emphasized further the proliferation of musical societies throughout the colleges:

and whereas at New College we could with difficulty in those days muster from the whole university sufficient musical talent to carry on the glee meeting, eked out with solos, duets, and occasional pianoforte performances, there are abundant materials in several colleges, which have no musical foundations, to form small associations ...[2]

[1] Maurice, *What shall we do with Music?*, 4.
[2] Ibid.

To the tradition of concerts featuring resident and visiting performers was now added an increase in the opportunities for student performance.

The strengthening of music 'within the walls' of the colleges was matched by a revival of University-wide concert promotion, following the hiatus in the Holywell series during the mid-nineteenth century. Some moves towards drawing together musical forces had already been made, for instance with Crotch's founding of the Oxford Choral Society in 1819. New university-based societies were formed partly in association with the trend to increase the academic value placed on music (as with Monk's, later Corfe's, Motett and Madrigal Society)[3] and partly under the influence of the developments in concert life generally in Britain. By the end of the century, both university and college music-making flourished. Far from signalling the decline of concert-giving in Oxford, the cessation of the Holywell concerts by the mid-nineteenth century (described in such vivid terms by Mee)[4] represented, when seen in retrospect, merely a lull before a great wave of concert activity in the second half of the century.

Late nineteenth- and early twentieth-century concert life in Oxford was characterized by the establishing of numerous college, university, and civic musical societies of diverse nature. Many institutions that were to be of lasting significance in Oxford's musical life were founded during this period, including the Oxford Symphony Orchestra (1902), the Oxford Chamber Music Society (founded 1898 as the Oxford Ladies' Musical Society), and the Oxford Silver Band (founded 1887 as the Headington Temperance Band). Among others that have survived to this day were the Oxford Bach Choir, which was founded in 1896 and in 1905 incorporated the Oxford Choral and Philharmonic Society (itself formed in 1890 from an amalgamation of the Oxford Choral Society founded by Crotch, and the Oxford Philharmonic Society founded by Stainer in 1865); and the Oxford University Musical Club and Union,[5] formed in 1916 from an amalgamation of the Oxford University Musical Club (1872) and the

---

[3] E. G. Monk was founder and first conductor of the society (from 1847); C. W. Corfe took over the conductorship from 1848. See Abdy Williams, *Degrees in Music*, 52; and, further on the society, Ch. 8, pp. 135–6 above.

[4] *Music Room*, ch. v: 'The End of the Music Room' (referring e.g. to the 'enterprise, so sturdily maintained . . .' coming to 'an inglorious end in 1840': cf. p. 175).

[5] Renamed in 1983 Oxford University Musical Society; now known as Oxford University Music Society (OUMS).

BALANCE SHEET.   January 1869.

Cr.	£.	s.	d.	Dr.	£.	s.	d.
Cash in hand at Audit, July 18, 1868.	0	9	9	Hire of Music Room, Lady Day to Mich.			
Mich. Term. 132 Subscribers at 5s.	33	0	0	1868.	10	0	0
Total Receipts from Concert, Dec. 9.	83	16	6	Hire of Chairs	2	17	6
Due from the Society	57	10	6	Mr. Russell—Expenses of Concert	6	1	0
				for Piano, two Terms	5	18	0
				Four Solo Singers	36	16	0
				Band, London and Oxford	38	17	0
				Putting up Orchestra	12	0	0
				Music	6	7	4
				Conductor, two Terms [*nominal fee to*			
				cover expenses]	10	10	0
				Advertising	12	18	0
				Refreshments	5	5	0
				Ellard	2	8	6
				Dicks	2	1	6
				Pianist	2	12	6
				Bowden, for Printing, &c.	10	19	0
				Small items	0	12	11
				Hire of Corn Exchange, Lighting and			
				Warming	8	12	6
	£174	**16**	**9**		**£174**	**16**	**9**

T. VERE BAYNE. (*Treasurer.*)

FIG. 13. Balance sheet, Oxford Philharmonic Society, January 1869

Oxford University Musical Union (1884), and using the Holywell Music Room (restored to its primarily musical function from 1901) as its base.

At the beginning of the nineteenth century, the tradition of Holywell concerts was still in existence. Certainly some notable changes, and indeed disruption, had set in after 1789: the period from the 1790s through to 1820[6] was characterized by fluctuating fortunes affecting the continuity of the concerts. Throughout, the stewards strove to keep a strong guiding hand on the proceedings: the pattern of their efforts, including periodically the introduction of various schemes to revive the concerts, can be derived from the regular advertisements in *Jackson's Oxford Journal*.[7] Sources of difficulties ranged from economic pressures to problems of decorum and personality clashes. In the latter regard, Philip Hayes's role

[6] A distinct chronological marker was created by the extent of the programme collections consulted by Mee (he described the two-volume set of Oxford Concert Bills in the Bodleian Library, Mus. 1 d. 64, as covering the years 1788–1819; in its present form it contains additional items). A further volume, Mus. 1 c. 74, covers 1823–36. In addition, the Bodleian has recently acquired a collection of programmes only partly duplicating the earlier holdings.

[7] The outline of this phase of the concerts is charted in Mee, *Music Room*, ch. iv, pp. 115–74. The problems of the concerts at this period were observed by Marsh, visiting his son ('for whom I subscribed', he noted) in 1801: see *The John Marsh Journals*, 727.

MUSIC ROOM, OXFORD,

FEBRUARY 4th, 1800.

THE Stewards of the Mufic Room are forry to be under the neceffity of reprefenting to the Subfcribers, and the Univerfity and City at large, that the prefent ftate of their fund is wholly inadequate to the neceffary expences of the Concert.

By the plan of the inftitution no fixed Salary is enfured to the Performers; but each depends intirely for what he is to receive upon the contingent produce of the fund: the fmall amount, however, of the Subfcriptions for the prefent year, (being only 141) and the little attendance given at the Concerts, do not hold out to them any profpect of fubfiftence.

The Stewards, therefore, are defirous, in juftice to the Performers and their families, to give this ftatement of the Finances of the Room, and they take the liberty of fubmitting to the confideration of the public—whether after a commodious Room has been built and furnifhed at a great expence, and the Orcheftra has been provided with a complete fet of Mufical Inftruments and Books; and after a Band of Inftrumental Performers, of acknowledged abilities in their profeffion, has been collected; they will fuffer the Room and its Furniture to be rendered ufelefs, and the Performers to be difperfed, by withdrawing their fupport from an Inftitution, which has been eftablifhed upwards of fifty years, and which provides fo much rational and elegant amufement, at an expence comparatively inconfiderable.

As a means of afcertaining the fentiments of the public, as to the line of conduct to be purfued under the prefent circumftances, the Stewards propofe to have two Concerts, on Monday the 10th and Monday the 17th Inftant, at the ufual price of admiffion on common nights; *when the attendance of every friend to the Society is earneftly requefted.* If the additional Subfcriptions and Attendance fhould not be found fufficient at the laft Concert abovementioned, to enfure the neceffary payments to the Performers, the Stewards muft be compelled to fhut up the Room, and the Subfcriptions paid for the prefent year will, if required, be returned.

Should the Concert be continued, a Female Performer of eminence will be engaged, as foon as it appears that the receipts are likely to anfwer the expence; and the Stewards cannot omit this opportnnity of requefting the refident families to affift in promoting the Subfcription, and to countenance the Concert by their attendance.

SIGNED,

B. TATE, *Magdalen, College.*	J. PARKER, *Worcefter College.*
H. KETT, *Trinity Coll.*	G. SCOBELL, *Balliol Coll.*
T. PEARSON, *Queen's Coll.*	R. T. COATES, *Corpus Coll.*
W. HOOPER, *Univerfity Coll.*	H. SISSMORE, *New Coll.*
J. DAVIES, *Jefus Coll.*	
D. BRYMER, *Wadham Coll.*	R. P. GOODENOUGH, *Chrift Church.*
H. HALLIWELL, *Brafe Nofe Coll.*	J. VINICOMBE, *Pembroke Coll.*
C. MAYO, *St. John's Coll.*	J. LANDON, *Oriel Coll.*

SUBSCRIPTIONS are received at the Bank, by Meffrs. FLETCHER and PARSONS; by Mr. JUNG, oppofite the Mufic Room, Holywell; and on Concert Nights at the Mufic Room.

₰ *A Lift of Subfcribers will be printed.*

PRINTED BY DAWSON AND CO. OXFORD.

FIG. 14. Appeal by stewards of the Musical Society, 4 February 1800

seems to have become diminished from 1793 onwards, thus removing a cause of continual friction: the Stewards of the Music Room took over 'the entire Management of the CONCERT'[8] and Crotch was appointed 'to preside at the Harpsichord' in place of Hayes.[9] With respect to the financial troubles that beset the concerts, rescue operations included—with a twist to the usual benefit concerts held for individual performers (and echoing the origins of the Room)—concerts for the benefit of the Music Room itself.[10] As Mee remarks, the success of such appeals is impressive 'considering the strain on the resources of the country at the time'.[11] Another angle on the function that music might have in those troubled times is represented by the concert in the Town Hall on 11 October 1798, 'FOR THE RELIEF Of the WIDOWS and ORPHANS Of those who fell in the late glorious VICTORY . . .', a 'Grand MISCELLANEOUS CONCERT' combining '*the Music Room and Military Bands*'.[12]

Amid the various changes reflecting local tensions and losses of personnel, and against the larger backdrop of the Napoleonic wars, the early nineteenth-century Holywell programmes retained partly the spirit of the eighteenth century. Handel's music, notably the oratorios (and also instrumental works, such as his concertos) remained a staple element in this and other Oxford contexts. As before, a variety of excerpts from Handel oratorios might appear in the regular weekly (or equivalent) programmes of vocal and instrumental music, and in benefit concert programmes,[13] while more substantial portions, or entire works, might feature in the termly 'Choral Nights'.[14] In the early years of the nineteenth century a series of

[8] Mee, *Music Room*, ch. iv, 123; cf. *JOJ*, 27 Apr. 1793.

[9] Mee, *Music Room*, 124; cf. Crotch, Malchair MS (Ob, MS Mus. d. 32), p. 48, and Rennert, *Crotch*, 39.

[10] Mee, *Music Room*, 127–8; cf. *JOJ*, 16 Apr. 1796: 'At a Meeting of the Stewards of the Music Room . . . to examine the State of their Finances, it was found absolutely necessary, in order to maintain the small Prospect . . . of continuing the Concert . . . That on *Wednesday* next the Twentieth Instant, will be a CONCERT . . . for the BENEFIT of the ROOM, As the only Means . . . to make up the Deficiency . . .'. This idea had been tried from at least 1789 onwards, as in the elaborate programme of 26 February 1789 for the benefit of the Music Room (with, 'Between the ACTS, (By particular Desire)' a Handel organ concerto played by 'Master Crotch': cf. Ob, Mus. 1 d. 64/1).

[11] Mee, *Music Room*, 128.

[12] *JOJ*, 6 Oct. 1798, referring to Nelson's great victory.

[13] For example, Miss Clarke's on 8 March 1804, when Mr Jackson (flute), Mr Marshall (violin), Mr Reinagle (cello), and Dr Crotch (organ) joined her in presenting a programme that included six Handel items of a total of twelve; and the special concert held on 9 November 1807 'to defray the Expences incurred in fitting up the Room' and featuring Mrs Salmon, with again six Handel items out of twelve altogether (beginning with the Introduction and opening chorus from *Deborah*, 'Immortal Lord of earth and skies'). Programmes in Ob, Mus. 1 d. 64/1; see also *JOJ*, 7 Nov. 1807.

[14] The pattern of these was altered periodically from 1776 (when they were replaced in Easter and

oratorios was presented at Holywell. *Messiah*, with the characteristic designation of 'the sacred oratorio', was announced as the Choral Music 'for
the present Term' to be performed on Monday, 16 February 1801 (thus in
its traditional Lent Term context); *Judas Maccabaeus*, also billed as a 'sacred
oratorio', on Monday, 8 March 1802, conducted by Crotch; and the
'SACRED ORATORIO OF SAMSON' on 28 February 1803, again conducted by
Crotch.[15] Typically these would be followed by a Grand Miscellaneous
Concert, as on Tuesday, 9 March 1802, when Madame Mara, Mr Hill,
and Mr Welch (who had featured among the soloists in *Judas Maccabaeus*)
were engaged to perform, and Crotch played an organ concerto of his
own composing.[16]

While the Choral Nights might show a greater preponderance of vocal
items, the term was often loosely interpreted at this period, so that their
contents (as in the successive concerts on 10 and 11 May 1804 referred to
below) might not be greatly differentiated from those of the Grand Miscellaneous Concerts that followed them. The range of Handel items within
one programme, or in a pair of successive concerts, could be collectively
very wide. Sources of pieces performed in the choral concert on Monday,
18 March 1805 and then in the Grand Miscellaneous Concert on Tuesday,
19 March 1805 were (for the 18th) *Joshua*, *Belshazzar*, and *Deborah*, and (for
the 19th) additionally the Coronation Anthems, *Athalia*, and the overture
to *Alcina*, with much emphasis generally on chorus.[17]

Another Oxford favourite, Haydn, was represented by the performance of his *Creation* (this also sharing with the Handel works the description 'A Sacred Oratorio') as the termly Choral Music, with Dr Crotch,
'PROFESSOR OF MUSIC', conducting, on Tuesday, 16 June 1801.[18] (The

Michaelmas Terms by 'Grand Miscellaneous Concerts') onwards; in the 1790s the pattern was of three
Choral Nights followed by three Grand Miscellaneous Concerts on successive nights (see Mee, *Music
Room*, 141), and this pairing persisted into the next century.

[15] *JOJ*, 14 Feb. 1801; 6 Mar. 1802; and 26 Feb. 1803 (programmes in Ob, Mus. 1 d. 64/1). It may be
speculated (although it is not documented) that Crotch conducted the first of these performances.

[16] *JOJ*, 6 Mar. 1802 ('Mr Welch' was the singer Thomas Welsh). Similar patterns of events are
observable in other years, e.g. on 16 and 17 June 1801 (*JOJ*, 13 June 1801): see below.

[17] Programmes in Ob, Mus. 1 d. 64/1.

[18] *JOJ*, 13 June 1801. The notice advertises *The Creation* (on 16th) and then a Grand Miscellaneous
Concert (on 17th), giving the programme for the latter and following this ambiguously with 'the whole to
be conducted by Dr. CROTCH'; the extant programme book for 16 June shows Crotch as conductor for *The
Creation* (Ob, Mus. 1 d. 64/1).

RECITATIVE.—POLYPHEME.

Whither faireſt art thou running,
Still my warm embraces ſhunning.

RECITATIVE.—GALATEA.

The lion calls not to his prey,
Nor bids the wolf the lambkin ſlay.

RECITATIVE.—POLYPHEME.

Thee, Polyphemus, great as Jove,
Calls to empire and to love;
To his palace in the rock,
To his dairy, to his flock,
To the grape of purple hue,
To the plumb of gloſſy blue,
Wildings which expecting ſtand,
Proud to be gather'd by thy hand.

RECITATIVE.—GALATEA.

Of infant limbs to make my food,
And ſwill full draughts of human blood.
Go, Monſter! bid ſome other gueſt,
I loath the hoſt, I loath the feaſt.

AIR.—POLYPHEME.

Ceaſe to beauty to be ſuing,
Ever whining love diſdaining,
Let the brave, their arms purſuing,
Still be conq'ring not complaining.

AIR.—CORYDON.

Would you gain the tender creature,
Softly, gently, kindly treat her,
Suffering is the lover's part;
Beauty by conſtraint poſſeſſing,
You enjoy but half the bleſſing,
Lifeleſs charms without the heart.

RECITATIVE.—ACIS.

His hideous love provokes my rage,
Weak as I am I muſt engage;
Inſpir'd with thy victorious charms,
The God of Love will lend his arms.

AIR.

Love ſounds the alarm,
And fear is a flying,
When beauty's the prize
What mortal fears dying;
In defence of my treaſure
I'd bleed at each vein,
Without her no pleaſure,
For life is a pain.

AIR.—DAMON.

Confider, fond ſhepherd,
How fleeting's the pleaſure
That flatters our hope in purſuit of the fair;
The joys that attend it
By moments we meaſure,
But life is too little to meaſure our care.

RECITATIVE.—GALATEA.

Ceaſe, O ceaſe, thou gentle youth,
Truſt my conſtancy and truth;
Truſt my truth and pow'rs above,
The pow'rs propitious ſtill to love.

TRIO.—ACIS and GALATEA.

The flocks ſhall leave the mountains,
The woods the turtle dove,
The nymphs forſake the fountains,
E'er I forſake my love.

POLYPHEME.

Torture, fury, rage, deſpair,
I cannot, cannot, I cannot bear.

ACIS and GALATEA.

Not ſhow'rs to larks ſo pleaſing,
Nor ſun-ſhine to the bee;
Not ſleep to toil ſo eaſing,
As theſe dear ſmiles to me.

POLYPHEME.

Fly ſwift, thou maſſy ruin, fly,
Die, preſumptuous Acis, die.

RECITATIVE.—ACIS.

Help, Galatea, help ye parent Gods,
And take me dying to your deep abodes.

CHORUS.

Mourn all ye muſes, weep all ye ſwains,
Tune your reeds to doleful ſtrains,
Groans, cries, and howlings fill the neighbouring ſhore,
Ah, the gentle Acis is no more.

SOLO.—GALATEA.

Muſt I my Acis ſtill bemoan,
Inglorious cruſh'd beneath that ſtone?

CHORUS.

Ceaſe, Galatea, ceaſe to grieve,
Bewail not whom thou can'ſt relieve.

SOLO.—GALATEA.

Muſt the lovely charming youth
Die for his conſtancy and truth?

CHORUS.

Call forth thy pow'r, employ thy art,
The goddeſs ſoon can heal the ſmart.

SOLO.—GALATEA.

Say, what comfort can I find,
For dark deſpair o'er-clouds my mind.

CHORUS.

To kindred Gods the youth return,
Thro' verdant plains to roll his urn.

RECITATIVE.—GALATEA.

'Tis done, thus I exert my pow'r divine,
Be thou immortal, tho' thou art not mine.

AIR.

Heart, the ſeat of ſoft delight,
Be thou now a fountain bright;
Purple be no more thy blood,
Glide thou like a cryſtal flood:
Rock thy hollow womb diſcloſe,
The bubbling fountain, lo! it flows;
Thro' the plains he joys to rove,
Murmuring ſtill his gentle love.

CHORUS.

Galatea, dry thy tears,
Acis now a God appears;
See how he rears him from his bed,
See the wreath that binds his head;
Hail! thou gentle murmuring ſtream,
Shepherd's pleaſure, muſe's theme,
Thro' the plains ſtill joy to rove,
Murmuring ſtill thy gentle love.

FIG. 15. Concert programme, *Acis and Galatea*, 18 February 1805, showing performers' names pencilled in

composer's billing as 'Dr. Haydn' reminded subscribers of his distinguished Oxford connections.) Mee cites Crotch's departure for London in
1806 (actually December 1805, according to Rennert) as the decisive factor
in the abandoning of complete performances of oratorios at Holywell.[19]
There may be some sign of compensation by way of including longer extracts among the miscellaneous programmes (although paired items—
for example, duet and chorus—had long been popular), as in Reinagle's
'ANNUAL BENEFIT CONCERT' at the Music Room on 19 March 1817: the final
item in 'Act 1' consisted of a recitative, trio, and chorus ('The Heavens are
telling') from *The Creation*. In at least one case, selections from the *Messiah*
formed a whole 'Act'. But besides these excerpts from oratorios, integral
performances continued to be advertised, as with *Messiah* at the Music
Room in March 1811 and 1812.[20] The stewards were able to draw on the
leading soloists in oratorio of the time; a programme for *Messiah* at the
Theatre Royal, Covent Garden for Lent 1804 features among the singers
Mr Braham, Mr Thomas Welsh, Miss Munday (who later became Mrs
Salmon), and Mrs Second, all of whom were also engaged regularly in
Oxford.[21]

The Holywell Band, under the new leadership of Mr Marshall from
1801,[22] continued to supply the orchestral forces for the subscription concerts, while star performers joined them as soloists for special events and
particular schemes, such as Crotch's series of twelve concerts.[23] As Mee

[19] *Music Room*, 165; cf. Rennert, *Crotch*, 51. As Rennert observes, Crotch continued to take part in
summer concerts in Oxford after this. With Crotch's withdrawal from regular conducting, Walter
Vicary's name appears, for example conducting the *Messiah* for the Choral Night on 13 February 1815
(Ob, Mus. 1 d. 64/2). Vicary was already listed by Jung (*Concerts*, p. xiii) in 1808 as conductor of the
Holywell Band

[20] *JOJ*, 2 Mar. 1811 and 7 Mar. 1812. Ob, Mus. 1 d. 64/2 includes a programme for the Music Room,
Tuesday, 5 Mar. 1811 with, inscribed in a 19th-cent. hand, 'On Monday, March 4, The Messiah was per-
formed'. Also in Ob, Mus. 1 d. 64/2 is a concert bill dated 7 March 1812 (printed by Munday and Slatter,
Oxford; incidentally, both names of musical families) announcing that 'The Sacred Oratorio of the
MESSIAH will be performed on Monday Evening'. (For a performance in 1815, see p. 160 below, and n. 68.)
During this period, as Mee observes, *Acis and Galatea* also 'retained something of its former vogue' (*Music
Room*, 165); see e.g. the programme of a complete performance, Monday, 18 Feb. 1805, annotated with
performers' names (Ob, Mus. 1 d. 64/1).

[21] In Ob, Mus. 1 d. 64/1.

[22] Marshall, succeeding Mahon (who was Alday's successor: see Mee, *Music Room*, 138–9), like some
of his predecessors evidently gave long service to the band, retaining the leadership until 1846 (*JOJ*, 31
Oct. 1846).

[23] Described by Mee (who attributed the scheme to Crotch) as a 'daring experiment', these large-
scale concerts in 1804–5, replacing the standard performances over the course of the year, were unsuccessful financially. After this failure 'the old plan of the concerts was restored . . . External aid was only

remarks, 'the performers engaged for special concerts during the first twenty years of the nineteenth century consisted, as in the eighteenth century, of the best singers and instrumentalists of their day'.[24] Established Oxford favourites appearing among these including the singers Mrs Billington, Signora Storace, and the once-controversial Madame Mara, and among the instrumentalists such names as Lindley (cello), Holmes (bassoon), and Madame Dussek (harp) had already featured in eighteenth-century Oxford programmes.[25] But, as Mee comments, 'on the whole there was plenty of enterprise and plenty of novelty'.[26] Soloists from the London stage and the international circuit included the celebrated Mr Braham, and the equally distinguished Madame Catalani, who both rapidly secured an Oxford following. The language in which Catalani was lauded locally is revealing in its attribution of superior quality to her performance in Oxford:

On Friday and Saturday . . . the Music Room was graced by Madame Catalani. This elegant Syren seems to have poured forth all the treasures of her sweet sounds . . . into the bosom of Isis; for never at the Opera, or in any of her Concerts, did she display more science, or warble with more native melody, than here . . .[27]

Concert advertisements typically referred to the singers' operatic connections (bringing an exotic aura to Oxford, where opera still was generally lacking). Thus it was announced, with reference to the Choral Music on Thursday and Grand Miscellaneous Concert on Friday, 10 and 11 May 1804, that 'Miss PARKE, and Signor MORELLI, Bass Singer, from the Opera

---

invoked for the "Choral Nights", the weekly concert being performed by the permanent staff' (Mee, *Music Room*, 150).

[24] Ibid. 162.

[25] An increased emphasis on both the harp and the pianoforte in solo as well as accompanimental role is noticeable in Oxford at this period. On 30 May 1805 'Madame DUSSECK' performed a 'SONATA, *Harp.*' by 'DUSSECK' (Ob, Mus. 1 d. 64/1). The programme for 6 February 1806 (ibid.) included, in Act II, 'SOLO, Piano Forte.—Mr. GRIFFIN. (*Consisting of a Capricio and Steibelt's Storm.*)' Also in Act II Mr Welsh sang Giordani's setting of J. Warton, 'The dart of Isdabel prevails', '*Accompanied on the Piano Forte by himself*'.

[26] *Music Room*, 162. As Mee points out (pp. 163–4), the 'minor celebrities', too, included excellent artists. A curiosity featured in Reinagle's Annual Benefit Concert at the Music Room on Wednesday, 19 March 1817 was a series of parodies: 'Mr. MATHEWS Will give a Variety of IMITATIONS of LONDON PERFORMERS, *Whose Names will be specified during the Performance*' (Ob, Mus. 1 d. 64/2).

[27] Mee, *Music Room*, 163–4, n. 1, quotes in full this paean to Madame Catalani's 'transcendent genius' (cf. *JOJ*, 5 Dec. 1807).

House, and Master MORI, a Child of seven Years old, as Concerto Player on the Violin' were engaged.[28]

Prodigy appearances such as Mori's in 1804 periodically formed one of the special attractions at Holywell, as they had done earlier. And child per-formers continued to feature regularly as soloists drawn from among the local choristers; one such choirboy selected to sing solo was 'Master Cox', probably George Valentine Cox.[29] Among the 'new blood' in the early nineteenth century were members of local families of musicians such as the Marshalls,[30] the Reinagles, father and son,[31] and the Mahons. Jung in 1808 listed three members of the Haldon family in the Holywell Band; two of these were recorded with obituaries in *Jackson's Oxford Journal* in 1829 and 1843 respectively.[32] Mrs Salmon, daughter of Mrs Munday (née Mahon) retained her local following over a long period, besides achieving fame more widely:

We learn with much satisfaction, that the Stewards of the Music Room have suc-ceeded in engaging our towns-woman, Mrs. SALMON, for the Choral Con-cert . . . on the 2d of February next . . . As it is probable the public will not have another opportunity of hearing this inimitable singer before her departure for the Continent, we have no doubt the room will be much crowded.[33]

The fashion for talented musical couples (seen to some extent in the pre-ceding century) was exploited by the stewards. Mr and Mrs Vaughan, Mr and Mrs Mountain, Mr Lacy and Madame Bianchi Lacy, and Signor de

---

[28] *JOJ*, 5 May 1804. Mori played a Viotti violin concerto in the second Act of the choral concert on 10 May, and a concerto by 'JARNOVICK' [Giornovichi] in the Grand Miscellaneous Concert following this on 11 May, again in Act II (programmes in Ob, Mus. 1 d. 64/1). In later years (now 'Mr Mori'. presumably the same) he continued to appear frequently as soloist in the Holywell concerts (cf. *JOJ*, 23 Feb. 1833, when Mori was billed to play 'a Concerto on the Violin' in Act I and a Fantasia in Act II). As a pupil of Viotti and leader of the Philharmonic Society orchestra he possessed distinguished credentials.

[29] For example, see the subscription concert programmes of 27 January and 3 February 1800, when Master Cox joined the line-up of vocal soloists (Ob, Mus. 1 d. 64/1).

[30] See Mee, *Music Room*, 184–6. William Marshall and his family continued to play an important part in Oxford concerts; on Monday, 4 January 1836 at least three members of the Marshall family took part in the concert arranged by Mr E. Marshall (flute), with Mr W. Marshall as leader, and Mr J. M. Marshall also playing violin (cf. *JOJ*, 2 Jan. 1836).

[31] Mee, *Music Room*, 186–7.   [32] Jung, *Concerts*, pp. xiii–xiv; Mee, *Music Room*, 159.

[33] *JOJ*, 15 Jan. 1820. Notwithstanding this marketing technique, she was in fact advertised as singing again subsequently on several occasions (cf. *JOJ*, 26 Feb. 1820). On an earlier appearance, see n. 13 above. Success did not guarantee later security; in 1842 the *Journal* carried an appeal for funds for Mrs Salmon, 'a native of this City', and 'once a charming singer, having for many years lost her voice, and being now a widow in very indigent circumstances' (*JOJ*, 6 Aug. 1842).

Begnis and Madame Ronzi de Begnis all appeared in the Holywell concerts, either separately or jointly, at various times. The Vaughans were considered a particular draw: '*Music Room*—The attractions of Mr. and Mrs. Vaughan produced the most respectable attendance at Monday and Tuesday's Concerts that we have witnessed . . .'.[34] Where several members of a famous musical family were known as performers, clearly the surname (*tout court*) occurring in the concert programmes over a protracted period may refer to different individuals; however, the possibility that, equally, such appearances may relate to the same performer is confirmed by the *Journal*'s comment regarding Lindley: 'He is well remembered by several lovers of music in this City, as occupying, nearly 50 years ago, the same position as he did on the present occasion.'[35]

Benefit concerts for leading individuals associated with the Holywell Band (principally Marshall and Reinagle in this period) continued to form an important part of the pattern of concerts, that also brought in distinguished performers from outside. These 'benefits' were the focus for special efforts, and possibly some rivalry among the musicians to produce ever more interesting programmes, as when in May 1799 it was announced that 'several performers from London' had 'promised their assistance' at the Benefit for Mrs Hindmarsh (one of the regular singers) and that 'Mr Salomon' had 'kindly offered her for that Night a GRAND MILITARY SYMPHONY [presumably No. 100], and a NEW MARCH, composed by Dr. HAYDN.'[36] Military music was obviously topical. Local compositions of this genre were featured earlier that year in the benefit concert for Francis Attwood (on Thursday, 28 February 1799): 'the first Act will finish with a MARCH, composed and dedicated to Lady MACKWORTH, by F. ATTWOOD, and the second Act with one dedicated to Colonel COKER and the Officers of the *Oxford University Volunteers*'.[37]

The programme of Attwood's Benefit is full of incidental interest and worth quoting from in some detail: 'In the Course of the Concert, Mrs.

---

34 *JOJ*, 23 Nov. 1811. The *Journal*'s report continues: 'We noticed among the company Lady Abingdon, Lady C. Bertie, Lady and Miss Bowyers, Mrs. and Miss Curson, &c, &c.' (H. Curson was Lieutenant-Colonel Commandant of the Oxford Loyal Volunteers).

35 *JOJ*, 8 July 1848.

36 *JOJ*, 18 May 1799.

37 *JOJ*, 23 Feb. 1799, also the source of the quotations in the paragraph that follows here. On music-making at the home of Sir Digby Mackworth, see Rennert, *Crotch*, 48.

HINDMARSH, Master MUNDAY, and Master COX, will sing a GLEE, composed on Purpose by the Marquis of BLANDFORD . . .'. And for the 'favourite GLEE, "Bragela,"' it was announced that 'Mr. Attwood has procured a Grand Piano Forte' (accompaniment for glees seems to have been a standard feature in Oxford). Mee's positing of a family connection with the Mozart pupil Thomas Attwood is strengthened by Francis Attwood's frequent programming of works by Thomas in his benefit concerts:[38] for that of 28 February 1799 he advertised the glee 'of Mr T. Attwood's, that met with so much Applause at his last Benefit, "In Liquid NOTES."' to be sung by 'Miss WHEATLEY, (a Pupil of Mr. T. Attwood's) Master MUNDAY, and Master COX'. (Vocal music seems to have dominated on this occasion.)

The marketing strategies developed in concert promotion during the preceding period are amply in evidence in this later phase, as Attwood's notice of February 1799 shows. There is the confident dubbing of named pieces as 'favourite' (investing them with established popular attraction), the assurance that they have been well tried and tested (having met with so much applause in this context previously) and at the same time the important promise of new and special items (for example composed 'on purpose' for the occasion by the Marquis of Blandford). The Holywell concerts from the end of the eighteenth through the early decades of the nineteenth century not only manifested elements in their programmes that loyal members of the audience would recognize as continuing from past patterns, but also showed new enterprise, designed, in combination with energetic advertising, to attract wider support. The continuing availability of *Jackson's Oxford Journal* as a vehicle for publicity, together with a variety of outlets for ticket sales (including individual musicians at their home addresses, local tradesmen, and the banking firm of Fletcher and Parsons) aided the stewards in their efforts to keep the concerts afloat during difficult times.[39]

In a number of respects, the Holywell repertoire at this period is distinctly marked off from its eighteenth-century precedents. Perceptible

---

[38] Mee, *Music Room*, 139 n. 5. These works were sometimes described as 'new', perhaps suggesting special access (but of course sharing that epithet with much else in the Holywell programmes).

[39] Forthcoming events were also advertised on current programmes. Ticket outlets announced, e.g. in January 1815 for the subscription concerts, included a stationer's (Mr Pearson, opposite the Market, High Street), Fletcher and Parsons's Old Bank, and Mr Marshall's Music Shop (*JOJ*, 28 Jan. 1815). Other sources included the *Journal*'s own offices, and Mr Carter (watchmaker) in Holywell (cf. *JOJ*, 29 Jan. 1820).

changes of taste reflected in the concert programmes include the greater emphasis on part-songs, made explicitly a matter of programming policy in 1811:

We understand it to be the intention of the Stewards to get up some of the old Catches and Glees, and to bring forward the strength of the Orchestra, in performing a constant variety of the valuable music which the Music Room possesses—a plan which we hope will succeed. The subscriptions are increasing rapidly.[40]

(Later, in 1828 when the stewards launched another rescue operation to re-establish the concerts with the local band, the repertoire was to be mainly confined to the 'chaste and beautiful productions of our Old Masters'.)[41]

Besides the 'old Catches and Glees', more modern composers are represented in the Holywell part-song repertoire: alongside Callcott (1766–1821) and Webbe (1740–1816), works by younger composers such as Horsley (1774–1858) and Knyvett (1779–1856) were featured, altogether presenting 'almost every famous glee of the best period in English glee-writing'.[42] In the operatic sphere, vocal numbers were drawn from a range of Italianate sources; these included Mozart more regularly in the early nineteenth century, and composers who achieved their successes from the 1790s onwards, such as Fioravanti and Nicolini; while the newly popular Rossini was represented from 1819 onwards by a series of operatic overtures (discussed further, below) and vocal items from his operas.[43] Amid all this established or currently fashionable continental repertoire, English solo song (including works by émigrés such as J. C. Bach and Rauzzini, both doyens of English concert life) was not totally submerged. A new name occurring increasingly frequently is that of Henry Bishop; his works were sung at Holywell long before his appointment as Heather Professor, and both he and Mrs Bishop (the singer Elizabeth Sarah Lyon) performed

---

[40] *JOJ*, 23 Nov. 1811.   [41] *JOJ*, 23 Oct. 1828.

[42] Mee, *Music Room*, 168. For an interesting essay on the glee by Bishop, see Northcott, *Bishop*, 102–4.

[43] *Figaro* continued to be a popular source of arias, such as 'Non più andrai' and 'Voi che sapete' (the latter e.g. sung in Marshall's Benefit Concert, Wednesday, 25 Feb. 1829: cf. *JOJ*, 21 Feb. 1829, and report in *JOJ*, 28 Feb.). Performers associated with the London premières of Mozart's operas in the early 19th cent., including Giuseppe Naldi (1770–1820) and Josephine Fodor (the first London Zerlina), were booked to sing at Holywell in that period. On 6 and 7 May 1805 Signora Storace sang a 'SONG' by Fioravanti and, with Mr Braham, a duet by Nicolini (Ob, Mus. 1 d. 64/1).

in the concerts.[44] (These appearances may have formed a part of the background to his eventual election as professor.)

On the instrumental side, what the *Journal*'s critic termed the 'strength of the Orchestra'[45] was represented in the symphonic repertoire associated with the earlier phase of the Holywell concerts—Haydn, Pleyel, Stamitz, and their contemporaries—together with a spate of operatic and dramatic overtures (this genre predominating now over the concert symphony) both from post-Revolutionary French opera and from modern Italian works: Cherubini's *Lodoïska*, Rossini's *Barbiere di Siviglia* and others, Paer, and Mayr.[46] Where Haydn, among the 'Viennese Classical' composers, had previously reigned supreme in Oxford in the orchestral sphere, Mozart and now also Beethoven took their place beside him.[47]

The performance of overtures was particularly praised: 'it is but justice to the instrumental Band to say, that the Overtures were given with a precision and effect that would do credit to a London Orchestra.'[48] Possibly the band had acquired an anthology of overtures at this period; for Marshall's Benefit concert of 1819 the programme featured a rash of works in the genre, including Beethoven's *Prometheus* (already scheduled at Holywell, for example in 1817),[49] Rossini's *Il Barbiere*, Cherubini's *Lodoïska*, and Gluck's *Iphigenia*.[50] By the 1830s, Auber and Hérold appeared among the overture repertoire, representing up-to-date taste.

A special element among contemporary repertoire in the programmes continued, as in the eighteenth century, to be formed by the introduction of the soloists' own (or their partners') compositions, most commonly in the form of solo song or instrumental concerto. Visiting singers might bring with them their own settings of topical poetry, for example Braham's evidently popular piece 'The Death of Abercrombie', which exudes the reasons for its popularity (see Ex. 9.1)[51] while the solo

[44] For details of Mrs Bishop's career see Northcott, *Bishop*, 6–8. She also sang in Oxford before her marriage, together with her sister; for example (billed as 'the two Miss Lyons') they performed alongside Braham in June 1808.

[45] Reference as n. 40 above.

[46] For the first of the two Commemoration Concerts at the Music Room, on Tuesday, 3 July 1821 the Rossini overture 'Il Turco in Italia' was billed as 'New' (*JOJ*, 30 June 1821).

[47] See Mee, *Music Room*, 166–7 on the 'tardy recognition' accorded these two composers.

[48] *JOJ*, 19 May 1821 on Marshall's Benefit Concert (14 May 1821).

[49] Also in Marshall's Benefit Concert: *JOJ*, 26 Apr. 1817.

[50] *JOJ*, 6 Nov. 1819 (which of the *Iphigenia* overtures was not specified, but *Aulide* is the likelier candidate).

[51] Performed at Holywell on 6 May 1805 (Ob, Mus. 1 d. 64/1) among other occasions. The words,

Ex. 9.1. John Braham, 'The Death of General Sir Ralph Abercrombie', 'Sung by M[r]
Braham . . . *The Words by* T. Dibdin *the Music by J. BRAHAM*. Pr. 1/6', London
*c.*1805, from the recitative and air

instrumentalists frequently performed concertos, sometimes fantasias or sonatas, which they had themselves written (presumably designed to display their instrument and their own prowess on it). The Holywell concerts also continued to serve as a showcase for local composers' talents.[52] Clearly the invited soloists introduced pieces reflecting their own repertoire as well as relating to the audience's taste; at the same time they will have helped to form that taste.[53]

All these elements combined to create a wide variety of music on offer. Certain fashions can be perceived, for example a Purcellian phase lasting through the first two decades of the nineteenth century, as Mee notes.[54] Mee is also right to draw attention to the habitual juxtapositions of incongruous items (although at the time these would have fitted programming conventions and expectations).[55] After the turn of the century, with the widening of the repertoire, the potential for such contrasts became more extreme. A 'snapshot' of the concerts from a point towards the end of each decade—1809, and 1819—gives an impression of the effect of these various trends. For the first Subscription Concert of the season, on Monday, 30 October 1809, the programme contained (in the customary two 'Acts') two groups of five items each, alternating instrumental with sung items in symmetrical arrangement.[56] The range of composers, genres, and performance settings here is, like the structure of the concert, exemplary of the contemporary tendencies. In Act I the glee 'Lawn as white as driven snow' by [Benjamin] Cooke, sung by Miss E. Bolton (who took a leading part in the event)[57] with Messrs Haldon and Liddell, was flanked on either side by a Handel overture, to '*Sampson*' [*sic*] and a Corelli concerto; Handel's 'Thou shalt bring them in and plant them' [*Israel in Egypt*],

printed in the programme, refer to 'brave Abercrombie' and Nelson's band achieving 'a glorious day'. Braham sang his 'Death of Abercrombie' as late as Feb. 1823 (cf. *JOJ*, 22 Feb. 1823).

[52] Crotch continued the tradition of presenting keyboard concertos at Holywell. Among popular compositions performed repeatedly was Reinagle's 'Battle of Salamanca' (Mee, *Music Room*, 171–3 and 145–6).

[53] Mrs Bianchi Lacy e.g. programmed solos by Lacy (cf. 31 Jan. 1815: Ob, Mus. 1 d. 64/2).

[54] Mee, *Music Room*, 167–8; Mee queried the attributions of 'Macbeth' and 'The Tempest' to Locke. I am grateful to Simon McVeigh for pointing out that the authorship of the version presented as Locke's 'Macbeth' music during the 18th cent. is currently a problematical issue. On the unclear situation regarding Locke's music and the extent of his contribution see particularly Fiske, 'The "Macbeth" Music', and Caldwell, *OHEM* i. 557–8.

[55] Mee, *Music Room*, 173–4.   [56] Ob, Mus. 1 d. 64/2.

[57] Mee (*Music Room*, 160) lists Miss E. Bolton among the singers employed annually and resident in Oxford 'during the term of their engagement'.

sung by Master Spence, was followed by a Pleyel symphony. Similar patterns prevailed in Act II, with a mixture of continental and British composers—Cimarosa, Avison, Shield, Borghi—and a Haydn 'Overture' (unspecified, and probably a symphony) to begin the Act. Essentially, then, a song recital (orchestrally accompanied) is here interwoven with an orchestral concert.

The programmes for the 'Third and Fourth Choral Concerts' in the current subscription, on Monday and Tuesday, 22 and 23 March 1819, show a striking mixture of old and new.[58] 'ACT I' on 22 March was described as 'Selected from ACIS and GALATEA', beginning with the Overture and chorus 'O the pleasure of the plains' and with soloists including Miss Travis (later Mrs W. Knyvett) as Galatea and Mr [Thomas] Vaughan as Acis. Act II featured two instrumental items, the overture to Gluck's *Iphigenia* (unspecified) and a 'Fantasia, Flute' on 'God save the King', with variations, played (and presumably composed) by Mr Weiss; each of these was followed by three vocal items. These ranged from Handel to contemporary English and Italian song: Mr Vaughan sang Bishop's ballad 'Native land! I'll love thee ever', and Miss Travis Zingarelli's Recitative and aria ('Rondo') 'Tranquillo io sono fra poco … Ombra adorata'.[59] With the final 'CHORUS. Handel. "Zadock the Priest"', the programme ended with the resounding 'Hallelujah! Amen'.

For 23 March the four soloists were joined by Haldon (a singer and instrumentalist in the band)[60] for a five-part glee; according to a handwritten annotation in the programme, possibly by one of the stewards, 'Master Marshall' substituted for Miss Travis. The mixture of Italian and English vocal items included dramatic music ascribed to Locke (a selection in each Act, from *The Tempest* and *Macbeth* respectively; the original attribution to Purcell has been partly corrected by hand) and Mozart (the trio 'La mia Dorabella', ascribed here to *Le Nozze di Figaro*).[61] Handel's Overture to *Esther* began Act I, while Haydn's 'OVERTURE, The Surprise' closed it; during Act II Mr Weiss performed a flute concerto, again presumably of his own composing. Airs and choruses from the final act of Handel's *Saul* ('In sweetest harmony') sat among Cimarosa, Webbe, and Haydn in

---

[58] Ob (new acquisition 2000).
[59] Niccolò Antonio Zingarelli (1752–1837): cf. *NG2* xxvii. 844–6.   [60] See Mee, *Music Room*, 159.
[61] *Così fan tutte* had been premièred in London in 1811, *Figaro* in 1812.

the first half of the concert. And in this case the second half ended with an operatic overture, that to Arne's *Artaxerxes*. The repertoire thus spanned the Restoration period, the 1730s, 1760s, and 1780–90s, as well as contemporary music.[62]

A lateral survey of the concert programmes across a period of several months shows that, together with a persistent loyalty to certain composers and genres, specific pieces were favoured. The popularity of these might be reflected, and established, by their repetition soon after the first performance. So Paisiello's 'AIR, with Variations—Mrs. SALMON', entitled 'Sul Margine d'un Rio', featured in the programme for Monday, 14 November 1814, recurs 'By desire' on Tuesday, 29 November 1814.[63] Besides the association of the performers with particular repertoire, there is a general sense of their loyalty to the Holywell enterprise. Thus at the foot of the programme for 29 November 1814 it was announced that 'Mrs. SALMON and Mr. BARTLEMAN having further offered their assistance for a CONCERT for the BENEFIT of the ORCHESTRA', this event would take place on Tuesday, 6 December (they sang on Monday, 5 December at the Music Room too)

The faithfulness shown by many of the invited performers to Oxford is striking. With their reputations firmly established and commitments elsewhere, they continued to return to Holywell. 'The famous Braham', for example, given 'amongst the men, the first place' by Mee,[64] and heard in Oxford as early as 1804, was constantly engaged for the Holywell concerts during the following decades, still appearing in the 1840s.[65] It is significant that Braham was billed in February 1804 alongside Signora Storace, whose own connection with Holywell had lasted since 1789.[66] Networking among musicians, whereby they introduced one another to the concerts, could well have been a strong factor in the patterns of engagement by the stewards. Other aspects included questions of geographical proximity, travel, and the performing circuit; a note at the foot of the programme for Monday, 25 November 1811 informed the public that 'the Stewards have

---

[62] Some of the earlier repertoire presumably survived in the collection of music from the 18th cent. (see Mee, *Music Room*, 54–62, and Ouf, rare books): for example, Arne's overture to *Artaxerxes*, and Locke's *Tempest*.

[63] Ob, Mus. 1 d. 64/2.   [64] Mee, *Music Room*, 163.

[65] *JOJ*, 18 Feb. 1804; Mee, *Music Room*, 199–200.

[66] Ibid. 118. Braham had toured the continent with Nancy Storace from 1797 to 1801, and was associated with her subsequently: see Levien, *Braham*, 18.

taken the opportunity of engaging Mr. and Mrs. VAUGHAN for next Monday's Concert, on their way to Birmingham'.[67] Some of the problems aired by the stewards will strike a chord with any impresario: thus an announcement similarly placed at the foot of the programme for Monday, 6 February 1815 (the first concert under a new system) stated that

The CHORAL MUSIC for this Term will be on Monday and Tuesday next, for which Mr. and Mrs. VAUGHAN are already engaged.—Mr. BUGGINS (Counter-Tenor) and Mr. BELLAMY have been written to, but their answers have not yet arrived.—*The Messiah* will be performed on the Monday evening.[68]

Turning from the regular miscellaneous concerts and Choral Nights to the annual Commemoration festivals held in the summer, we encounter in the latter many of the same elements of repertoire—*Messiah*, glees and ballads, symphonies and overtures—together with, often, the same visiting soloists; Braham, Bellamy, Mr and Mrs Knyvett, and many other familiar names appear.[69] Obviously the Commemoration events were on a grander scale. The practice of calling in reinforcements, established in the preceding period, persisted (and indeed seems to have escalated): for the 'GRAND MUSICAL FESTIVAL' in the Theatre on Monday, Tuesday, and Wednesday, 28, 29, and 30 June 1813 it was announced that

In the course of the Concerts will be introduced CONCERTOS by the principal Instrumental Performers: and the most celebrated GLEES, DUETTS, TRIOS, &c. as performed at the Ancient and Vocal Concerts, London. CHORUSSES from *Handel, Mozart, Haydn, Pergolesi*, &c. . . . *The* BAND *will consist of* 120 *performers.* The CHORUSSES will be sustained by the Members of the OXFORD CHOIRS, assisted by other Performers from LONDON, BIRMINGHAM, WINDSOR, &c. &c. &c.[70]

The vocal soloists on that occasion included Madame Catalani, Mrs Vaughan, and Messrs Goss, Vaughan, and Bellamy, together with local performers—Miss Darby and Master Hobbes;[71] the instrumental list simi-

---

[67] Ob, Mus. 1 d. 64/2.

[68] Ibid. They presumably agreed, as their names appear on the programme for 13 Feb. 1815.

[69] The connections were strengthened by the stewards assuming a new (although claimed as an old) role in the proceedings: 'We are informed, from good authority, that the Stewards of the Music Room are very desirous of taking upon themselves, according to ancient custom, the management of the musical performances in the Theatre, at the ensuing installation; the profits arising from which were formerly appropriated to the benefit of the Radcliffe Infirmary and the Musical Society in Oxford' (*JOJ*, 23 Dec. 1809).

[70] *JOJ*, 19 June 1813.

[71] For Miss Darby see Mee, *Music Room*, 160.

larly mixed imported and resident talent, with 'Mr Cramer' as leader and Marshall principal second violin, conductor Walter Vicary 'Mus. Bac.', and many other local names—Reinagle, Woodcock, Mahon, Tebbett—besides the favourite outsiders such as Mori and Lindley, as well as some more exotic imports, including Messrs Petrides on horns, Mr Schmidt as principal trumpet, and Signor Mariotti on 'Double Trombone'.[72] The *Journal*'s critic reported the following Saturday that the 'Musical Festival, comprising nearly all the vocal and instrumental talents of the country' had given '*eclat* and vivacity to the Commemoration of this year . . .'.[73]

The term 'Musical Festival', or 'Grand Musical Festival', had become customary for these events by the early nineteenth century. Echoing the pattern of their eighteenth-century predecessors, they generally consisted of three concerts on successive days of the Commemoration week in late June, as with the concerts at the Theatre on 25, 26, and 27 June 1805 for the Grand Musical Festival of that year. A Ball—or sometimes two Balls—usually formed part of the week's proceedings.[74] Characteristically *Messiah* was performed on the first day of the festival (as happened on 25 June 1805, with Braham among the soloists).[75] Its attractions remained undiminished: the *Journal* offered a description of *Messiah* (performed at the Commemoration in 1818) as a 'wonderful composition . . . without parallel in . . . that sacred pathos which goes immediately to the feelings and electrifies the heart'.[76] An interesting insight into the audience culture surrounding this perennial favourite is given by the advertisement in the *Journal* at Commemoration time in 1844, for:

HANDEL'S MESSIAH. Unique and portable Edition, imperial octavo, edited by E. J. WESTROP. Price, bound in cloth, 10s. *** To persons frequenting the public

[72] For the full list cf. *JOJ* (n. 70 refers); for individuals see Mee, *Music Room*, 158–65. A more exotic range of instruments, too, began to appear in the late 18th and early 19th cents., including serpent (*JOJ*, 30 June 1810) and double bassoon (used here).

[73] *JOJ*, 3 July 1813.

[74] Cf. *JOJ*, 30 May 1818: '*There will be a BALL at the TOWN HALL, on . . . the 4th of June, being the last day of the Grand Musical Festival, for which an excellent Band has been provided*' (tickets at 10s. 6d., including tea and coffee, were available from the usual outlets); and 7 June 1823: 'The STEWARDS of the MUSIC ROOM respectfully announce to the public, that TWO BALLS, for which *Payne's Full Quadrille Band* has been engaged, will, by permission of the Mayor and Council, be given in the Town Hall . . .' [on the Tuesday and Thursday evenings of Commemoration week].

[75] Programme in Ob, Mus. 1 d. 64/1.

[76] *JOJ*, 6 June 1818.

performance of this sublime work, the above edition, from its beautiful clearness and portability, presents a desirable acquisition, as it may be taken without incumbrance and referred to during the performance. London: Z.T. Purday, 45 High Holborn; and to be had of all Music and Booksellers.[77]

In that year the stewards of the Music Room were still in charge of the proceedings:

OXFORD GRAND COMMEMORATION
MUSICAL FESTIVAL
THE STEWARDS of the MUSIC ROOM beg to
announce that there will be
THREE CONCERTS in the THEATRE,
DURING THE WEEK OF THE
GRAND COMMEMORATION,
THE THIRD WEEK IN JUNE NEXT.
Sir HENRY R. BISHOP has been engaged as Conductor.[78]

As with the regular Holywell programmes, so also with the Commemoration concerts, Bishop appeared as composer and conductor for many years before his appointment to the Heather Professorship. At the two Commemoration concerts on Tuesday and Wednesday, 3 and 4 July 1821, the *Journal* reported, 'N.B. Mr. BISHOP, THE COMPOSER, has kindly offered to accompany his Pupil, Miss GREEN'.[79] For the 'CHORAL and COMMEMORATION CONCERTS' at the Music Room on Tuesday and Wednesday, 22 and 23 June 1819, Bishop's 'Echo Song' ('What airy sound floats sweetly round') was programmed 'By desire' alongside Mozart's 'Vedrai carina', a Rossini aria sung by Mrs Dickons (née Poole), and Handel, together with a variety of orchestral items including an 'OVERTURE. (New. MS.)' by A. R. Reinagle, Haydn's Military Overture (Symphony No. 100) and Handel's overture to 'Sampson'. For these concerts, in addition to Mrs Dickons, Miss Stephens, Messrs Vaughan and Bellamy were engaged to sing, and were joined in the glee by Master W. Marshall (who had made his Oxford début in his father's Benefit Concert in 1815).[80] The *Journal* referred subsequently to the 'meritorious exertions of our own home performers' and

---

[77] *JOJ*, 15 June 1844 (also featuring the vast programmes for the concerts). By this date the transport arrangements were advertised in terms of the new railway: from the Angel, Star, Mitre, and Roebuck Hotels in Oxford there would be 'OMNIBUSSES to and from the Railway Station to meet every Train'.

[78] *JOJ*, 17 Feb. 1844.   [79] *JOJ*, 30 June 1821.

[80] For programmes, 22 and 23 June see Ob, Mus. 1 d. 64/2, also for the programme of Marshall's

☞ The STEWARDS of the MUSIC ROOM, with much regret, announce to the Subscribers and the Public, that Miss STEPHENS is under an absolute necessity of returning to her Engagements in Town To-Morrow. Thus situated, she has liberally proposed to give her services without remuneration This Evening; and Mrs. DICKONS, on the shortest notice, has handsomely offered to supply her place in the Concert on Wednesday Evening.

FIRST

Choral and Commemoration CONCERT.

Music Room, Oxford,

TUESDAY, JUNE 22, 1819.

ACT I.

OVERTURE, *Sampson*. - - - - - - - Handel.
CHORUS. "Awake the trumpet's lofty sound." - - Handel.
SONG—Mr. BELLAMY.
DUET—Miss STEPHENS and Mr. VAUGHAN. - - Graun.
"Te ergo quæsumus."
OVERTURE, *Prometheus*. - - - - - - Beethoven.
GLEE. "Blest pair of Syrens." - - - Stafford Smith.
Miss STEPHENS, Master W. MARSHALL, Messrs. HALDON, VAUGHAN, and BELLAMY.
SONG—Mr. VAUGHAN.
SONG—Miss STEPHENS. "Thou didst blow." - Handel.
CHORUS. "The depths have covered them." - - Handel.

ACT II.

OVERTURE (Military). - - - - - - - Haydn.
GLEE. "With sighs, sweet rose." - - - - Callcott.
Messrs. HALDON, VAUGHAN, WILKINS, & BELLAMY.
THE ECHO SONG—Miss STEPHENS. (By desire.) Bishop.
"What airy sound floats sweetly round?"
SONG—Mr. BELLAMY.
CHORUS. "O Father, whose almighty power." - - Handel.
GLEE. "Now the bright morning star." - - Greville.
Miss STEPHENS, Master W. MARSHALL, Messrs. HALDON, VAUGHAN, and BELLAMY.
OVERTURE (in D.) - - - - - - - Romberg.
SONG—Mr. VAUGHAN.
SONG—Miss STEPHENS. "Vedrai carina." - - Mozart.
CHORUS. "When his loud voice." - - - Handel.

Admission to Non-Subscribers, 7s. 6d.

Tickets may be had of Messrs. HALDON and LOWNDES, Stationers, &c. Journal Office, Corn Market; of Messrs. LODER and GUNNER, and at Mr. MARSHALL's Music Shop, High-Street; and at the usual places.

GROSVENOR AND HALL, PRINTERS.

FIG. 16. Concert programme, 22 June 1819

the 'brilliant attractions resulting from the vocal powers of Miss Stephens, Mrs. Dickons, and Messrs. Vaughan and Bellamy', who were 'deservedly honoured' by a maximum capacity audience.[81] Others who received praise at such times included the stewards, in a bouquet to 'the good taste, and kind and sedulous exertions of those Gentlemen who superintended the arrangement of the Festival', and the conductor: 'the selection of Music . . . does infinite credit to Dr. CROTCH, the conductor, who may be said to have taken the *cream* from each composer.'[82]

Besides advertising the proceedings, the *Journal* played an increasing role during the first half of the nineteenth century in carrying criticism of these and other concerts. The Commemoration events attracted particularly full coverage:

OXFORD, *Saturday, July* 3 [1824]. Our Commemoration Week opened with two excellent Concerts at the Music Room, on Monday and Tuesday. The Room was much thinner than on former times, and we cannot but think that the late brilliant Concerts at our Town Hall, where we had the pleasure of hailing the "divine Catalani," greatly affected them. Mr. Sapio sung in his usual chaste and manly style. It is no undeserved compliment to that Gentleman to say, he excelled in every thing he undertook. Of his ballads we need only mention that the pretty Scotch air of "Kelvin Grove" was rapturously *encored*, as it was at the Town Hall, where he was engaged with Madame Catalani. We are happy here to have an opportunity of thanking Mr. Sapio for the introduction of Bishop's song, "Orynthia, my beloved." . . . Miss Stephens can receive no addition to her fame . . . It is enough to say, that she again sung, as we have always heard her, with that sweetness, and delicacy of taste, which those only know how to estimate who have had the pleasure of hearing her.[83]

The sense of a loyal and admiring (indeed discriminating) following in Oxford is especially strong here.

In spite of the occasional downturn in attendance, the impression is that these events were generally well supported. Annotations to the pro-

---

Benefit concert (Monday, 24 Apr. 1815) featuring 'CONCERTANTE—*Two Violins obligato*. Pleyel. Mr. and Master MARSHALL, (his first public performance in Oxford)'. In 1820 a notice of Marshall's Benefit included 'Master William Marshall (of his Majesty's Chapel Royal)' among the singers (*JOJ*, 22 Apr. 1820).

[81] *JOJ*, 26 June 1819.

[82] On the stewards, see *JOJ*, 6 June 1818; on Crotch see ibid.

[83] *JOJ*, 3 July 1824. The language in which the criticisms were couched became noticeably 'Romanticized' as the century progressed (cf. the notice of the *Messiah* quoted above (n. 76 refers)).

grammes, as well as reports in the press, record audience numbers, and even if only approximate these give an idea of the scale: 'present about 800' (26 June 1805), 'Present about 1300' (27 June 1805: both referring to the Theatre) and, apropos *Messiah* on Tuesday, 25 June 1805, 'In the Theatre, at the performance, there were present about 1100'.[84] The venue for the Commemoration concerts varied among the Music Room, the Sheldonian Theatre, and the Town Hall.[85] The periodic refitting of the Music Room was on occasion connected with the Commemoration, as when it was reported in 1821 that:

In addition to the great improvements which have been lately made in lighting the Orchestra of our Music Room, we understand that at the ensuing Commemoration Concerts a superb chandelier, which has lately been purchased at Birmingham, will be exhibited for the first time. Its structure is, we hear, splendidly elegant.[86]

On such occasions the Room was as much 'on show' as the performers and their programme.

Refurbishment of the room was one of the sources of expense to which the stewards repeatedly referred. The emphasis in this was very much on audience accommodation and comfort, as well as general embellishment: in November 1822 the stewards announced that 'great expences have been incurred in carrying several improvements into effect', including a new staircase and doorway 'into the Gallery' and removal of a stove and chimney-piece, allowing 'nearly 50 new Sittings', together with improved heating and ventilation. In that same month it was made clear that if the number of subscribers did not soon reach 150 'it will be impossible for the Stewards to continue to engage London Performers of such distinction as have hitherto attended the Oxford concerts'.[87] The distinguished 'London Performers' indeed continued to appear, and the stewards were able to commend the Room to their audiences for its warmth: 'Mr. Sylvester's plan of warming the Music Room having completely succeeded, no apprehension need be entertained of taking cold in the Room'.[88]

[84] Ob, Mus. 1 d. 64/1.
[85] Mee, *Music Room*, 194–8, gives a summary outline of the concerts at Encaenia, indicating location.
[86] *JOJ*, 23 June 1821.
[87] On the improvements, see *JOJ*, 2 Nov. 1822; on the subscriptions, see *JOJ*, 9 Nov. 1822.
[88] *JOJ*, 22 Feb. 1823.

Either the fortunes of the concerts were considered newsworthy, or the stewards had established a permanent slot in the *Journal* (or both); announcements of falling subscriptions, presumably published in the hope of eliciting the necessary additional support, as well as reports recording the success of schemes for the continuation of the concerts, regularly appeared in the *Journal's* pages.[89] The 'Oxford news' column for 8 November 1823 carried a notice to the effect that:

We understand the new subscription to the concerts is filling very rapidly, the list of subscribers already exceeding that of last year, by a considerable number. Madame Caradori and Mr. Sapio were selected for the first two concerts, on Monday and Tuesday last, and the audience were delighted with some of the finest productions of Rossini, Mozart, &c. Mr. Harper likewise played, each night, a concerto on the trumpet, (in which instrument he stands unrivalled) and was highly applauded.[90]

The year that followed, however (1824–5), produced a crisis: in a notice dated 28 October 1825 the stewards regretted to inform the public

that they are compelled at present to abandon all idea of opening a subscription for Concerts, during the ensuing year, in consequence of the great failure in their receipts during the last. The number of Subscribers was so small, and the support . . . so inadequate, that there remains a balance of more than One Hundred Pounds against the Room at the close of last year's accounts.

Two choral concerts were planned, 'For the Benefit of the Music Room', on Monday and Tuesday, 14 and 15 November 1825, with 'Madame CARADORI' and 'MR. PHILLIPS' (the former in much larger capitals than the latter).[91]

The lure of current attractions was characteristically linked with a sense of the strong historical dimension of the concerts to appeal to the public's responsibility for supporting the Holywell events, as with the stewards' announcement of the twelve-concert scheme in 1804 in place of the 'usual engagement with the Performers' for the ensuing year, declaring themselves 'anxious . . . that the UNIVERSITY should not be deprived of the

---

[89] In the earlier phase of the concerts the stewards' announcements had been published from time to time.

[90] *JOJ*, 8 Nov. 1823, 'Music Room'.

[91] *JOJ*, 29 Oct. 1825. On the stewards' ensuing struggles to maintain the concerts, see Mee, *Music Room*, 178–81.

Rational Amusement of a CONCERT, which has been established upwards of Fifty Years'.[92] But it was not until almost 100 years after the start of the Holywell concerts that their demise was finally signalled. By 1840 the stewards' tenancy of the Music Room had ceased,[93] and W. A. Dicks inserted a notice in the *Journal* 'respectfully' informing 'the Members of the University and the Inhabitants of Oxford and its vicinity' that he had 'taken a LEASE of the MUSIC ROOM, in Holywell-street, for the purpose of such Exhibitions and Concerts as may be approved of by the Vice-Chancellor', adding that he intended 'selling by Auction every description of Property . . .'. An adjacent advertisement declared

TO BE SOLD BY AUCTION,

By Mr. DICKS,

At the Music Room, Holywell-Street, Oxford, early in the week after next, of which due notice will be given in bills,—A quantity of GOODS, consisting of Books, Prints, square Piano Forte, Bookcases, ancient Carved Chairs, easy ditto, Sofa, Ottoman, &c. the property of a gentleman, late a Member of this University. Catalogues may be had in due time of the auctioneer, 94, High-street, Oxford.[94]

A number of reasons have been suggested for the decline of the Holywell concerts during the 1830s. Mee to some extent blamed the stewards, perhaps picking up from some of their own remarks the idea that 'the stewards had neglected to keep up their own orchestra of men living in the place and had relied too much on performers imported from London'. Mee was more inclined, however, following Tuckwell's *Reminiscences*, to ascribe the change in outlook to the influence of the Oxford Movement.[95] While his assertion here that an 'almost complete lack of interest in musical art . . . fell upon Oxford soon after 1825' overstates the case, its gist is echoed by the lament printed in the *Journal* early in 1836:

Oxford. SATURDAY, FEB. 20.

Our readers will imagine that the taste for music must be very much on the decline in Oxford, when they learn that the two excellent concerts given in our Music Room on Tuesday and Thursday evening were so feebly supported . . .[96]

[92] Notice dated 29 May 1804 in Ob, Mus. 1 d. 64/1 (the scheme was due to begin on 15 Oct.).

[93] Mee, *Music Room*, 181.

[94] *JOJ*, 9 May 1840. On Dicks's improvements to the Room see Mee, *Music Room*, 199.

[95] Mee, *Music Room*, 182–3.

[96] *JOJ*, 20 Feb. 1836. Fewer than 100 on average were in the audience each evening, although the

Thewlis noted the rise of new concert societies in the early nineteenth century as a 'disintegrating' influence on the Holywell concerts, taking the view that the 'rival societies' in the colleges and the town 'struck a severe blow' to the activities of the Musical Society. He also identified professional absenteeism as a contributory factor.[97]

Two distinct trends can be observed in the development of Oxford's concert life in the period leading up to and following on from the cessation of the Music Room concerts in the late 1830s. On the one hand, the growth of individual enterprise becomes noticeable. A new venue, the Star Assembly Rooms,[98] formed the setting for occasional series of concerts such as Marshall's, and Sharp's, from about 1838 onwards. Marshall's concerts included (besides various members of the Marshall clan) performers associated with the Holywell concerts: F. Cramer and W. Cramer (violins), Lindley and Reinagle (cellos), and Dragonetti and Haldon (double basses). Clara Novello appeared among the singers; W. Marshall, 'Mus. Bac.', conducted. Sharp's concerts also featured contributions from the Marshall family, together with various imported players. The programmes generally covered a broad repertoire ranging from early Romantic orchestral music (Mendelssohn, Overture to *A Midsummer Night's Dream*) and contemporary Italian opera (Pacini, Bellini) to modern British and continental composers (Onslow, Balfe) as well as the glees, ballads, Mozart opera and Handel oratorio extracts that had become established fare at Holywell. Corelli and Rossini were juxtaposed; Schubert songs were featured alongside Avison concertos. Particular experiments included Marshall's subscription concerts launched in 1839 'upon the plan of the classical quartett concerts in London' with Mozart, Haydn, and Beethoven in the repertoire (although 'a quartett, by Krommer' was reportedly 'the gem of the evening . . . performed with a precision that would have done credit to the first professors in London'); 'W. Marshall, M.B., organist of Christ Church, &c. presided at the grand piano forte, and sang . . .'. The *Journal* continued to serve as an outlet for

performers, Mrs Bishop, Mr Hobbs, Mr Parry, and the 'inimitable' W. Nicholson (flute) were much applauded.

97 Thewlis, Notes, iv. 859, 874.

98 The Star, an ancient inn, was given a new façade in 1783 (*EO* 94); Thewlis (Notes, iv. 860) documents its concert room opening in October 1832.

advertisements and reports, its critic expressing the hope that these ventures would 'lead to a revival of the declining musical taste' in Oxford.[99]

On the other hand, a new force for concert life was the formation of societies promoting musical performances. The University Amateur Musical Society (UAMS) gave termly concerts, with the Lent Term event consisting of 'a sacred concert, for which the Choristers of Magdalen and New College assisted'.[100] By 1840 the UAMS was involved in the music for Commemoration week: reporting the proceedings, the *Journal* noted that 'The University Amateurs gave a concert at the Star Assembly Rooms' on the Monday evening, when 'a large and fashionable audience attended, and expressed their entire approbation of the performances'. And where previously the concerts given by individuals such as William Marshall were still described as taking place 'with the permission of the stewards of the Music Room' (even if held elsewhere),[101] in November 1841 Marshall's concert at the Star Assembly Rooms was billed as 'under the patronage of the University Amateur Musical Society'. (It was on this occasion that Mr Henry Cooper performed on the violin 'a Grand Sonata on One String only . . . written expressly for him, and dedicated to Paganini' (possibly by De Bériot).)[102]

The University Motett and Madrigal Society put on regular 'open nights' conducted by C. W. Corfe during the 1850s, with programmes devoted to Renaissance vocal music: Dowland's 'Awake, sweet love', Gibbons's 'The Silver Swan', Wilbye's 'Flora gave me fairest flowers', and other gems of the English and Italian repertoire.[103] For Marshall (senior)'s Benefit concert at the Star Assembly Rooms in 1850 acknowledgement was made to 'the members of the Oxford Choral Society, who have kindly given their services on this occasion', under the conductorship of Dr Elvey.[104] By 1854 the 'Oxford Society for the Study of Plainsong' was

---

[99] *JOJ*, 23 Feb. 1839; for the quartet concerts see also 9 and 16 Feb. The taste for chamber music became established; by 1846 the *Journal* reported encouragingly on 'Mr. and Mrs. REINAGLE's first Quartet Concert' (*JOJ*, 31 Oct. 1846) and in 1847 it was felt that 'We must not omit to notice Mr. & Mrs. Reinagle's third concert, on Monday evening last, although the auditors, owing to the heavy fall of snow, were few in number. We can bear witness to the excellence of the programme, and the performance was, as usual, of a first-rate character'.

[100] Thewlis, Notes, iv. 859. Thewlis dates the earliest programme to 30 May 1829.

[101] Cf. Mee, *Music Room*, 181.

[102] Thewlis, Notes, iv. 887 with reference to *JOJ*, 13 Nov. 1841.

[103] At least some of these events took place at the Music Room: cf. *JOJ*, 2 July 1851.

[104] *JOJ*, 2 Nov. 1850.

meeting to sing Gregorian chant.[105] When, in the 1870s and 1880s, the Oxford University Musical Club and the University Musical Union were founded, this was against a strong background of university societies.

In the middle decades of the nineteenth century a host of college musical societies sprang up also, so that again when, in the 1880s, the Balliol concerts were launched, these—although a special case—were part of a larger scene in which college musical resources had been harnessed into societies of both a generalized and a more specific nature. Thewlis identified the St John's College Musical Society as an early example of the 'secession from the domination of the Music Club [the organization run by the Holywell stewards] by the formation of a separate College Musical Society': the earliest extant programme is dated Friday, 12 December 1816; the next dates from Friday, 21 March 1817, and later in that year the society was billed as 'a Musical Club consisting of some Undergraduate Members of St John's College'.[106] Among others noted by Thewlis as in existence by the mid-nineteenth century were the New College Glee Club and the Worcester College Philharmonic Society. These, too, attracted attention in the press.[107]

During the 1850s and 1860s the patterns of both individual enterprise and collective effort continued. For the annual Commemoration celebrations the University Amateurs generally provided musical entertainment, as in 1850 when 'a concert at the Star Assembly Room by the University Amateur Society, formed a most agreeable finish to the day's enjoyment'.[108] Thewlis notes that the UAMS was increasing in importance during this period; in March 1856 its Lent Term performance of Handel's *Samson* was attended by approximately 800 'of the *elite* of the University and City'. (The Orchestra of some 150 performers was described as 'most complete'.) Several eminent instrumentalists from London, and vocal soloists from the London Sacred Concerts, performed on this occasion together with the Oxford musicians.[109] And for the June Commemoration in 1856 it was remarked in connection with the UAMS concert at the

---

[105] Thewlis, Notes, iv. 918.

[106] See ibid. iv. 803; and Ob, MS Mus. 1 d. 64/2.

[107] Thewlis, Notes, iv. 898, 913. For further discussion of the college music societies see also Ch. 10 below.

[108] *JOJ*, 11 June 1850.

[109] Cf. Thewlis, Notes, iv. 921; *JOJ*, 5 Mar. 1856.

Town Hall the previous Saturday that 'so great was the demand for tickets, that the Committee were obliged to limit the number to about 900. The Hall was crowded in every part . . .'.[110] Typically, as in this programme, the society performed 'selections' from eighteenth- and nineteenth-century composers, especially of the Austro-German traditions (and Handel, whose place in the repertoire continued to be assured).[111] In December 1857 the *Journal* recorded with a new slant on audience and function that the UAMS had given a concert to 'the Members of the Oxford Working Men's Educational Institution'.[112]

Among individuals putting on concerts in the middle decades of the century (besides the ubiquitous Marshall family) new names emerging included that of Mr (James) Russell, who in November 1853 announced his series of 'Celebrity' concerts, beginning with Sims Reeves.[113] In 1859 Russell's team of invited performers at the Town Hall featured Madam Viardot Garcia, Signor (Giulio) Regondi, and the pianist Miss Arabella Goddard.[114] (Like the Holywell stewards in earlier days, Russell in engaging his artists showed a keen sense of the leading musical talent to be found on the British concert scene.) For his 'Grand Concert' in the Town Hall in November 1860, Russell arranged a farewell performance to mark Clara Novello's last appearance in Oxford; she was accorded 'a wonderful reception'.[115] The post-Holywell phase allowed scope for experiments in repertoire, and in concert planning and structure. 'Mr James Russell's Grand Concert' at the New Corn Exchange in November 1863 offered

---

[110] *JOJ*, June 1856. Thewlis tracks the UAMS through until 1867 (Notes, iv. 945).

[111] Handel (especially, but not only, the choral music), remained popular generally: *Acis and Galatea* and *L'Allegro ed Il Penseroso* featured in 1854 and 1861 respectively (noted in Thewlis, Notes, iv. 917 and 934); Bishop Mitchinson of Pembroke remembered singing at this period with the UAMS in *Samson, Alexander's Feast*, and *Acis and Galatea* under Stephen Elvey ('Oxford Memories' (unpublished memoirs), PCA, MS 60/15/83, p. 20).

[112] *JOJ*, 5 Dec. 1857.

[113] *JOJ*, 26 Nov. 1853. The music businesses of James Russell and Sydney Acott were eventually amalgamated in 1951, at 124 High Street, to form the (sadly no longer) shop of Russell Acott. On Sims Reeves see *NG2* xxi. 77.

[114] Thewlis, Notes, iv. 933. Regondi had been popular in Oxford for some years (for his career and importance see *NG2* xxi. 122; for Arabella Goddard see *NG2* x. 70). A series of fashionably virtuosic pianists was heard in Oxford during the middle decades of the 19th cent., and critical appreciation heaped on them: Thalberg appeared often, and Liszt arrived in November 1840 when his performance during the Grand Concert at the Star Assembly Rooms, 'upon one of Era[r]d's Patent Grand Piano Fortes', was pronounced 'perfectly astonishing' (*JOJ*, 28 Nov. 1840).

[115] *JOJ*, 17 Nov. 1860.

selections from 'Mr Gounod's celebrated Opera of Faust'.[116] Another entrepreneur, Mrs Reinagle, proposed to give a series of six solo piano recitals at the Music Room in that same year; her miscellaneous programmes presented selections from a wide range of composers, including Bach, Handel, Scarlatti, and Couperin as well as Haydn, Mozart, Clementi and Dussek, Beethoven and Field.[117] Such enterprises as Russell's and Mrs Reinagle's brought new music (or newly revived old music) in new venues or new formats to Oxford audiences. The sense of experiment was seen also in the developments in college concerts, which from 1850 onwards proliferated, especially, although not exclusively, during the Commemoration season in May and June each year.[118]

A highlight during these decades in terms of public interest, attention in the press, and subsequent literature, was the appearance of Jenny Lind. Her first performances in Oxford took place in 1848 at a 'Grand Miscellaneous Concert' in the Sheldonian Theatre, '*Under the Sanction of the Rev. the Vice-Chancellor*', on 1 December. This obviously constituted a huge event: 'As soon as it was publicly announced that Jenny Lind would appear in Oxford, and sing in the Theatre, the most lively interest was manifested throughout the University and City, and the concert has been, during the week, *the* topic of conversation in all circles.'[119] The 'FULL ORCHESTRA' included 'Mons. Nadaud' as leader, Signor Piatti as principal cello, and Mons. Lavigne and Signor E. Belletti on oboe and clarinet respectively; vocal soloists listed after 'Mademoiselle Jenny Lind' were Signor F. Lablache, and Signor Belletti ('*BASSOS, FROM HER MAJESTY'S THEATRE*'): there were no other female vocalists to compete with Jenny Lind for the limelight, or to detract from her share of it. The whole was conducted by Mr. Balfe. Other than Weber's overture to *Oberon*, which opened the concert, no music with English connections was featured; the mainly

---

[116] *JOJ*, 7 Nov. 1863 (conducted by Signor Arditi). On the Corn Exchange, and Cornmarket Street, see *EO* 102–4.

[117] *JOJ*, 17 Oct. 1863. Mee (*Music Room*, 187) describes Mrs Reinagle (née Orger) as 'a good pianist, and one of the first lady composers'; on the series of 'Classical Chamber Concerts' she gave, with her husband Alexander Reinagle (e.g. in 1846–7), see Thewlis, Notes, iv. 902 and n. 99 above.

[118] See especially Ch. 10 below.

[119] *JOJ*, 2 Dec. 1848; see also 25 Nov. for advertisement. Cox, *Recollections* (365) mentions that the use of the Sheldonian Theatre on this occasion was conditional upon the ticket prices being kept at a moderate level (they were 10s. 6d.) and notes that Jenny Lind left £100 of her profits to be applied to 'Oxford Charities'.

JENNY LIND.

*Under the Sanction of the Rev. the Vice-Chancellor of the
University of Oxford.*

IT is respectfully announced that a GRAND MIS-CELLANEOUS CONCERT, with full Orchestra, will take place on FRIDAY MORNING NEXT, December 1, at the **THEATRE**.

VOCALISTS.

MDLLE. JENNY LIND,

Signor F. LABLACHE, and Signor BELLETTI,

(Bassos, from her Majesty's Theatre.)

CONDUCTOR, Mr. BALFE.

INSTRUMENTAL PERFORMERS.

Leader of the Orchestra—Mons. Nadaud.	Piccolo—Mr. King.
	Oboe—Mons. Lavigne.
Principal First Violin and Solo Performer—Mons Herrmann.	Clarinette—Signor E. Belletti.
	Bassoon—Signor Tamplini.
Principal Second Violin—Mr. Oury	Horn—Herr Sleglick.
Principal Viola—Mr. Hughes.	Trumpet and Cornet-a-Piston—
Principal Violoncello—Sig. Piatti.	Herr Zeiss.
Principal Contra Basso—Signor Anglois.	Trombone—Mons. Marin.
	Drums—Mr. R. Hughes.
Grand Flute—Mons. Remusat.	

(Selected from her Majesty's Theatre.)
Music Librarian, Mr. Mapleson.

PROGRAMME.
PART I.

Overture *(Oberon)*	Weber.
Duo—Signori Belletti and F. Lablache, "Se pur giungi" *(Marino Faliero.)*	Donizetti.
Recit. and Air—Madlle. Jenny Lind, "Prendi Prendi." *(Elisir.)*	Donizetti.
Solo—Oboe, Monsieur Lavigne.	
Duetto—Madlle. Lind and Sig. Belletti, "Per piacere."	Rossini.
Aria—Signor F. Lablache, "Miei Rampolli." *(Cenerentola.)*	Rossini.
Solo—Violoncello, Signor Piatti. (Aria and Variations from "Linda." ..	Donizetti.
Aria—Signor Belletti, "Vi raviso." *(Somnambula.)*	Bellini.
Scena—Madlle. Lind, "Casta Diva." *(Norma.)* ..	Bellini.
Pot Pourri—Orchestra.	

The Solo Parts by Signor Piatti (Violoncello), Signor Anglois (Contra Basso), Monsieur Remusat (Flute), Monsieur Lavigne (Oboe), Signor E. Belletti (Clarinette), Signor Tamplini (Bassoon), Herr Sleglick (Horn), and Herr Zeiss (Cornet-a-Piston.)

(AN INTERVAL OF TEN MINUTES.)

PART II.

Overture.	Rossini.
Solo—Violin, M. Herrmann. (Introduction & Variations.) *(Carnival of Venice.)*	Paganini.
Trio—Voice and Two Flutes, Madlle. Lind, Monsieur Remusat, and Mr. King, (composed expressly for Mdlle. Lind.) *(Camp of Silesia.)*	Meyerbeer.
Duetto Buffo—Signor Belletti and F. Lablache. "D' un bell' uso."	Rossini.
Solo—Clarinette, Signor E. Belletti.	
Cavatina—Madlle. Jenny Lind. *(Der Freischutz.)* ..	Weber.
Aria—Signor Belletti, "Non piu Andrai." *(Nozze di Figaro.)*	Mozart.
Swedish Melodies—Mademoiselle Jenny Lind.	
Grand Finale.	

₊ Doors open at Twelve o'clock—to commence at One.

PRICES.—Semicircle, One Guinea; other parts of the Theatre, 10s. 6d.—Tickets of Admission will be sold on Monday next and three following days, between the hours of Two and Four, at the Theatre.—No money taken at the doors.

FIG. 17. Advertisement for Jenny Lind's concert
(*Jackson's Oxford Journal,* 25 November 1848)

nineteenth-century operatic items included a trio by Meyerbeer 'composed expressly for Mademoiselle Jenny Lind', and the programme further gained a special flavour through the inclusion of a set of three Swedish songs (provided with English translations—as indeed, unusually, were the various German and Italian texts—in the programme-book).[120]

Jenny Lind's 1848 concert did not fit the customary Oxford format (no Handel, nor even Haydn; and no choral music). Although billed as a 'miscellaneous' concert it concentrated much more on a single swathe of repertoire, and on one performer, than had been usual. The genuine sense of miscellany present in the regular Oxford concerts was lacking; in its place a showcase for a star (seemingly a 'superstar' of her time) was created, and the audience responded with enormous enthusiasm. The culmination came in a glittering Commemoration festival of 1856 featuring 'Madam Jenny Lind Goldschmidt' and Madame Viardot Garcia, when it was announced that Jenny Lind would sing 'in Oxford (for the last time) during the Grand Commemoration Week, in the Theatre'; the *Journal* commented on the rapturous welcome she received.[121] A particular draw was the performance of Haydn's *Creation* on 4 June. Prince Albert, Prince Frederick William of Prussia, and the Prince of Baden were present at this event, which reportedly allowed Jenny Lind's 'exquisitely beautiful and silvery high notes' to be 'heard to perfection in "Thy marvellous work"', and "With verdure clad"'.[122] (Jenny Lind Goldschmidt in fact returned to perform in subsequent Commemoration concerts.[123])

In general it is clear that by the late 1850s the decline earlier lamented by commentators on the Oxford concert scene had been reversed. Oxford music was exciting and vibrant during the middle decades of the century on its own terms, as well as through the periodic injection of glamour afforded by spectacular visits such as those of Jenny Lind. In 1846 the *Journal* reported that 'MR. E. MARSHALL's concert, which was the most spirited affair we ever had in Oxford . . . was attended by upwards of 500 persons, embracing most of the heads of houses and their families, and gentry of the neighbourhood'. Marshall played flute; Herr Koenig, on the cornet

---

[120] Ob, new acquisition 2000.
[121] *JOJ*, 7 June 1856.
[122] Ibid. (cf. Thewlis, Notes, iv. 922).
[123] Cf. ibid. 934–5 (1862).

('cornet-à-pistons') was 'rapturously encored'; and the conductor was 'Monsieur Jullien', with his 'celebrated band'; the *Journal*'s critic summed up the event as a 'great musical treat'.[124] A further series of 'Mr Jullien's Grand Concerts', overwhelmingly well attended, followed in 1847. Mee (in view of the scope of his book) took his outline list of the Commemoration concerts up to 1844 only, and with the entries 'No concerts [at Commemoration]' for 1840–3 gave an impression of the decline of this tradition, as well as of the Holywell concerts, at this period.[125] But had he been able to follow the Commemorations through to 1860 he would have seen that, besides Jenny Lind in 1856, many internationally famous performers graced the Sheldonian on these occasions. In 1844, where Mee's entry simply reads '"Messiah". Two miscellaneous concerts. Bishop conducted', Madame Caradori Allan, Signor Salvi and others sang, and the string-players included Signor Sivori (violin), Mr Lindley (cello), and Signor Dragonetti (double bass).[126] Mr Cramer and Mr Loder led;[127] Marshall was principal second violin, and Reinagle played among the cellos. Bishop, conducting on this occasion, was billed as 'Conductor of Her Majesty's Concerts of Ancient Music', a reminder of his serious credentials.

The documentary records of the Oxford Commemoration concerts offer a vivid picture of an aspect of nineteenth-century British festival culture.[128] Almost every one of these events forms a source of special interest. At the 'Commemorative Musical Festival' of 1852, when Mendelssohn's *St Paul* was heard (and was apparently a success in spite of the competing efforts of a brass band parading down Broad Street)[129] the instrumental performers at the concerts in the Sheldonian Theatre included 'Herr Joachim' on violin and 'Signor Bottesini' on double bass. (Marshall was leader of the band, and Bishop, as Professor of Music, conducted.) Joachim 'delighted the audience' (reportedly 1,200 were present); it was noted in the *Journal* that 'extra trains' from Paddington, Euston and

---

[124] *JOJ*, 7 Feb. 1846. Thewlis (Notes, iv. 914) took a dim view of Jullien's appearances in Oxford.

[125] Mee, *Music Room*, 198.

[126] On Bishop and Dragonetti see Northcott, *Bishop*, 133. Sivori is described in *NG* (xvii. 357) as 'the most exciting violin virtuoso after Paganini'.

[127] John David Loder.

[128] See my article, 'The Oxford Commemorations and nineteenth-century British festival culture' (in preparation).

[129] Thewlis, Notes, iv. 915.

Banbury would be put on for the occasion.[130] As so often happened with visiting performers, Oxford adopted Joachim. It also, at this same period, adopted Mendelssohn's oratorios and other works, to some extent with the kind of canonic status earlier granted to Handel. Both Joachim and Mendelssohn had family connections with Oxford. Joachim's nephew, Harold Joachim of Balliol, was to become a Fellow of Merton College (1897) while Mendelssohn's grandson Paul Victor Mendelssohn Benecke later became a Fellow of Magdalen College.[131] To mark the fiftieth anniversary of Joachim's public career in 1889, he was presented with a laurel wreath at the Oxford University Musical Club's open concert in the Sheldonian Theatre. Dr Stainer commented: 'the young President [Mr Benecke] who presents this wreath to you is himself the grandson of the immortal Mendelssohn.'[132]

Among the many diverse musical associations formed during the second half of the nineteenth century, the founding of the OUMC in April 1872 (with Charles Harford Lloyd as its first President) launched an initiative 'which was to play a very great part in the musical life of Oxford, especially in the University'.[133] Mitchell-Innes later wrote to Lloyd, recalling: 'It was the intense pleasure which I derived from those delightful string quartets in Wild's Rooms (at Christ Church) which made me regret that a larger audience could not share the pleasure, and this suggested the idea of a Club which you took up so keenly and carried into effect.'[134] Chamber music was moving increasingly during the nineteenth century from the private or domestic into the public domain, and Oxford concerts in general reflected this trend. But the Club's focus related more to the earliest history of concerts in Oxford: the *Journal* referred in 1873 to OUMC as consisting of 'the leading amateurs of the University' who met weekly in Term to play together.[135]

The launching of the OUMC in 1872, followed by the Oxford University Musical Union (OUMU) in 1884, above all secured a strong central focus for student music-making. For the OUMU, two commemorative vol-

[130] *JOJ*, 19 June 1852.
[131] Cf. Crum, 'Deneke Mendelssohn', *BLR* 12 (1987); Deneke, *Benecke*.
[132] *JOJ*, 16 Mar. 1889.
[133] Thewlis, Notes, iv. 953.
[134] Ibid. iv. 954.
[135] *JOJ*, June 1873. The popular 'Public Classical Concerts' later run by OUMC (from 1891 onwards)

umcs provide particularly valuable documentation of the first twenty years of its existence. Continuity was created by the involvement of Dr Mee; a founder member, together with W. H. Hadow and others, he was evidently regarded warmly by his colleagues, and was the only one among the several compilers who contributed his expertise to both volumes of proceedings, 1884–94 and 1894–1904.[136] During 1890–1 Mee gave to the Club an organ (with two manuals and pedals) which was 'found to be of great practical use to members'.[137] By 1904 Mee and Kemp reported the move to new premises—the Holywell Music Room—mentioning that Mee's history of the Music Room was in progress.

Again echoing at two centuries' distance the activities of the earliest documented Oxford musical society, the Club lent or hired out music, books, and instruments. Members on leaving Oxford donated scores, sheet music, or books; and during 1891–2 Mr Taphouse 'with characteristic generosity' offered his library to supplement the Club's collection.[138] Also evocative of the earlier Musical Society were the OUMU's club rules, which imposed fines for infringement of these regulations, including 'disturbing the performance of music by talking, striking matches, writing with a quill pen . . .'. Under Rule IX the Committee would 'have power to expel any member . . . for conduct that is in their judgment unbecoming in a gentleman', and while under Rule XIII strangers might be admitted to performances by leave of the Committee, such leave would not be granted 'to any lady' (nor could dogs be brought into the Club-room).[139] The Club seems to have filled a widely felt need; starting with fifty members, 'much larger support' materialized than originally expected and by 1894 the authors of *Ten Years* reported a membership of over 100. The Club's

offered large-scale programmes of orchestral as well as chamber music and acted as a forum for new works; at the Public Classical Concert held in the Town Hall, 8 Feb. 1912, one of the two works premièred (when 'Dr. Allen's Orchestra rendered an interesting programme', and Tovey 'played the pianoforte', with 'much brilliance') was Butterworth's *Two Idylls on English Folk-Tunes* (cf. *Oxford Chronicle*, 9 Feb. 1912).

[136] Mee's co-editors for *Ten Years*, P. C. Buck of Worcester College and F. C. Woods of Exeter College, adapted the well-known lines: 'Men may come and men may go, but he goes on (we hope) for ever' (ibid. 9).

[137] Ibid. 6.

[138] Ibid. 2; p. 7. For a catalogue of the library's holdings see pp. 48–58 (modified in Kemp and Mee, eds., *Ten More Years*, 197–228). Taphouse was for many years a leading Oxford music shop, established 1857 (cf. *EO* 448).

[139] *Ten Years*, 11–12. In connection with the forming of the OLMS, Woodgate (*Oxford Chamber Music Society*, 5) notes that a 'particular reason for setting up a ladies' society was that membership of the Oxford University Musical Club . . . was open only to men from the University'.

attraction to members will have been enhanced by its non-profit-making policies, with subscriptions kept at a low rate and no extra charge for concert tickets.[140]

An emphasis on chamber music particularly characterized the OUMU. Indeed it was claimed that when, 'in Lent Term, 1885, the first Invitation Concert was held in Balliol College Hall', it was 'worthy of note as throwing some light on the good influence of the O.U.M.U. on University music in Oxford, that at that time a professional string quartett had not been heard in Oxford for five years'. It was further noted that 'at the very first meeting a String Quartett was performed, and there have been very few meetings since at which this typical species of chamber music has not been represented'.[141] The Club offered its members the chance not only to put on weekly 'smoking concerts' but also to benefit from professional coaching, with a weekly class 'for practice under professional teaching'; from January 1886 the ensemble coach was Mr G. H. Betjemann. It also, importantly, gave members regular opportunity to have their own compositions performed: from the first concert of compositions by members of the Club, in December 1885, onwards, the plan was reported both to have 'been found to give the composers much useful experience' and also to have been 'the means of bringing forward many charming compositions in the highest branches of musical art'.[142] Obviously those student members who were music graduates (or aspiring graduates) of the university, such as S. Spooner-Lillingston, would expect to be involved in composing.[143]

Standards of performance in OUMU were reputedly high, and it was stressed that these depended on members rather than outsiders: in 1892–3 an 'exceptional number of excellent performers were in residence and almost all the most important chamber music of the great composers was heard in the course of the year'. Naturally the compilers of *Ten Years* (which was distributed free to members) in celebrating the 'brilliant suc-

---

[140] On membership and financial arrangements, see *Ten Years*, 1–2. The entrance fee of one guinea and termly subscription of half-a-guinea were maintained at this level during the twenty-year period charted in *Ten Years* and *Ten More Years* (the fine for breaking the rules about disturbing the performance was 5s.).

[141] *Ten Years*, 1–2.

[142] On coaching, and concerts, see ibid. 1, 3–4.

[143] Mentioned in *Ten Years*, 32 *et seq.*

cess' of the Club were inclined to emphasize their point that 'the excellence of the weekly musical meetings' had been 'steadily maintained . . . entirely by the performances of members'. But their glowing commendation is balanced by the delightful attribution of the successful atmosphere to 'a spirit of the truest criticism . . . that does not ignore faults but seeks first for merits to applaud', as well as to 'student life' with its spirit of good humour (which apparently carried the Club through various fierce controversies).[144] What emerges most strongly is the formative role the Club played in the musical experience of its members at a key stage in their careers.

The Club's membership contained names of importance on the Oxford scene—besides Mee, H. M. Abel of Merton College (later a medical practitioner) was among the founding members—and those who were to become distinguished in the musical and educational professions: Hadow, R. R. Terry, E. H. Fellowes of Oriel College (specially mentioned for 'services rendered' to OUMU), and Frederick Bridge: when the new Club room was opened in Michaelmas Term 1887, the first programme (19 October) 'consisted of Mendelssohn's Octett for Strings and Schumann's Pianoforte Quintett', and 'Dr. J. Frederick Bridge . . . present as a visitor, was so pleased with what he had heard that he at once became a candidate for membership'.[145] An important element was the Club's connection with its Cambridge counterpart; Cambridge University Musical Club was established in 1889–90 and reciprocal visits were arranged annually.[146]

An influential follow-up to this was the Oxford and Cambridge Musical Club (founded 1899), based in London with initially about 300 members. Dr Horace Abel was its first Honorary Secretary and the three earliest Presidents were Joseph Joachim, Arthur James Balfour, and W. H. Hadow. Among 'distinguished Non-Performing Members' were Hugh Allen (1903) and E. M. Forster (1905).[147] The early concert programmes show an emphasis on chamber music, with Haydn 'much in favour' and some rare, and some very up-to-date, items: a scholarly element appears, too (Purcell's *Chaconne* in G minor was played in 1909, 'from an unpublished

[144] *Ten Years*, 7–8.   [145] Ibid. *passim*, esp. pp. 4, 7.   [146] Ibid. 5–6.
[147] For information on the early years, see Laurie Pettitt in Thorne, *Oxford & Cambridge Musical Club*, 9–23.

manuscript in the British Museum').[148] Writing in the eightieth anniversary history, Pettitt noted that 'This Week's Composers' on Radio Three (30 January–3 February 1978) included Moeran and in the same week 'works by Donald Tovey, Thomas Dunhill, George Butterworth, and Patrick Hadley were broadcast, and Sir Adrian Boult conducted Vaughan Williams' London symphony. All Club members . . .'.[149]

While OUMU and its satellite, the OCMC, were aimed especially at 'promotion of knowledge of [instrumental] Chamber Music' amongst members of the university (although singers were featured), the Oxford Bach Choir, founded also in the late nineteenth century, was designed to promote knowledge of the major choral repertoire among university members—undergraduates in particular.[150] And it enabled men and women to work together in this cause: an early member of the choir was the young Dorothy Sayers, who came up to Somerville College in 1912 as an undergraduate, joined the choir in that year, and continued to sing in the Bach Choir under Allen until 1919. The Oxford Bach Choir was also characterized by its 'mixed town-and-gown membership'.[151]

In the years around the turn of the century, concerts were harnessed to the war effort: the first of the Children's Concerts for charity given by the OLMS in the Town Hall on 13 December 1899 was 'in aid of the Transvaal War Fund'.[152] Thewlis deduces that the relatively few concerts given in 1900 can be explained by 'many Oxford men being away at war in Africa'.[153] In her founding speech to the OLMS Mrs Burdon-Sanderson had remarked: 'it may possibly be thought by some people that a new Music Society ought to have a very substantial raison d'être. I have indeed heard it whispered that we have already too much music in Oxford . . .'.[154] Certainly, as 'the domination of the Music Room [concerts] gave way to the rise of independent Societies, both in Town and University' during the

[148] Thorne, *Oxford & Cambridge Musical Club*, 47–56.

[149] Ibid. 23; and cf. pp. 14–15 for a list of 'Distinguished Professional Musicians who were Performing Members'.

[150] On the aims of OUMU, see *Ten Years*, 10. For a discussion of OBC under Hugh Allen, see Ch. 11 below.

[151] *EO* 300 ('Oxford Bach Choir'); cf. Wollenberg, 'Music in Oxford in the Time of Dorothy L. Sayers' (1993).

[152] Woodgate, *Oxford Chamber Music Society*, 10.

[153] Thewlis, Notes, iv. 981. Thewlis also points out (ibid. 983) that in 1901 the usual concerts were suspended because of Queen Victoria's death as well as the war in South Africa.

[154] Quoted in Woodgate, *Oxford Chamber Music Society*, 6.

nineteenth century,[155] opportunities to perform, compose, and listen to music in a variety of locations and cultural contexts seemed ever more plentiful.

In February 1914 the Oxford University Musical Club marked its 1000th concert with a reception hosted by the Principal of Brasenose (President of the Club) and Miss Heberden, and a dinner, in addition to the concert itself on 10 February. Edmund Fellowes recalled this 'memorable event':

Under Basil Harwood's conductorship on that occasion, I led the band to accompany the Bach Concerto in C for two pianofortes, played by Parratt and Hugh Allen, successively the University Professors of Music. The Andante of Mozart's Sonata in D for two pianofortes was played by the Vice-Chancellor and an ex-Vice-Chancellor, both of them Heads of Colleges, Dr. T. B. Strong, Dean of Christ Church, and Dr. C. B. Heberden, Principal of Brasenose. This marked an astonishing change in the academic outlook towards music in university circles during the previous half-century. Heberden was an accomplished pianist . . .[156]

Later in that year Hugh Allen and Mary Venables were involved in giving concerts for the War Relief Fund; these marked the beginning of a period in which it was felt generally in Oxford that 'the war has made concerts here almost an impossibility'.[157] Yet the strong foundations established for Oxford music in the preceding era enabled many of the ventures started then to flourish in the post-war period.

[155] Thewlis, Notes, iv. 981.   [156] Fellowes, *Memoirs*, 183.   [157] Thewlis, Notes, iv. 990.

10

~~❦~~

The Colleges, II

In the early nineteenth century, music could be woven in many ways into the daily lives of the college residents, as Egerton's diary shows with reference to New College:

[1826: 26 March, Sunday chapel]: Bennett is an admirable organist & has improved the Choristers wonderfully.

[29 March]: . . . Dined in Hall—at seven went to . . . a Practising Fiddling Party. Young Reinagle led: a very clever Fellow. He plays the Violin & Violoncello capitally.

[31 March]: Dined in Hall, & at eight o'Clock had a Musical Party for Practice in it. Reinagle led—& though the Echo in Hall is rather too great the Music sounded beautifully. Haydn's symphonies went particularly well—Three Violins, a Tenor & two Basses, one of which I played.—gave the party some supper there afterwards & after it there were Glees. Very pleasant evening.

[1 April]: Had a singing lesson from Bennett at nine o'Clock . . .

[15 April]: Bennett our Organist took me to see the new Pedal just put to our Chapel organ—It is a Row of Keys for the Feet, & supplies the place of a Third Hand. He played & the effect was excellent.

[Thursday, 15 June]: First of all we had some sacred Music in the Chapel for an Hour & very well it was performed by the Choir. Then we adjourned to the Hall, where we had a Concert—Marshall, Reinagle, young Jackson & some more, about seven Instrumentalists & there were plenty of Glees & songs.[1]

Egerton's involvement in music-making continued to centre on string ensembles and singing. In May 1827 he noted:

Returned by Defiance [coach] to Oxford—where I had engaged to get up a Quartette for Blanco White. He dined with me and afterwards in S[enio]r. C.[ommon] Room he joined Sharp, Reinagle & Aldrich of Exeter [College], who is very musical—he played the Tenor this Eve[ning]—very well indeed. Several Pieces from Haydn, Beethoven, Pleyel, & Mozart went beautifully—Blanco plays very well & has a beautiful toned Amati—He seemed much pleased—went away at ten . . .[2]

The practice of singing glees in the college Hall became established. On Friday, 27 October 1826 Egerton recorded: 'Had a Glee Party in Hall: The commencement I hope of a regular meeting—we had some supper & kept it up very late', and again on Wednesday, 1 November: 'Dined in Hall—& we had another Glee Party in it . . . & all went off capitally.'[3] By early December Egerton was referring to 'Glee Practice' and 'our Club Musical meeting in Hall'; on the latter occasion some visitors came to listen and 'liked the singing very much', and the 'Musical Practice of the Club' on Tuesday, 12 December was followed by a 'Club open night' on 13 December, 'the singing all good'.[4] By March 1827 Egerton noted 'A large Party in Hall to hear our Glee Concert, a great proportion Ladies . . .'[5] and the Glee Club meetings continued in this vein with regular practices and open nights.

For John Henry Newman music was a constant occupation during his undergraduate years at Trinity College (he was a keen violinist). In February 1820 he wrote to his sister of his involvement with the recently founded society at St John's College: 'Our music club at St John's has been offered and has accepted the music room for our weekly private concerts.'[6] The

[1] Diary of John Egerton (Fellow of New College, 1815–28): cf. Cheshire County Council, DDX 597/3; pp. 18–60. On the organ, Bursar's invoices for 1826 show a sum of £15 paid for 'Making New Pedals' to the Organ in Chapel and connecting the Choir and Great organ manuals (NCA, 11, 411: Apr. 1826).

[2] Diary, p. 175. Joseph Blanco White (1775–1841) was a clergyman and theological writer of Spanish origin who settled in Oxford, at Oriel College from 1826.

[3] Ibid. 128–30.   [4] Ibid. 145–6.   [5] Ibid. 164 (Friday, 30 Mar.).

[6] Quoted, from J. H. Newman, *Correspondence*, ed. A. Mozley (1891), in Thewlis, Notes, iii. 589–90. On the St John's Club see also Ch. 9 above; and on Newman's involvement in music see Bellasis, *Cardinal Newman*, esp. 7–10.

process of evolution from private gathering to more high-profile club as documented by Egerton was echoed elsewhere: the nineteenth-century expansion of the colleges, together with the increase in student numbers, was accompanied (in the context of the proliferation of clubs generally in Oxford) by a noticeable growth in opportunities for organized music-making within the individual colleges. Pembroke College, for example, showed at this period, especially under Jeune's Mastership (1843–64), a 'transformation': 'matriculations increased sharply, to the point where they were, at one stage, the third largest in the University; the college buildings were doubled in size'.[7] John Mitchinson, later Master of Pembroke (1899–1918), recalled how as an undergraduate he was involved in musical activity in the college as well as the university:

Music bulked largely in my recreations. I had a fairly good tenor voice and could read music fluently. I belonged to Dr Corfe's Motett & Madrigal Society ... and also to the Amateur Musical Society ... This Society gave concerts, and very good they were ... I must not forget our own little musical club in College. I hatched it, and for a while they were content with me as their instructor. Ere long, like the Israelites under Samuel, they wanted to be like the surrounding nations, and hankered after a professional instructor. So I gracefully retired in favour of M^r. A. Barrett, a music vendor in a small way. We knew him among ourselves as Signor Barretti. He taught us quite well, and though we never broke out into a concert, we had our full measure of profit and pleasure from our weekly practice lesson in the good old English men's voice glees.[8]

By the 1860s and 1870s the 'little musical club' founded by Mitchinson had evolved into the college Glee Club and the college Musical Society, and these were putting on concerts.[9]

During his mastership of Pembroke, Mitchinson ensured that music in the college chapel was maintained on a secure basis. At other colleges, musical societies developed partly as an extension of, and perhaps also as an antidote to, the chapel music. Among the rules of the New College Glee Club in its later phase of existence (documented from 1839 onwards) as agreed at a meeting held in the college hall on 11 February 1867, was 'That the Organist be ... ex-officio Conductor ... to preside at the

---

[7] *EO* 320 ('Pembroke College').
[8] Bishop Mitchinson, 'Oxford Memories' (unpublished memoirs), PCA, MS 60/15/83, pp. 20–1.
[9] Concert programmes are extant in PCA, 58/1–3.

Piano-forte and to assist the Stewards of the Music' (rule 6).[10] And it had previously been established that the conductor would have the power to veto any music for which the choristers' voices would be unequal to taking the treble part.[11] (Apart from the trebles, the singing members were divided into contratenors, tenors, and basses.) The repertoire at this period, as in Mitchinson's undergraduate musical club, focused on English part-songs:

> Rule 1:   That the New college Glee club shall have for its object the performance of Glees, catches, rounds, canons, and Madrigals, or any similar kind of English music, provided always that it be a piece for not less than three voices.[12]

The earlier rules make reference to 'open nights' when programmes would be advertised and members could bring guests.[13] The programme of the Glee Club's first meeting (14 March 1839) survives.[14] The composers represented in the Holywell part-song repertoire are prominent here too: Webbe ('Glorious Apollo' and 'Come live with me', for example), Horsley, Mornington, Callcott, and Bishop ('Mynheer Vandunck', a popular theatrical song that the composer somewhat regretted), among others.[15] The final item, 'Non nobis Domine' by 'Bird', clearly suggests a wish to temper the secular nature of the programme, if only briefly. But the mixture of items also echoes (more extremely than had been customary) the juxtapositions noted by Mee in relation to the Holywell concerts, as well as anticipating to some extent the concerns of the later Motett and Madrigal Society.[16]

Membership of the New College Glee Club was open to present or former members of the college. Similarly, Fellowes described the 'Magdalen Vagabonds' as 'an organization of past and present academical clerks, as the choral scholars of Magdalen were termed'.[17] By 1892, when Fellowes was invited to join their concert tour, the Vagabonds had

[10] NCA, 3523.   [11] Ibid. rule 14 (passed 1846).   [12] Ibid. (1867).

[13] Ibid. (1839). The disciplinary clauses echo long tradition, with 'any member talking during the performance of any piece of music' being fined sixpence (rule 15) and all singing members not present after quarter of an hour to be fined (originally one shilling, later sixpence).

[14] NCA, 3523.   [15] See Northcott, *Bishop*, 58–9.

[16] Cf. Ch. 9 (on Holywell) and (on the Motett and Madrigal Society) Ch. 8 above. On the history of the misattribution of the canon 'Non nobis Domine' to William Byrd, see *The Byrd Edition*, 16 (*Madrigals, Songs and Canons*), ed. P. Brett, pp. viii–ix.

[17] Fellowes, *Memoirs*, 62.

established 'the habit of making tours lasting for four or five days, giving the proceeds of their concerts to charities'.[18] Audiences in Leeds (the Albert Hall), Birmingham, Hereford, Lincoln, Worcester, and other cities heard these representatives of the Oxford choral tradition; on the tours Fellowes participated in (as violinist, to provide 'variety to the programmes') the sums raised for charity were 'gratifying'.[19]

In other cases the college societies cultivated the symphonic repertoire and the larger-scale choral works, taking over some of the character of the now defunct Holywell concerts. On the occasion of the fiftieth anniversary of the Eglesfield Musical Society at Queen's College in 1910, in surveying the society's history it was noted that

It has proved impossible to recover many of the earlier programmes, but in 1860 Mozart's Symphony in C major [? the 'Jupiter'] and Rossini's 'La Gazza Ladra' Overture, and in 1868 Haydn's Symphony in D major, No. 1, Mozart's 'Figaro' Overture, and Rossini's 'Il Barbiere' Overture were performed. In 1871 a somewhat larger . . . fine orchestra . . . proved such a success that it was followed by a similar performance in 1873, when Sterndale Bennett's 'May Queen' was performed.[20]

Apparently 'the celebrated singer Madame Goldschmidt (Jenny Lind) was present' on this last occasion. Apart from 1874, when the annual concert 'accidentally fell through', and 1881, when 'a sad fatality, in the shape of the drowning of an undergraduate . . . just before the Concert, caused its abandonment', the chronicler in 1910 recorded that every year since 1872 had been marked by a concert. It was characteristic of the Society that it drew on 'graduate and undergraduate members of the College, aided by other Oxford residents'. Among its conductors were Dr T. W. Dodds, organist of the College, Dr F. Iliffe, organist of St John's College, and Dr G. G. Stocks of St Edward's School. It was further noted that 'for many years the Society has performed works for men's voices and orchestra', and in this connection Dr Mee once again appeared as the recipient of a warmly appreciative tribute:

There has been no one who has spent himself more freely in the interests of this Society than the Rev. J. H. Mee, D. Mus., formerly Scholar of the College. Not

---

[18] Fellowes, *Memoirs*, 62.   [19] Ibid. 62–3.
[20] QCA, News cuttings album, p. 23: programme booklet (16 June 1910, 8.15 p.m.).

only has he composed works for the performances, [and] financed the Society through days of difficulty, but has . . . been a member of the chorus in every concert since 1872.[21]

(Mee was listed in the programme booklet as Treasurer of the Eglesfield Society.) In the preface to the booklet the committee (which also included G. B. Cronshaw), giving a short account of the Society's 'artistic work . . . in the past', identified as its original aim the offering to guests of an entertainment in the form of 'a Concert of high-class music rendered in the best possible way', and claimed that this idea had been 'so extensively imitated' since (presumably implying within colleges) that it was difficult now to realize its 'boldness'.[22]

The fiftieth anniversary programme (conducted by G. G. Stocks) was certainly very substantial for its time and context. Part I began with Mendelssohn's Overture 'Das Märchen von der Schönen Melusine', Op. 32, and continued with Schubert's *Gesang der Geister über den Wassern*, Op. 167. For the latter item the chorus of men's voices was 'divided into eight parts' (the programme book listed the names of twenty tenors including Cronshaw, and thirty-nine basses). Finally before the interval Beethoven's Symphony No. 8 in F major was heard. In Part II Handel's 'Concerto Grosso for Strings in B minor' (from Op. 6 of 1739) was performed in full; the remaining works were Wagner's *Siegfried Idyll*, followed by part-songs (Mee's 'Love's name' and Elgar's 'Feasting, I watch') and the 'Old English Suite' of Granville Bantock.[23] The programme notes, too, are extensive (in fact constituting a rare example, among the various nineteenth- and early twentieth-century collections of Oxford concert programmes, of prose descriptions).[24]

[21] QCA, News cuttings album, p. 23 (cf. n. 20 above).

[22] Ibid., preface.

[23] This last item consisted of five 'Elizabethan pieces' (by Gibbons, Byrd, and others) 'arranged for a modern small orchestra'. The composer's statement ('in a preface to the score') that he had not hesitated to 'alter a harmony, or a note or two', making no claim to 'pedantic antiquarianism', conveys the principles on which it is based.

[24] In style the commentary has a Toveyesque quality: 'the critics have agreed to find in it [Beethoven's Seventh] a great deal of Beethoven's rough humour . . . The "double bar and repeat" is not invariably, as may be supposed, a cheap way of lengthening a movement nor of preserving its balance . . .'; and there is much vivid programme note writing here, for instance in the reference to a subject 'rescued' from 'alien territory' but seeming 'determined to go astray'.

By the early decades of the twentieth century the colleges had become the setting for concerts of considerable distinction. Two examples survive from New College: a poster and a programme booklet, respectively.[25] The poster advertised, for Saturday 16 June 1906 at 9 p.m.:

    1. Overture – "Melusina" (Op. 32) – *Mendelssohn*.

    2. Ballad for Chorus and Orchestra – *C. Hubert H. Parry*.
        "The Pied Piper of Hamelin"
        Conducted by the Composer.

    3. Piano Concerto in B flat (Op. 83) – *Brahms*.
        Piano – Mr. DONALD FRANCIS TOVEY.

    4. Overture – "Die Zauberflöte" – Mozart.

    Tickets (5/- each) to be obtained only through Members of New College.

For the concert on Saturday, 22 June 1907 at 9.15 p.m. the programme featured:

    (1) Rhapsodie for Alto Solo and Men's Chorus, Op. 53 – *Brahms*.
          Solo – Miss MABEL PRICE.

    (2) Rondino for Wind Instruments in E flat – *Beethoven*.

          —————————

    (3) Songs, with Orchestral Accompaniment – *C. V. Stanford*.
                             R. Vaughan Williams.

          Solo – MR. H. PLUNKET GREENE.
          ("Trottin' to the Fair." (A.P. Graves); "The Vagabond."
                            (R.L. Stevenson))

          —————————

    (4) Symphony in F ('Cambridge') – *C.H.H. Parry*.
          Conducted by the Composer.
          Andante sostenuto, allegro moderato–Scherzo, molto
          vivace – Andante – Allegro vivace.

    (5) Songs of the Sea, for Solo Voice and Men's Chorus, Op. 91
                                 – *C. V. Stanford.*

[25] NCA, 2801.

Solo – MR. PLUNKET GREENE.
Conducted by the Composer.
("Drake's Drum.", "Outward Bound.", "Devon,
O Devon, in Wind and Rain.", "Homeward Bound.",
"The 'Old Superb.' ")

A survey of concert activity at various colleges, contained within a selected decade, and of one particular college sampled over a few years, shows some of the range of music-making that developed. Taking the general survey from 1860 (the year of the Eglesfield Society's founding) through to 1870 we find examples of intercollegiate co-operation: a Merton College concert in January of that year, featuring 'Madrigals, Part songs, and Glees', was conducted by Dr Hayne, organist of Queen's College. In May 1860 the Christ Church choir and others joined with the choristers of St Mary's College, Bampton in 'Two Grand Concerts' at the Star Assembly Room in aid of St Mary's College. A concert at Exeter College Hall for the Hullah Fund, in February 1861, raised £42. 14s. 0d.[26] In December of the same year Exeter College Musical Society's termly concert attracted an audience of 200; these concerts continued to be held regularly during the 1860s, their contents varying from selections from oratorios (in March 1862, for instance, from *Elijah*, *St Paul*, and *The Creation*) to piano duets (as in December 1869, when Parry played, with Mr Powell, and Stainer conducted the concert).[27] Parry was prominent as a pianist at these events: in December 1868 his piano solos at an Exeter College concert were described as played 'with very great taste; and . . . loudly encored'.[28] The concerts also featured Parry's compositions, as in June 1868 when the programme included his 'Quartett. "Pure Spirit, O where art thou now?"', billed as 'composed especially for this occasion', and his ' "Gnome Song." Etude', for piano solo.[29]

A novelty appearing in the 1860s were the promenade concerts in col-

---

[26] Thewlis, Notes, iv. 934. (For the 1860–70 college events generally, see ibid. 931–51.)

[27] Ibid. 950. [28] Ibid. 949.

[29] Ibid. 948. Further on Parry's activities at Exeter see Dibble, *Parry*, 56–7. Commenting on Parry's 'appetite for Schumann', Dibble notes that 'the piano works such as *Carnaval*, the *Romanzen*, *Faschingsschwank aus Wien*, and *Phantasiestücke*. . .dominated the short recitals he gave as soloist in the Exeter College Musical Society concerts' (Dibble, *Parry*, 70).

lege gardens during Commemoration week. These were part of the whole series of college concerts on offer during the celebrations. In 1863, for example, on Monday of Commemoration week a 'Promenade Concert in Merton Gardens' was advertised, from 10 until 12 o'clock; on the Tuesday a concert was held in Worcester College at 8 p.m., and there were also concerts at St John's and New College during the week, in addition to an Exeter College event and a performance by the University Amateur Society. The Promenade Concert at Trinity College in June 1864 was 'assisted by the City Rifle Corps Band': during that particular Commemoration week there were concerts at over half a dozen colleges including Wadham, Pembroke, Queen's, Exeter, New College, Magdalen, and St John's. These college concerts were part of a well-established pattern. In June 1866 the Magdalen College concert was postponed owing to the death of Revd W. J. Sawell, described as 'a devout lover of music, and who always rendered efficient assistance at the College concerts'.[30]

Besides the concerts at Commemoration time and in the period approaching Christmas, Lent Term remained a popular time for college events: within ten days in March 1867 a concert by 'Trinity Glee Club' was followed by concerts at Pembroke and Queen's. (The typical venue for these was the college Hall.) Particular individuals contributed to various college efforts, as with C. H. Lloyd, who was very active as a conductor and was associated with both the Choral Society and the Philharmonic Society; in 1870 Lloyd, described as 'of Magdalen Hall', played and conducted at concerts in Magdalen and in Pembroke College.[31] Sampling the concerts organized by one specific college during a shorter period of time, we find overall a lively variety of music-making. In February 1865 the Maltese Glee Club of Magdalen College put on in the Holywell Music Room a 'Private Concert given by Edw. Handley, Commoner of Magd. Coll' and conducted by Stainer, college organist, with a characteristically light programme of short, mainly vocal items, including a 'Part Song' by Handley himself.[32] The owner of the extant programme has noted the occasion as 'very good', in spite of the fact that Miss Fanny Armytage (soprano)

[30] Thewlis, Notes, iv. 943. Bishop Mitchinson of Pembroke remembered 'Sawell the Chaplain', together with 'Blyth the organist' at Magdalen, as 'both Lovely Tenors' (Mitchinson, 'Oxford Memories', PCA, MS 60/15/83, p. 19).

[31] Thewlis, Notes, iv. 951.

[32] MCA, MS 983 (printed programme with handwritten additions).

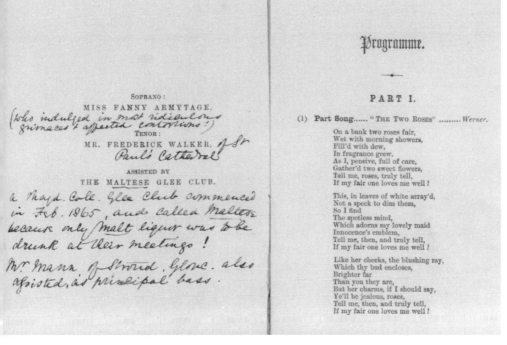

FIG. 18. Concert programme, Maltese Glee Club, 23 February 1865

apparently 'indulged in most ridiculous grimaces & affected contortions!' A Christmas concert given by the Magdalen College Madrigal Society on 30 November 1865 shows a more substantial content.[33] The three Mendelssohn items (of a total of nine) included his setting of Psalm 42, 'As the Hart pants', in Part I (which opened with his overture 'Athalie'). A Mozart 'motett' (*Splendente Te Deus*) and a Handel chorus, the latter ending Part II, were juxtaposed with Christmas carols by Pearsall. The madrigals in the programme ranged from Palestrina ('When flowery meadows') to Stainer. The attractions of Stainer's madrigals sparked the publication in about 1865 of his set of eight madrigals ('composed by John Stainer, B.A. and Mus. Bac./Organist to the University of Oxford & Magdalen College') to which numerous Oxford friends, colleagues (including Handley, Hayne, and the Savilian Professor of Astronomy, W. F. Donkin), and institutions, subscribed. At their best these settings achieve a fine blend of traditional skills in part-writing with more modern melodic and harmonic

[33] MCA, MS 984.

style (see Ex. 10.1). Magdalen College Choir put on concerts in 1868 and 1870 with songs, glees, madrigals, and choruses (including Stainer's song 'Jilted' and Pearsall's ballad 'The King sits in Dunfermline town' (both in 1870) and (in 1868) Sullivan's setting of 'Sigh no more, ladies').[34]

The documentation of college concerts in the second half of the nineteenth century shows a trend towards the involvement not only of senior members of the college but also of their wives and daughters. (Before the founding of the women's colleges from the 1870s onwards, the all-male precincts represented by the colleges were counterbalanced in the sphere of musical entertainment by the mixed audiences and performing groups in the University and city, while within the colleges a domestic aspect to this mixed society now became apparent.) Thewlis found the first mention of a concert in Christ Church Hall on 1 December 1863; the custom then continued, and on 24 May 1864 Dr Corfe presented a 'Grand Vocal and Instrumental Concert' at which 'the solos, choruses and duets, were sustained by 12 lady amateurs, pupils of Dr Corfe, and [by] members of the University. A powerful band was engaged, led by Mr Blagrove and conducted by Dr Corfe'.[35] The *Journal* commented that 'the appearance of the ladies was a novelty . . . and added not a little to the attraction'.[36] At the 'Grand Concert of Sacred Music' in Christ Church Hall in March 1868, given to 'a most distinguished company' of 400–500 persons 'comprising a happy admixture of University, County and City families . . .', Mrs Liddell (wife of Dean Liddell) was the 'leading spirit' and played harp accompaniments, while at least one of the Misses Liddell sang in the largely Mendelssohnian programme (Part I consisted of his 'Hymn of Praise', a favourite item in Oxford programmes).[37] And for a Merton concert on 2 December 1887 the Revd J. H. Mee sang tenor, with Mrs Mee among the altos, and the Hon. Edith Brodrick, the Warden's niece (who

[34] MCA, MS 985 (i) and (ii): 10 Dec. 1868 (a seasonal concert in the Radcliffe Infirmary) and 22 June 1870 (during the Commemoration week featuring the installation of the Marquis of Salisbury as Chancellor of the University).

[35] Thewlis, Notes, i. 41.

[36] Ibid.

[37] Thewlis, Notes, i. 42–4. The Philharmonic Society (conducted by Stainer), from which numerous amateur performers assisting on this occasion at Christ Church were drawn, had included among the ladies taking part in its first concert in 1866 Mrs Liddell, together with Mrs Mostyn Owen, Mrs Acland, Mrs Donkin, Mrs Stainer, the Misses Cox, and others (cf. ibid. 42).

also sang in the altos) played a piano solo, the Valse Allemagne (*sic*) of Rubinstein.[38]

Amidst these varied manifestations of college musical enterprise, from their inception in 1885 the Balliol concerts displayed a uniquely consistent quality as well as the particular impress of the college organist, John Farmer. These Sunday evening concerts were, to borrow the phrase applied to the Eglesfield Society, 'high-class music rendered in the best possible way', mingled with remnants of Farmer's German training, most famously the chorale with which by convention each concert ended. The prominence of organ music within mixed chamber recitals was also unique (Jowett had furnished the college hall with a Willis organ in 1885 at his own expense and seemingly at Farmer's insistence). The Balliol concerts' consistently more serious aspect, compared with the generality of college concerts at the time, appeared in the emphasis on Baroque (Corelli, Bach, and Handel) and on the central Austro-German repertoire (from Haydn, Mozart, Beethoven, and Schubert to Schumann, Mendelssohn, and Brahms), together with the inclusion of multi-movement works in full (Grieg's Sonata for Violin and Piano, for example), as well as the more usual extracts.[39] The Balliol concerts also featured imported 'artistes' of high quality and renown, in addition to local musicians.

The comment (referring to modern-day Oxford) that 'nearly every college now has its own musical society, organizing concerts and recitals, and generally fostering musical activity among its members'[40] could equally have been made of Oxford in the late nineteenth century. (It was noted of John Farmer at Balliol that 'his design is mainly educational, and that he proposes to make music more an integral part of college life than it has hitherto been'.)[41] Similarly, most colleges now have provision for chapel music, with organ scholars and possibly also choral scholars; and this too

[38] Programme in Merton College Archives, Q.2.36; cf. Wollenberg in *HUO* vii. 439.

[39] Programmes and other documentation in Balliol College Archives. See also Burns and Wilson, *The Balliol Concerts*. The influence of the OUMU (founded 1884) may have been a factor in their development. Their Sunday placement was not universally approved of, but was maintained steadily nevertheless. Others besides Farmer who made a strong impress on the Balliol concerts included D. F. Tovey and Ernest Walker.

[40] *EO* 267.

[41] Thewlis, Notes, iv. 970–1. The newly founded women's colleges joined in the trend: Somerville had a 'Practising Society (to keep up Music)' available in 1889. Cf. Adams, *Somerville*, 128.

was a late nineteenth- and early twentieth-century trend. At Merton College, for example, an organ scholarship was initiated in 1907.[42] At Pembroke, choral music developed in the college chapel from the late 1860s on, 'probably after the departure of Master Jeune, a low Churchman'.[43] In 1868 the Governing Body voted £20 per annum towards the support of the chapel choir; the 'triumph of the High Church movement' in the college, 'marked by Kempe's transformation of the chapel (1884) was followed by an appeal to raise monies for a chapel organ. Bishop Mitchinson, elected Master in 1899, paid the organist's salary ...'.[44] In 1906 the title 'organ Exhibitioner' was used of one appointment, with a termly honorarium of £5. The level of remuneration (and perhaps performance) was naturally more modest than that of the larger choral foundations.

At these latter establishments the choirs went through considerably chequered periods during the nineteenth century, but had re-emerged in generally fine form by the close of this period. The appointment of a new Head of House might again seem to mark a turning-point, for example at Christ Church: in 1856 it was noted in the *Journal* that

in addition to making the Cathedral worthy of its name, and giving increased effect to its services, the present Dean, Dr Liddell, in that spirit of progress which has ever been his characteristic, aims at putting Christ Church Cathedral ... on the same footing as other cathedrals, with regard to the public, who will, for the future, enjoy the same facilities of attending its services as are now possessed in other cathedral towns.[45]

The newly fitted Cathedral (with seating for at least 300 persons) was opened on 12 October 1856 and declared to be 'a wonderful improvement'. The service on that occasion included Corfe's anthem *Thou O God*. The advent of Corfe as organist in 1846 had already instigated musical and liturgical improvements (for instance, in encouraging the chaplains to

[42] Martin and Highfield, *Merton College, Oxford*, 360. Mark Curthoys has suggested (in a personal communication) that Exeter College may have been the first to found an organ scholarship (in 1859), on the opening of its new chapel; Keble College followed suit in 1876.

[43] Personal communication from Aidan Lawes.

[44] Ibid. PCA, 4/17/1 (Ledger) contains records of regular payments to the organist as well as special payments, for example £10 to Mr Boughton on 15 June 1906 (possibly for a Gaudy), and recurrent small sums paid to the organ blower.

[45] *JOJ*, 23 Aug. 1856 (quoted in Thewlis, Notes, i. 36).

'revive the practice' of intoning the service), but it was felt that with Dean Liddell in 1855 an increase in the spiritual effect of the services was secured. Cox affirmed that

This year [1856] began with a great and obvious improvement in the Cathedral Service at Christ Church, under the auspices of Dean Liddell. The prayers 'at 10 and 5' (which had been, for years immemorial, *read* by the chaplains, while the choir responded in a slovenly monotone) were now chanted or intoned; not well, of course, at first, the chaplains being new to the work, but still the Service was made more like what Cathedral Service should be. It is no longer hurried through, for a congregation consisting of a single Canon and the choir, but is carefully performed before an increasing number of persons, strangers and residents, well-seated and civilly treated by the vergers.[46]

By 1858 the choir was described in the *Journal* as 'one of the best among the many of which Oxford can boast'.[47] Attendance at the Cathedral services now formed one of the highlights of the Commemoration: 'In the afternoon the Cathedral attracted the largest numbers, both on account of the great facilities afforded to the public by the Dean and Chapter, and the high character of the choral service there . . . nearly 1000 people were present.'[48]

Taking a special occasion (the 500th Commemoration of the Founder, in 1879) for which the order of service survives, Hale found evidence of a distinct contemporary slant in the repertoire at New College:

At Morning Prayer . . . the Canticles were sung to Parry . . . in D. The Anthem was *Now my God, let, I beseech Thee* by William Sterndale Bennett . . . At Evening Prayer . . . the Canticles [were] . . . sung to Garrett (1834–79) in D, and the anthem was *Sing, O Heavens* by Arthur Sullivan . . . All this service music was remarkably modern at the time and shows considerable progress from the music lists of only a few years before.[49]

[46] Cox, *Recollections*, 414–15. See also Thewlis, Notes, i. 36.

[47] Ibid. i. 38.

[48] Thewlis, Notes, i. 38 (Sunday service in 1862).

[49] See Hale in Buxton and Penry Williams, *New College, Oxford*, 284–5. Among contemporary liturgical documentation, a printed order of service from Magdalen College (MCA, MS 795, belonging to James Elwin Millard) gives detail on the 'Order of Daily Service, as chanted in the chapel of St. Mary Magdalen College, Oxford', together with festival responses. Further on college service music at this period, and its dissemination, an edition of the Magdalen Psalter (ed. L. S. Tuckwell and Sir J. Stainer, and printed by W. R. Bowden, Oxford) belonging to J. V. Roberts, college organist (MCA, MS 794), indicates among the advertising matter at the end the use of the psalter at various colleges including Christ Church, besides Magdalen; and at the Metropolitan churches, at most Anglican churches of Oxford and the locality, and most of the large public schools, as well as at Sandringham, commenting that 'it has long enjoyed popularity'.

A characteristic layer in the musical holdings of the college choirs continued to be provided by custom-made compositions: thus Ouseley's 'Festival Anthem' of 1869, *Ascribe ye greatness unto our God*, was dedicated to the President and Fellows of Magdalen College, Oxford (who acknowledged it gratefully).[50] Its style presumably reflects the choir's skill, and suggests, under Stainer's conductorship, a highly trained body of singers. Ouseley's anthem combines a sophisticated modulatory technique with rigorous contrapuntal working-out. The extended fugal section following the declamatory opening is set almost in species-style counterpoint, developed in rhythmically stylized manner and following strict fugal procedures. The 'stile antico' element here—with its associations of stability and timelessness—seems particularly well suited to the words: 'He is the Rock, His work is perfect' (see Ex. 10.2). This piece makes its effect impressively through a kind of confidence in applying various techniques as well as in conveying its verbal text.

Even allowing for the rhapsodic feelings of a participant in a Gaudy, the description of the service at New College by a visitor in 1865 shows (as well as a distinctly non-utilitarian churchman) that the musical element was perceived as substantial and impressive:

Last Thursday week was the gaudy-day at New College; to which as Wykehamist, I had an invitation ... The old Bishop of Winchester was there looking extremely well ... The music at New College is as good as ever, if not better ... the organ powerful but not *over* powering; filling the whole of that vast chapel (for including the ante-chapel it is vast) with volumes ... every note, whether from organ pipe, or lips of chorister or chaplain, reverberated with a peculiar depth and mellowness of tone among the lofty pillars ... yet so as to betray no effort; such are one's impressions. But then again ... they have been continuously for five hundred years working at their chapel services, and never without ample resources ... However there is more than that; the building, music, and all force on you the thought that after all there is a grandeur in the human soul.[51]

Against this sweeping enthusiasm for the product of the choir's and organist's efforts can be set the background documented in various college

[50] Score with dedication in MCA, MS 410; dated 5 Oct. 1869. Orchestral version in Ob, MS Tenbury 1187 (*c*.1881).

[51] *Letters of Thomas Arnold the Younger (1850–1900)* (ed. J. Bertram, Oxford, 1980), letter of November 1865 to John Henry Newman: extracts quoted by H. Reid in the *New College Record* (1983).

Ex. 10.2. Frederick Ouseley, anthem, *Ascribe ye greatness unto our God*, 1869, bars 25–42 (MCA, MS 410, pp. 4–6)

[* original barring separate for organ part]

records of the management of the choir. Warden Sewell of New College took a particularly strong interest in the arrangements for the chapel music and services, as his personal letter-books and college Discipline Books show.[52] He was concerned to regulate the attendance of chaplains and choral scholars in order to facilitate 'the decent performance of divine service'.[53] The Warden was driven to suggest that '*all* the members of the Choir should meet together at least once a week for the purposes of practice & rehearsal'.[54]

A long series of complaints and recommendations over many years convey Warden Sewell's persistence (possible viewed as interference) in matters relating to the chaplains, choristers, clerks, choral scholars, and college organist's duties. For example, he noted reasonably that lay clerks should not 'absent themselves from Chapel to attend Concerts' and that 'the Choral Service requires the co-operation of the whole Choir' (together with punctuality and decorum at services, this was a recurrent preoccupation): '[it] must lose in efficiency, & character, if those who are appointed to sustain the parts in it, & especially the principal parts are allowed to leave their places unfilled in order to make engagements elsewhere'.[55] Besides these essential aspects, his concern for details of proced-

[52] NCA, 8666–7 and 8561 ('Letters and other memoranda concerning Discipline', 1860–71).

[53] NCA, 8561, p. 17 (24 Jan. 1861).

[54] Ibid. 22 (13 Apr. 1861).

[55] Ibid. 148–9 (2 May 1867). The Warden specifically mentioned that the many visitors attending services in this term might form a wrong impression of the choir.

ure seems also to have been inexhaustible. It is clear that for Warden Sewell, musical performances in chapel constituted a branch of college discipline as well as of religious observance and propriety:

New College Chapel.

It is particularly requested, that all persons remaining in the Chapel after the end of the Service will refrain from walking about, or conversing, while the Voluntary is played.

J. E. Sewell. Warden. May 26. 1883.[56]

Lay clerks were regularly admonished or dismissed from the choir for such offences as absence without leave, and insobriety: 'Mr John Kendall, Lay Clerk, was distinctly warned, that in case of any falling again into a state of incapacity to fulfill his proper part in the Chapel Service, through inebriety, his place would be immediately vacated.'[57]

One element in the work of the choral foundations that seems to have become more stringently controlled during the nineteenth century was the selection (as well as the training and education) of the choristers. Looking back many years later on his school and college life at Magdalen, one (anonymous) former chorister recalled how 'in 1834, when I was not quite eight years old, I got a nomination to a Choristership at Magdalen, and having been coached a little in scales, and having something of a voice and ear, after a very slight examination I was passed as satisfactory'.[58] He also described the lax educational standards, commenting that 'about the year 1842 some of the Fellows instituted a yearly examination of the School, very much against Mr. W. [the Headmaster]'s inclination'.[59] (He left the school in about 1844 and in 1845 was elected to a Demyship at the college (reading for a degree in Lit. Hum.); subsequently he was given a Fellowship and after various curacies became Vice-President of Magdalen before accepting a living.[60])

By the close of the period voice trials were being held (and advertised) more systematically, and the schooling had fallen more into line with the

---

[56] NCA, 981 (Discipline 1872–1901), loose paper in front.

[57] Ibid. 17 May 1893. See further, Wollenberg in *HUO* vii. 436. Sewell's efforts were part of a general trend; Tuckwell (*Old Magdalen Days*, 8) credited Dr Bloxam of Magdalen with bringing about 'a remarkable reformation as regards the order and decency in the conduct of the Chapel Services'.

[58] 'A Hundred Years Ago', the *Oxford Magazine* (27 Jan. 1938), 321 (copy held in MCA, MS 1005).

[59] Ibid. 323.   [60] Ibid.

generality of schools: thus 'with expanding provision and demand for secondary education' it was felt at New College that it was important 'to
ensure that the boys were properly prepared for education after choristership. This meant . . . developing a school which would give the boys the
same opportunities as their peers', a process which was 'only really
achieved by 1900'.[61] For the nineteenth, as for the eighteenth, century,
Bloxam's documentation of Magdalen gives valuable information on
career paths for choristers and singing clerks.[62] A musical career, and entry
into the church, need not be the only paths subsequently taken; George
Valentine Cox (1786–1875), after a choristership and clerkship at Magdalen (1793–1802; 1803–7) and having graduated BA in 1806 (later MA, in
1808) became not only [Head] Master of New College School (1807–57)
but also Esquire Bedel of the University in Law (1806) and subsequently in
medicine and arts (1815) as well as coroner to the University.[63]

The proximity of boy choristers and older students in the colleges gave
cause for worry. Concerns about fraternization were voiced during this
period: at New College Warden Sewell wrote of Mr Tuckwell (Master of
New College School, 1857–64) 'I quite approve of the principle which he
has acted upon in discouraging communications between the boys under
his care, and members of the University not actually related to them, &
having no special interest in, or claim to acquaintance with them.'[64] And at
Magdalen a notice put up 'on the door of Magd. Coll. Hall', stated that
'Any undergraduate detected speaking to a Chorister will be sent down &
the Chorister expelled. Or if found asking a chorister to his room will be
expelled'.[65]

For the students residing in the colleges the expectation of opportunities to practise and perform (and indeed compose) music, and to listen to
it, was potentially higher by the end of the nineteenth century than probably ever before. The signs were read positively by the critics and
commentators. In 1879 apropos of Pembroke College's Commemoration
concert the *Journal*'s critic commented that 'the Pembroke concert was

[61] Edmunds, *New College Brats*, 40. Further on recruitment and education see ibid. 51–2.

[62] Bloxam, *Register*, i–ii.

[63] Ibid. i. 205, cf. *DNB* xii. 411. There are conflicts regarding dates of appointments among the
sources for Cox's biography (including the obituary in *JOJ*, 27 Mar. 1875).

[64] NCA, 8561, p. 8 (letter from J. E. Sewell to a member of Brasenose, 14 Nov. 1860).

[65] MCA, MS 881 (among loose papers facing p. 81).

most creditable for a small college . . . Mr Cumberledge played some solos by Schumann with great delicacy. Not many years ago such a concert would have taxed the strength of every College in Oxford combined'.[66] The following year a correspondent wrote to the *Musical Times*: 'in few places is the musical progress more clearly visible than in Oxford. The existence of such a state of things at a University where so many of our upper and middle classes are being trained is assuredly one of the fairest auguries for the future of music in England.'[67] And echoing Maurice's earlier claims, the *Journal*, summing up the year 1883, opined that 'the love of music has steadily increased of late years in Oxford—especially among the undergraduates—where a dozen years ago there was one piano to a college, there are now two or three to a staircase'.[68]

The formats for music-making ranged from the popular, informal 'smoking concerts'[69] to the large choral and orchestral performances; and from the chapel music heard by increasing numbers of visitors, as well as college members, to the celebrity recitals incorporated in college concert series, as at Balliol. Individual attainments varied from the 'musical neighbours' recalled by Warden Spooner from his undergraduate days:

The man in the room under me practised on the violin, but he knew only one tune and broke down in that always at the same point, which, having reached, he began it all over again. My neighbour on the other side kept an harmonium, and I remember his going right through Psalm CXIX on a chant played with one or two fingers . . .[70]

to the fine pianism of Parry in the Exeter College concerts. For men like Ouseley and Parry their undergraduate experiences of music helped form musical careers ultimately of great distinction, representing a breakthrough in social attitudes towards music as a profession.

---

[66] *JOJ*, 12 June 1879.   [67] Quoted in Thewlis, Notes, iv. 961.   [68] Ibid. 964.

[69] Fellowes (*Memoirs*, 62) recollected the ubiquitousness of these events: 'there was hardly a college at which I did not play at least once at smoking concerts'.

[70] NCA, 11, 334: Warden Spooner, 'Fifty Years in an Oxford College' (Spooner came up to New College as an undergraduate in 1862).

I I

~~~

Personalities: Bishop, Ouseley, Stainer, Parry, Parratt, and Allen

Sir Henry Bishop's comparatively brief spell as Professor of Music at Oxford (1848–55) following Crotch's incumbency has traditionally been regarded as unsatisfactory. Thewlis crossed out his original assessment 'was little more than a charlatan' and substituted 'but an indifferent musician', summing him up as 'an indefatigable arranger of other men's work'.[1] Such descriptions fail to do justice to the range of Bishop's abilities, the development of his career, and the effect of his personal circumstances. Bishop's knighthood was at that time (1842) a rare distinction for a musician; Northcott mentions only three precedents (and these bestowed by Lord-Lieutenants of Ireland) and Bishop himself referred to the unusual significance of this honour:

Hard have been my toils, many and severe have been my trials, but eminently distinguished indeed have been my rewards. I have lived to receive from my Queen the honour of knighthood, an honour of a peculiar distinction . . . from the circumstance of its never having been previously conferred by the hand of the sovereign on any musician in this kingdom . . . it was reserved for our own Queen . . . for the first time to place British musicians in that respect on a level with great British painters, sculptors, and other eminent men.[2]

[1] Thewlis, Notes , ii. 330.
[2] Northcott, *Bishop*, 114–15.

While in the course of a long association with London's theatres Bishop indeed contributed to numerous arrangements and pastiche productions, and while inevitably the first named composition of Bishop's to come to mind is 'Home, sweet home', his creative work, especially in the field of English vocal music, was acknowledged as possessing higher quality than these might suggest. Northcott observes that 'it was the Prince Consort who, recognising his artistic worth, advocated the honour of knighthood being conferred on him'.[3]

One factor that may have affected Bishop's later reputation could be the popularity of his works. The composer himself remarked indirectly that his songs were 'upon every pianoforte in the United Kingdom'.[4] But besides his contribution to popular culture Bishop was active in the higher spheres of musical endeavour. Having been involved in the establishment of the Royal Academy of Music in 1823 he was chosen to serve as Professor of Harmony and Composition in that institution (admittedly characterized by Northcott as a position 'of an honorary character, for he gave little or no instruction').[5] He was also one of the 'prime movers' in the founding of the London Philharmonic Society in 1813; and after beginning his association with the Ancient Concerts as a composer, then conducting, he was appointed 'permanent conductor of the Concerts' in 1841.[6] There is some evidence that Bishop was considered an 'intellectual' composer: Moore (author of the 'Irish Melodies') wrote to Power 'pray keep Mr. Bishop's learning down as much as you can' and further referred to Bishop's 'display of his science'.[7] Bishop carried out, at Oxford and elsewhere, some investigation into national song, as his letters show; he searched in the Bodleian Library for the origins and history of various 'old tunes'.[8] Other aspects of his career suggest that he was not without historical interests. When he commenced lecturing at scientific institutions and philosophical societies in the early 1820s his subjects (accompanied by musical illustrations) included the 'Origin and Progress' of opera in the seventeenth and eighteenth centuries.[9] And he was involved, with Crotch,

---

[3] Northcott, *Bishop*, p. ii. For a sympathetic evaluation of Bishop's work, see Caldwell, *OHEM* ii. 177–8.

[4] Letter of 25 Oct. 1833 to the music publisher Mackinlay: printed in Northcott, *Bishop*, 122–3.

[5] Ibid. 63.   [6] Ibid. 13; 109–11.   [7] Ibid. 45–6.

[8] Ibid. 142–3.   [9] Ibid. 59.

in the Handel Society's (aborted) plans for a Handel edition; Bishop edited the chamber duets and cantatas.[10]

In addition to these concerns with music of the past, Bishop was sensitive to the needs of British composers for the future. His pronouncements on the desirability of instituting an English National Opera were compellingly argued:

> It is considered by eminent Continental musicians as a singular anomaly that with the acknowledged advance of musical acquirement, and with the decided manifestations of an improved taste on the part of the public, there should be no theatre exclusively appropriated to the performance of Opera in our own language . . . In other countries the National Opera Houses are supported by large annual grants of money, as well as by liberal private subscriptions, but individual speculation has been hitherto the sole and precarious chance of support for an English Opera House.[11]

He spoke strongly of the benefits of such an organization; unfortunately his vision was not matched by the necessary backing. In this, as in his views on the ideal resources to support an academic musical establishment such as at Oxford, Bishop saw what was needed but was unable to create the means to implement his ideas in either case.[12] In spite of this failure, it remains true that he allied himself with progressive and informed opinion on the path that British music and musical education should take.

A more personal factor in Bishop's attitude to his work was the need to support his family. (It is clear from his letters that he was frequently short of money.) Here it is important to appreciate the peculiar circumstance of his concern for his children. Bishop's second wife, the singer Anna Rivière (whom he married after the death of the first Mrs Bishop) left him and their three children abruptly in 1839 to travel with the harpist Nicholas Bochsa: 'from that time to his death, she took no further interest in Bishop beyond occasionally singing his "Home, sweet home" '.[13] The composer's letters hint at the strain this defection placed him under:

> Latterly, I have suffered much from the usual fatigues of the season, and particularly from expressive depression of spirits, arising from reflections on a sad event now little more than a twelvemonth old, and feelings which mastered me, and

---

[10] Northcott, *Bishop*, 116.

[11] Quoted ibid. 112–13.   [12] See Ch. 8, p. 135 above.   [13] Northcott, *Bishop*, 90.

which, though I shall probably carry them with me to the grave (and they have hitherto 'passed outward show') I must strive against for my own and dear children's sake.[14]

Bishop's warmth of feeling for his children is evident in the letters. The need to provide for them may have spurred the composer to accept some of the 'hack work' with which he has traditionally been reproached for associating himself. As Northcott notes, by a 'sad coincidence' on the morning of Bishop's death the following appeared in *The Times* (30 April 1855):

> The friends of Sir Henry Bishop feel a painful and unavoidable necessity for announcing that this estimable composer is at this moment labouring under pecuniary embarrassment; they feel deeper regret in stating that he is also suffering from acute bodily infirmity, without the slightest means for meeting his own immediate necessities or for making any provision for his two youngest children . . . It is, therefore, proposed to open a subscription for raising a fund . . .[15]

This appeal, signed by Sir George Smart among others, closed with a touching tribute to Bishop, wishing to convey to the composer on his 'bed of sickness' the assurance that 'his sufferings meet with the deepest sympathy, and his great abilities as a genuine English composer are universally allowed and warmly appreciated'.

In reconstructing the impression of key figures in the history of Oxford's musical life, the distancing effects of time can partially be offset by the relative immediacy of contemporary descriptions. In the case of Ouseley, immense value is represented by the documentary compilation assembled by Havergal in 1889 as a memorial tribute to Ouseley in the year of his death.[16] F. T. Havergal was Ouseley's colleague in the diocese of Hereford; his older brother, H. E. Havergal, served as chaplain at New College and Christ Church, 1842–7, and was a singer and double-bass player. Ouseley's connections with the Havergals included sociable music-making: Canon John Rich recalled to F. T. Havergal how Ouseley 'and your brother Henry E. Havergal, and others, often sang glees in the summer evenings, in the Hall staircase at Christ Church . . .'.[17]

---

[14] Letter of 3 Sept. 1840 to Mackinlay (Northcott, 128–30).

[15] Quoted ibid. 120 (also source of the quotations below).

[16] Havergal, *Memorials of Ouseley*. The *Life of Ouseley* by Joyce benefited from the Joyce family's close acquaintance with Ouseley.

[17] Havergal, *Memorials of Ouseley*, 61.

The two strands of Ouseley's career that had most impact on British musical life and music in the church are summed up in Havergal's styling of Ouseley as 'Doctor and Professor of Music in the University of Oxford; Precentor and Canon Residentiary in the Cathedral Church of Hereford; Founder of St. Michael's Tenbury, and First Incumbent of that Church'.[18] These institutions—the University of Oxford, and the college and church of St Michael's, Tenbury—were central to Ouseley's work as a musician and churchman. Among the list of subscribers to Havergal's volume were canons, bishops, archdeacons, and numerous other clergy, as well as many leading musicians and distinguished colleagues. These included W. Alexander Barrett, Mus.D.; Basil Harwood, then organist of Ely Cathedral; C. H. Lloyd, organist of Christ Church, Oxford; A. H. Mann, organist of King's College, Cambridge; the Revd J. H. Mee, whose address was given as Kettel Hall (later Trinity College, Oxford); Sir Herbert Oakeley, of Edinburgh University; Hubert Parry; J. V. Roberts, of Magdalen College, Oxford; Revd J. E. Sewell, Warden of New College, Oxford: Sir John Stainer, Ouseley's successor as Professor of Music at Oxford; and James Taylor, of New College.

Although some family reminiscences are gathered among the items in Havergal's collection, the majority of the material derives from Ouseley's professional life. An interesting insight into his creative ability is yielded by Barrett's observation that, while Ouseley 'knew every knot and subtlety of contrapuntal art' (which suggests a predominantly written technique of composition), his imagination was conveyed most vividly through his extempore playing: 'in this, competent judges have expressed their opinion that he was unrivalled by any musician of the present century'.[19] Personal friends knew this side of his musicianship best. Its roots were in his prodigious early development; George Elvey remembered hearing him extemporize 'in the most surprising manner' at the age of about 12.[20] The

---

[18] Havergal, *Memorials of Ouseley*, title-page. The grandeur of the original consecration service at St Michael's in 1856 is evoked by the press reports reprinted ibid. (pp.64–5): 'Such a busy stir as there was at Tenbury on Monday last has never before animated that usually peaceful town . . . Carriages rattled to and fro to the spot with an increased rumble. By eleven o'clock there must have been 600 or 700 persons present, and later in the day between 300 and 400 persons — clergy and laity — partook of the Holy Communion.' Further on St Michael's, Tenbury see Watkins Shaw, *Ouseley and St Michael's, Tenbury* and Bland, *Ouseley and his Angels*.

[19] Havergal, *Memorials of Ouseley*, 64. For a well-balanced account of Ouseley in the Oxford context as well as in the general context of church music see Gatens, *Victorian Cathedral Music*, ch. 8.

[20] Havergal, *Memorials of Ouseley*, 61. On Ouseley's early compositions see p. 62, including Basil

placing of a high value on improvisation is perhaps associated more with earlier music, but the art continued to have importance for the nineteenth- and early twentieth-century musician, especially among organists.[21]

Ouseley's musical sympathies were wide-ranging. Canon John Rich recalled Ouseley's 'getting up the "Messiah", in the Town Hall, at Oxford, for the benefit of the Irish, in the famine of 1845', and composing a glee, 'Sweet Echo', whose proceeds went to the same cause.[22] The printed obituary notices stressed the extent to which Ouseley 'enriched the reper- tory' of liturgical music, for example with his eleven services and numer- ous anthems; his editing, with Dr [E. G.] Monk, of 'Anglican Psalter Chants'; and his contributions to 'Hymns Ancient and Modern'.[23] The in- tensity of the personal commitment informing these ventures was well recognized by contemporary commentators: 'The central aim of his life was to promote the interests of the Church he loved so well . . . and as to the musical element in the Church, his whole soul was in it'.[24]

Beyond Oxford Ouseley represented the University, generally, through his service to other institutions, including the RAM (of which his father, Sir Gore Ouseley, had been one of the chief founders). In connection with practical music-making, Southgate noted Ouseley's membership of the Committee of the Musical Union, describing its activities in hyperbolic terms: 'This institution, which Ella directed with so much skill and success for forty years, gave concerts of string music by the great masters, played to perfection by the best artists of the day . . .' and summing up its direc- tor's qualities in words which have an authentic ring: 'The venerable Professor Ella was an autocrat.—he was practically the institution . . .

Harwood's reference to 'a book containing a March in C and an Air in A♭, both written by him at the age of 6'; and further, p. 67. The March is reprinted in Shaw, *Ouseley and St Michael's, Tenbury*.

[21] See 'Improvisation', *NG* ix. 50, §I, 4: (iv); and Temperley, *The Romantic Age*, 437.

[22] Havergal, *Memorials of Ouseley*, 61. The first of these seems to refer to the performance by the 'Ama- teur and Professional Gentlemen' of 'Handel's Oratorio the Messiah' on Tuesday and Wednesday, 9 and 10 March 1847, 'for the benefit of the distressed poor in Ireland and Scotland' (*JOJ*, 6 Mar. 1847). Ouseley's five-part glee 'Sweet Echo' was dedicated to the UAMS and written for their concert in June 1845, whose profits went to the Irish poor (see Thewlis, Notes, iv. 898).

[23] Havergal, *Memorials of Ouseley*, 22 (from the *Hereford Times*). Joyce (*Life of Ouseley*, 256–7) lists thirteen items in the category of Services. Ouseley's anthems and services were published in his lifetime in several collected volumes. The *Hymns Ancient and Modern* first appeared in 1861.

[24] Havergal, *Memorials of Ouseley*, 22. Shaw (*Ouseley and St Michael's, Tenbury*, 24) observes that Ouseley felt 'his service to the Church must be through his musical gifts' (see ibid. 13, for a discussion of the influ- ence of the Oxford Movement and the work of John Jebb in the 1840s when Ouseley first came up to Oxford as a Gentleman Commoner).

However, he paid some deference to the opinions of Ouseley, and frequently listened to his advice in the arrangement of the eclectic programmes, and the engagement of the performers.'[25]

Ouseley's influence on the development of music as an intellectual discipline was felt partly through his leading role in the Musical (later to become the Royal Musical) Association, founded 1874 following preliminary discussions between Stainer and Pole: 'Sir Frederick Gore Ouseley was unanimously elected to the post of President, and right well he performed his duties.'[26] As Southgate remarked, 'most of our representative musicians and acousticians belong to the Association'; the president was expected to be prominent in the profession and to represent 'all branches of the art', to possess wide sympathies and 'general culture and qualifications' fitting him 'to preside over the meetings of a learned society of this nature'.[27] Ouseley also read occasional papers at the meetings of the association; an account of selected papers, ranging from early music theory to the use of musical instruments in churches (Ouseley favoured the church orchestra, and his talk was followed by a lively debate) is provided by Southgate.[28]

The profundity of Ouseley's musical scholarship, and his 'singular linguistic powers', are demonstrated by his interest in Italian and Spanish treatises of the fifteenth to the seventeenth centuries, 'a subject' (as Ouseley noted in one of these papers) 'which has never been much attended to in this country, probably on account of the excessive rarity of the works in question'; but which 'possesses a great deal of interest, when viewed in connection with the History of Musical Art'. (Southgate adds that 'in order to illustrate the subject, Sir Frederick had upon the table several of these rare ancient treatises, thoughtfully brought from his splendid library . . .'[29]) These papers, too, were followed by extensive discussion.[30] In a series of invited lectures given to the meetings of the Church

[25] Havergal, *Memorials of Ouseley*, 52.
[26] Ibid. See also Cobbe, ' The Royal Musical Association', on the early phase.
[27] Havergal, *Memorials of Ouseley*, 52.
[28] Ibid. 53–6.
[29] Ibid. 53–4. The core of the famous Tenbury collection is now, appropriately, housed in the Bodleian Library. Further on Ouseley's musical library, see ibid. 21–2 and Shaw, *Ouseley and St Michael's, Tenbury*, ch. 10, pp. 93 ff. (E. Fellowes).
[30] Among those participating on various occasions in these discussions were W. Chappell, W. H. Cummings, J. Hullah, W. Parratt, W. Pole, and Sir John Stainer, as well as Southgate himself.

Congress, Ouseley brought his wisdom and experience to bear on 'the "music question" . . . in which he took very great interest . . .'.[31] The impact of these is summed up by Southgate: 'Many clergymen must have carried away from these meetings suggestions and hints of how to employ music in our services that have borne good fruit in many a town and quiet country church in our land.'[32] In this, as in other aspects of Ouseley's career, a sense that he could 'speak with special authority' is strongly felt.[33]

Ouseley was evaluated in retrospect as a major figure in that raising of the status of music and musicians which motivated so many leading thinkers in the profession during the second half of the nineteenth century:

During the thirty-four years that he held this distinguished post [the Heather Professorship], the knowledge and the practice of the art has advanced amazingly. That advance is mainly owing to the precept and the encouragement of the late Professor . . . Undoubtedly he has left music, both as to its public performance and the estimation in which it is now regarded, in a very different condition from that which obtained when he first commenced his official work at the University.[34]

Ouseley had adopted Stainer as his protégé, appointing him as organist at St Michael's, Tenbury in the early days (when Stainer was still in his teens). But the connection reached back further, as Stainer later reported: 'I first made his [Ouseley's] acquaintance when a small chorister boy in St Paul's Cathedral. He came to examine the choir boys and a few words of kindness, advice and encouragement which he spoke to me on that occasion were valuable to me for the rest of my life.'[35]

As Ouseley's successor in the post of Heather Professor at Oxford, Stainer—to some extent groomed by Ouseley—was amply fitted to continue the distinguished link with the sacred tradition. But besides his credentials as a church musician, as a composer, and as an organist of the highest calibre, Stainer applied his scholarly skills to the production of important publications on early music. His reputation and influence in this field were secured by his *Dufay and his Contemporaries* (1898) and *Early Bodleian Music* (1901). A wider readership was addressed with his educational and reference works, including the *Dictionary of Musical Terms* (with W. A. Barrett, 1876; revised editions 1898 and 1912).

[31] Havergal, *Memorials of Ouseley*, 57.   [32] Ibid. 58.   [33] Ibid. 57.
[34] T. L. Southgate, ibid. 27.
[35] Presidential speech to the RCO (29 Apr. 1889), quoted in Charlton, *Stainer*, 18.

In his practical musicianship he contributed to the improvements in liturgical performance which characterized the later Victorian period generally, and Oxford particularly: the *Manchester Guardian* 'commented much later on his great success at Magdalen College, asserting that it was there that his extraordinary ability as a choirmaster had really become apparent and "he raised the choir to a higher standard than had hitherto been known in the Anglican Church" '.[36] Charlton also notes the importance of Stainer's appointment, on the death of Stephen Elvey, to the organistship of the University Church of St Mary (Stainer was then aged 20) and suggests that the association of this church with the Oxford Movement 'directly influenced the order of services in St Paul's Cathedral in the 1870s'. As organist and choirmaster of St Paul's (1872–88) Stainer, 'as a pioneer', achieved 'a great work in creating at St. Paul's a standard for the choral celebration of the Holy Communion Service in cathedral worship'.[37]

Beyond the chapel and the organ loft, Stainer was energetic as a conductor. Surveying this aspect of his work in Oxford during the 1860s and early 1870s, Charlton lists the conductorship of the Magdalen College Musical Society, the Oxford Philharmonic Society and Oxford Orpheus Society (choral societies founded by Stainer in the mid–1860s), the Oxford Choral Society (which Stainer revived), the University Amateur Musical Society, and Exeter College Musical Society, whose failing strength Stainer turned around with notable success.[38] (It was through this last-named, particularly, that Stainer's connection with Parry was first forged.) The range of musical repertoire that Stainer conducted was very wide. In this regard Charlton mentions particularly Stainer's adaptation, in an English version, of Schumann's *Das Glück von Edenhall* (The Luck of Edenhall); Stainer, with Parry accompanying on the piano, conducted 'the first public performance of this cantata in this country'. He also

[36] Charlton, *Stainer*, 24–5. See also the judicious evaluation of Stainer's work in Gatens, *Victorian Cathedral Music*, ch. 9.

[37] Fellowes, *English Cathedral Music*, 223. Assessments of Stainer's contribution in this sphere tend to value the church musician more than the composer. Charlton (*Stainer*, 124) links these two aspects carefully: 'the need for new church music was evident and he, like many of his fellow cathedral organists, helped to provide an extensive repertoire. From this period—between Goss and Stanford—relatively little remains in use; but . . . [it] served an important role in bringing order and high standards to Anglican worship.'

[38] See Charlton, *Stainer*, 28–9.

conducted Parry's own compositions on various occasions; much
Mendelssohn, including the oratorios *Elijah* and *St Paul*; and Handel and
Haydn. As a performer, often together with Parry, Stainer gave numerous
piano duet renderings of the orchestral repertoire, among them
Mendelssohn's Andante from the 'Reformation' Symphony, 'first time
heard in Oxford and almost new to London'.[39]

On the lighter side Stainer founded the Maltese Glee Club at Magdalen
(1865) and became its first conductor, as well as succeeding Blythe (the previous organist of Magdalen) as conductor of the college Madrigal Society.
His interest in madrigals and glees extended to the production of his own
compositions in the genre.[40] He was also connected with the Magdalen
Vagabonds, again conducting, until he was succeeded by Parratt: 'For
some years Dr Stainer joined us on our wanderings; and we do not know
which to admire most in this gentleman, whether it was his distinguished
musical talents, or the quiet and unaffected manner in which he displayed
these talents.'[41] Hugh Allen considered that Stainer was 'to be remembered during his first Oxford period particularly for the way he improved
college musical life, not only in chapel but in secular music also'.[42]

It is clear that Stainer's return to the University as Heather Professor in
succession to his mentor Ouseley was regarded as greatly fulfilling the
requisites and hopes that commentators such as Southgate invested in this
election. Hadow welcomed the appointment in relation to educational
aspirations for music at Oxford; Parratt, 'lecturing on Oxford music
twenty years after Stainer's appointment', considered that 'no worthier
successor to Ouseley could have been found than Stainer', and mentioned
both Stainer's discipleship ('not only his [Ouseley's] friend but to some extent also his pupil') and the effects of his 'vivifying personality' on music
generally and church music particularly.[43] Fellowes recorded that Stainer
as Professor was 'an excellent lecturer, and he did much to raise the status
of the Professorship of Music at Oxford while he held the Chair', adding
that 'he also did much valuable work in the field of musicology'.[44]

39 Charlton, *Stainer*, 29–30.
40 Ibid. 30; and see Ch. 10, pp. 191 ff. above.
41 Quoted from Hall, *The Magdalen Vagabonds*, in Charlton, *Stainer*, 32.
42 *PMA* (1921–2), quoted in Charlton, *Stainer*, 36.
43 Ibid. 89.
44 Fellowes, *English Cathedral Music*, 223.

Fellowes's insight into Stainer's achievements rested on his personal experience of Stainer's work at Oxford: as Fellowes later recorded,

Another organization to which I belonged was known as the Professor of Music's Choir. It was conducted by Dr. Mee in his official capacity as 'Coryphaeus' of the University . . . The purpose of the choir was to sing illustrations for Stainer's lectures as Professor of Music. This gave me opportunity for getting to know some music of a different character, for Stainer dealt with unusual subjects and was a fine musical scholar.[45]

Within the ten-year span which now became a standard tenure for the post, Stainer established as far as was possible the systematic instruction and 'official influence' on music that Southgate had hoped for from the appointment to the Professorship.[46]

When Stainer resigned the Heather Professorship in May 1899, Parry (who had been thought of as a possible successor to Ouseley in 1889, when Stainer was appointed to the Chair) was 'the most favoured candidate', and as Parry described it Stainer 'stood over him "like a gaoler"' until he had submitted his application.[47] Parry's reputation has become so well established that it comes as a surprise to read the grudging account of his achievements in a widely respected study of the social history of British music:

A gentleman by birth who, like Ouseley, had fought family opposition to his profession, he . . . composed much dead music, and published books which are said to have helped restore music 'to the place in literary, university and national life that it had lost for more than two centuries'. His most stalwart advocate also attributes to him, with apt prevarication, 'the accepted but unacknowledged leadership of the musical profession'.[48]

Recent work has brought out the vital qualities perceived in Parry's music, and musical scholarship, in his own time: as Dibble has noted, at the end of the Scherzo in the final rehearsal of Parry's Piano Quartet in 1879 Dannreuther turned to the other performers and 'said loudly, "Superbe Satz". The slow movement they expressed emphatically "magnifique",

---

45 Fellowes, *Memoirs*, 56.

46 Further on Southgate's views, see Ch. 7 above. For a valuable résumé of Stainer's teaching and other activities as Professor see Charlton, *Stainer*, ch. 6, pp. 90–105.

47 Parry: diary entry, 9 Nov. 1899 (quoted in Dibble, *Parry*, 367).

48 Ehrlich, *Music Profession*, 140.

"ganz himmlisch" . . .', while the author of the programme notes for the première of Parry's Second Symphony in F (1883) discerned that 'something of the composer's immensely happy, yet romantically turbulent life at Oxford, with all the uncertainties of what lay beyond, are contained therein'.[49]

Parry's writings on music belonged with the new wave of informative historical and analytical literature designed to make music accessible, and to communicate musical scholarship, to a wide readership. As Grove expressed it:

Music is now performed, studied and listened to by a much larger number of persons, and in a more serious spirit, than was the case at any previous period of our history. It is rapidly becoming an essential branch of our education . . . and a strong desire is felt by a large, important, and increasing section of the public to know something of the structure and peculiarities of the music . . . the natures and histories of the instruments on which it is performed . . . the biographies and characteristics of its composers . . .[50]

It was in the light of this modern trend that Parry published, for example, his *Studies of the Great Composers* (1886) 'accompanied by a preface explaining their purpose was to help "people of average general intelligence to get some idea of the positions which the most important composers occupy in the historical development of the art" '.[51] (The notions of a hierarchy of composers, and a developmental progression of the art of music, were among the contemporary orthodoxies held by the leading writers on the subject.) As Dibble points out, Parry's essays were informed by the latest scholarship, such as Grove's pioneering work on Schubert. His *Summary of the History and Development of Medieval and Modern European Music* (1893) was produced to fulfil the need for 'a new and more authoritative reader for young musicians'.[52] Besides his Bach biography, Parry's contributions to Grove's *Dictionary* and to the *Oxford History of Music* (1902) placed his scholarship centrally, in publications of lasting importance and influence.[53]

---

[49] Dibble, *Parry*, 167; p. 209. While Parry's choral works have remained firmly in the repertoire, his instrumental works have been revived in recent years.

[50] Grove, *Dictionary*, preface to vol. i.

[51] Dibble, *Parry*, 223.

[52] Ibid. 282. Its popularity led to a second edition in 1904.

[53] Parry was commissioned by Hadow and the OUP to write vol. iii of the *Oxford History* (*The Music of the Seventeenth Century*). His *Johann Sebastian Bach* appeared in 1909.

His *Style in Musical Art* (1911) was 'based on a tightly organized series of lectures given during his occupancy of the Heather Professorship at Oxford' (and also on material from lectures given at the Royal Institution and elsewhere); its title was derived from Parry's Inaugural Lecture at Oxford in 1900 (published in pamphlet form by the Clarendon Press). As Dibble observes, the later book of 1911 goes beyond 'largely impartial' technical discussion to consider 'the influence of audiences, methodical and conceptual antitheses . . . and, most didactic of all, quality'.[54] Parry's combination of searching scholarship with a strong and enduring commitment to composition, as well as teaching and administrative duties (he served as director of the RCM, succeeding Grove in this post from 1894, and as president of the Musical Association 1901–8), was fully in the Oxford professorial tradition. But as a composer he achieved higher stature than his predecessors: Fellowes viewed Parry's *Prometheus Unbound* (performed at Gloucester, 1880) as sparking a new revival of British music.[55] *Grove* (1994) refers to his 'revitalizing influence on English musical life in the late 19th century'.[56]

Apart from the more public aspects of Parry's work during his long connection with Oxford, he forged an intimate link with the musical life and with the musicians of the University. Among the strong impressions left by his experiences of Oxford music-making was the tradition of brilliant organ-playing maintained by successive college organists: 'Went to Magdalen 5 o'clock service . . . We had S. Elvey in A and "The Lord spake the word". Stainer played the last 3 movements of the Sonata in B flat (Mendelssohn) afterwards most gloriously; and brought out the "Tuba mirabilis" tremendously in the last strain.'[57] At the latter end of his career, when he returned to organ composition, Parry (during a trip to France in 1910) promised C. H. Lloyd, organist of Christ Church, that he would write a set of chorale preludes for him. 'During their composition in 1911 he submitted them to Lloyd, Parratt and Stanford, for criticism': his uncertainty over their effect ('having been away from the instrument for so long') was ungrounded. The pieces explored 'a significant range of sensibilities' and made 'full use of the possibilities of Romantic registration'.

54 Dibble, *Parry*, 444; p. 378.
55 Fellowes, *English Cathedral Music*, 233.
56 *NGCDM* 598.
57 Parry: diary entry, 20 May 1866 (quoted in Dibble, *Parry*, 40).

Their success led to the composition of the three Chorale Fantasias (1915) as well as the revised version of his earlier Fantasia and Fugue (published in 1913, and dedicated 'To my dear friend Walter Parratt').[58]

Chamber music, strongly pursued in university circles at Oxford, left an early impression on Parry. On his first day in Oxford he was 'delighted to be invited to attend a musical party at the home of Professor Donkin, himself a proficient amateur violinist'. There he met various 'leading figures' including Ouseley, Stainer, and James Taylor, organist of New College: Parry noted that 'the Donkins performed a quartet of Sir Frederick [Gore Ouseley]'s which he had composed for them'.[59] Taylor often performed as pianist in piano trios and piano quartets at the Donkins' home. His own household was a focus of chamber music, as Parry recorded: 'At Taylors. Quartetts. When I got there they were playing one of Mendelssohn's. We had Duos and Quartetts and solos and songs. They played for me Mendelssohn's Quartett no. 1 for Pianoforte, Violin, Viola, and Cello.'[60] From these new experiences of chamber music Parry took encouragement to explore the genre, and to compose string quartets which he tried over with friends. He too wrote works for Donkin.[61] And the Exeter College concerts offered opportunities to try out vocal chamber as well as choral music, while the period of Parry's undergraduate involvement in Oxford's musical scene additionally saw the infusion of new life into the university choral societies, especially under Stainer's influence. (Parry also joined the Exeter chapel choir.[62])

An appropriate point at which to highlight Parry's long association with the Oxford choral tradition is that of the composition and first performances of his *Songs of Farewell*. In particular, the Oxford Bach Choir—along with its significant links with contemporary composers—preserved a strong connection with Parry. And Hugh Allen, the Bach Choir's conductor, 'conducted some of the first performances of Parry's works, sometimes in semi-private trials in Oxford, where the first four *Songs of Farewell* were "tried over" in the Chapel of New College, with Allen's help, in 1915'.[63] The sixth and final setting, of Psalm 39 ('Lord, let me know mine

[58] Dibble, *Parry*, 446–7.
[59] Parry: diary entry, 4 Dec. 1866 (quoted in Dibble, *Parry*, 42).
[60] Parry: diary entry, 8 Feb. 1867 (quoted in Dibble, *Parry*, 49).
[61] Dibble, *Parry*, 62.   [62] Ibid. 48.
[63] Cf. Wollenberg, 'Music in Oxford in the Time of Dorothy L. Sayers', 28.

end') in a monumental version for double choir, was performed 'in the chapel of New College, Oxford by the Oxford Bach Choir, again under the baton of Allen, on 17 June 1917. "They sang "Lord let me know mine end" beautifully. The first time I had heard it . . .", Parry wrote in his diary shortly afterwards. Sadly, he never heard the motets sung as an entire set.'[64] The sixth motet, 'Lord, let me know mine end', was reportedly dedicated to Hugh Allen and the Oxford Bach Choir.[65] The *Songs of Farewell* were eventually heard, complete, in the programme of the Memorial Service for Parry held at Exeter College on 23 February 1919, with 'a picked Choir consisting of members of the [Oxford] Bach Choir, and the choirs of Christ Church and New College and members of the Oxford Orchestral Society [formerly Dr Allen's orchestra]'.[66]

In 1908 when Parry resigned the Heather Professorship, 'great efforts were made' to persuade Parratt to succeed him. The joint letter to this effect from Frederick Bridge and others must, as Geoffrey Parratt observed, have acted strongly in this:

March 21st, 1908

Dear Sir Walter,

Without wishing to press the matter of the Oxford Professorship unduly upon you, we should like to assure you that your appointment would give great and widespread gratification . . .[67]

And on his election to the post, Parry wrote warmly to his friend:

though a glimmer of a hint reached me that you might allow yourself to be nominated it had never been confirmed to a certainty. But it is most right proper and every way a joyful consummation that it should be so. Everybody will rejoice out of affection for you and . . . concern for the University, upon which you will confer distinction.[68]

---

[64] Dibble, *Parry*, 479.
[65] Bailey, *Allen*, 45.
[66] Thewlis, Notes, v. 358. The programme also included Parry's organ chorale preludes played by H. G. Ley, organist of Christ Church.
[67] Tovey and Parratt, *Parratt*, 110–11.
[68] Ibid. 112.

Among other letters he received, Parratt must have been left in no doubt, 'if by that time he had any, of the rightness of his decision to accept the post' by Parry's and also by Elgar's words:

Naples,
May 8th, 1908

My dear Parratt,

We are just embarking for England but I must send you one line to congratulate you and Oxford and to say how delighted I am that the U. has made such a super-lative choice . . . splendid for them and I hope gratifying to you . . .

Kindest regards,
Ever yours sincerely,
EDWARD ELGAR.[69]

Parratt, an organist of distinction ('the foremost English organ exponent of his time')[70] was also active as a conductor; in Oxford this included conducting numerous college musical societies (*Grove* (2001) lists Exeter, Trinity, Jesus, and Pembroke colleges).[71]

Although Parratt is not remembered as a scholar or composer, as Parry so strongly is, his son emphasized that Parratt's Oxford lectures did not take 'the easiest way' (by using musical illustrations as a peg to hang them on): the subjects on which he lectured included the growth of the modern orchestra, and the effect of 'the temper of the times' upon art, as well as historical topics and an appreciation of Ouseley, Stainer, and Parry. With characteristic modesty Parratt 'often expressed surprise and pleasure at the size and attentiveness of his audiences, and he was grateful for the great help received from Sir Hugh Allen, who succeeded him in the chair'.[72]

Hugh Allen made a definitive mark on Oxford, and on English music, long before his election to the Heather Professorship of Music in 1918. A number of aspects characterizing his contribution to Oxford's musical life in the period leading up to his appointment as Heather Professor were already strongly indicated in his early career and education. Before his appearance on the Oxford musical scene, when he took up his post as

[69] Tovey and Parratt, *Parratt,* 112.
[70] *NGCDM* 597.   [71] *NG2* xix. 149.
[72] Tovey and Parratt, *Parratt,* 114.

organist of New College in 1901, he had acquired a varied experience of organs and choirs in locations ranging from Reading (where he served as organist of St Saviour's from the age of 11) to St Asaph's cathedral in Wales, via Cambridge, Chichester, and Ely. As his biographer, Cyril Bailey, expressed it: 'The variety of his early experiences contributed . . . to his adaptability and capacity to tackle any job or deal with any situation which might arise.'[73] While this might suggest the makings of a generalist, rather than a specialist, Allen was noted for his interest in particular composers: Dent remarked that 'he was a great force in propagating Bach and Brahms'.[74] A formative influence was that of his teacher F. J. Read, who performed Bach at Chichester; as organ scholar of Christ's, Cambridge (1892–7), Allen included Bach in the choir's repertoire, introducing others to the profundities of Bach's style at a time when it was not generally appreciated.[75] His contemporary R. G. K. Lempfert, referring to Allen's work for the CUMS during this phase of his career, summed up the principles that governed his performances, recalling how 'not merely to make music himself, but to help others to appreciate the joys of music-making . . . seemed at that time to be his mission in life'.[76] Allen met Brahms in Vienna during a visit in winter 1897–8. At Ely (1898–1901) both the 'Matthew Passion and Brahms's Requiem were among the earlier performances' directed by Allen;[77] Dent annotated his diary entry for December 1898, referring to 'the concert in the Ely Town Hall . . . at which Allen performed the *Schicksalslied* [of Brahms] twice over in order that the audience should get to understand it',[78] a point which brings out the contemporary character of Brahms's music at that stage.

Among modern British composers of his own time Allen devoted special attention to Parry. Again, Read was influential; at Chichester he arranged for Parry to come over and conduct his *Judith* (1888), thus beginning a long friendship and musical collaboration with Allen: 'It fell to my lot after that first encounter to be associated with him in many other performances of his works, and eventually to be privileged to give the first performance of a considerable number of his later works . . .'[79] The years before his Oxford appointments also provided contacts with performers who later assisted Allen in Oxford, among them Marie Fillunger; and gave

[73] Bailey, *Allen*, 7.   [74] Ibid. 22.   [75] Ibid.   [76] Ibid. 18.   [77] Ibid. 29.
[78] Ibid. 31.   [79] Ibid. 11–12.

him experiences of particular works which inspired him subsequently to put on Oxford performances, as with *Fidelio*.[80] The accounts of Allen's formative years lead to the conclusion that in appointing this risky candidate to the organistship of New College, the selectors acknowledged in him an exceptionally strongly formed musical talent.[81] The college's confidence in his capacities was further affirmed when in 1908 he was offered a fellowship at New College, a distinction which, as the *DNB* notes, was 'at that time a most unusual recognition of a mere musician'.[82] This counteracts the unscholarly impression attached to some of the commentary on Allen's earlier career.[83]

In Oxford during the years prior to his taking up the Professorship, Allen's aim of giving 'every generation of undergraduates . . . the chance of singing in the B minor Mass or the St Matthew Passion or in the Beethoven Mass in D'[84] was centred on his work with the Oxford Bach Choir. It was in fact with Allen's conductorship of the choir (from 1901) that the B minor Mass began to appear regularly in the programmes. The Oxford Bach Choir under Allen played a pioneering role in the context of the English Bach revival. It is clear that Allen was not merely a local figure in this respect; as Hale writes, 'by 1920 Allen was acknowledged to be perhaps the greatest conductor in the country of Bach's choral music'.[85] Of his charismatic and idiosyncratic style at rehearsals, Dorothy Sayers has written particularly evocatively.[86] His début with the choir was in a performance of Brahms's Requiem in the Town Hall on 14 March 1901: the *Oxford Chronicle*'s critic remarked that 'Dr Allen, who made his first appearance in Oxford as a conductor, is a man of strong personality, full of genuine enthusiasm, and with ample control of his forces . . .'[87]. Those

---

[80] Bailey, *Allen*, 31 and 60. See also Ch. 12 below.

[81] For an insight into the circumstances of the appointment, see Bailey, *Allen*, 33. The then Precentor, Nowell Smith, commented: 'How easily might we, modest amateurs, only concerned to safeguard our musical tradition, have taken the safe and obvious course!'

[82] *DNB*, Suppl. (1941–50), 11. In that same year Allen was appointed Director of Music at Reading University (a post he retained until 1918: see Bailey, *Allen*, 7).

[83] Bailey remarks that 'there is no record of phenomenal scholastic success, but his natural love of music developed early' (ibid. 5) and that 'his Cambridge career appeared to his college dons "uneventful and undistinguished" ' (ibid. 23).   [84] Ibid. 44.

[85] Buxton and Penry Williams, *New College, Oxford*, 286.

[86] Quoted in Bailey, *Allen*, 51–3. On the importance of rehearsals to Allen the *DNB* notes (Suppl. (1941–50), 11) that 'at rehearsals he could talk and teach, at performances he could only glower and frown when he was not satisfied'.

[87] *Oxford Chronicle*, 15 Mar. 1901.

forces included, on this occasion, to the critic's evident bewilderment, the combination of 'organ, two grand pianofortes, and kettledrums' to replace the orchestra. The critic's hope that 'in future, as in the past, the Bach Choir will call in proper orchestral aid' was subsequently realized by the formation of Dr Allen's orchestra, led for many years by Miss Mary Venables, 'whose fine playing and sensitive leadership were an inspiration to the whole orchestra'.[88] As with his singers, Allen called forth the best from his players.

Besides the regular rehearsals and concerts, notable highlights of this period of Allen's career included his three-day Oxford Bach Festival (13–15 May 1914) with four programmes featuring organ chorale preludes, cantatas, motets, the Magnificat and other items, and culminating in a fine performance of the B minor Mass in the Town Hall. H. G. Ley 'rendered excellent service at the organ', as reported in the *Oxford Chronicle* (22 May 1914); Dr Allen's orchestra was (as was customary in larger works) supplemented by professional wind players from the LSO; and the trumpet parts were played by two college servants on 'Bach trumpets' specially procured for the Festival.[89] In this and other efforts, Allen stamped Oxford's cultivation of Bach with a strong character.

[88] Bailey, *Allen*, 56.
[89] See also Bailey, *Oxford Bach Choir*, [5]. Further on Sayers, Allen, Parry, and the Bach Choir see Wollenberg, 'Music in Oxford in the Time of Dorothy L. Sayers', 28 and *passim*.

12

Epilogue: The Tradition
after *c.*1914

In the years of the First World War, 'the role of music was intensified (though its practitioners were diminished in number)'; one commentator in the local press in Oxford observed that 'among the by products of war time must be reckoned the impulse it lends to art, literature and music'.[1] Another comment to the effect that 'the exigencies of war time' had 'deprived . . . the present generation' of the experience of large choral performances alluded to the Oxford Bach Choir as an exception. 'The particular occasion was 25 February 1915, at the Sheldonian Theatre, when Hugh Allen conducted a concert "in memory of those who have fallen in the war".' Included in the programme was Parry's *The Glories of our Blood and State* (originally composed in 1883). 'There was a vast audience, "not a seat being vacant", and many standing.'[2] Dorothy Sayers's poem 'To Members of the Bach Choir on Active Service' commemorated the continuing work of the choir as well as its absent members:

> From singer to singer the space is wide
> Where knee pressed knee once, side pressed side.[3]

[1] Cf. Wollenberg, 'Music in Oxford in the time of Dorothy L. Sayers', 28.

[2] *Oxford Chronicle*, 26 Feb. 1915, quoted ibid.

[3] Printed copy in Thewlis, Notes, v. [355]–[6] (interleaved), headed 'Reprinted for Members of the Oxford Bach Choir and Choral Society only, by Courtesy of the Editor of the Oxford Magazine', Feb. 1916. The poem was later reproduced in Bailey, *Oxford Bach Choir*.

Hugh Allen, as Heather Professor of Music from 1918, presided over the post-war recovery of music in Oxford. Among memorable markers in this process was the occasion in June 1919 when 'Oxford celebrated the 250th anniversary of the opening of the Sheldonian Theatre; an honorary D.Mus. was conferred on Vaughan Williams', and Allen conducted the Oxford Bach Choir in 'magnificent performances of works by Parry (*Blest Pair of Sirens*) and Vaughan Williams (*Sea Symphony*)'.[4]

A penchant for commemorating anniversaries, and particular composers, became characteristic of Oxford's musical life thereafter. Among the series of festivals, symposia, and exhibitions marking composers' anniversaries were the Haydn commemorations in 1932 and 1991 (the latter for the bicentenary of his Oxford visit); Bach and Handel in 1935; Parry in 1948; and Wellesz in 1985. The anniversary of the Heather Professorship was celebrated in 1926 and 1976 (the revised date of 1627 for its founding was established only recently).[5] Among many festival projects, the English Bach Festival originated in Oxford in 1963; an annual 'Handel in Oxford' Festival began in 1985; and an annual Oxford Contemporary Music Festival was launched in 1994. So much has developed in Oxford's concert life and in the academic musical sphere since 1914–18 that only two particularly crucial points can be addressed here. First, attention must be drawn to the belated emergence of fully-fledged opera performances in Oxford. Here too, Allen was influential. 'Twice . . . he made operatic ventures': in Beethoven's *Fidelio* (1910) with the soloists including Campbell McInnes and Adrian Boult, Allen 'had trained the chorus of fifty voices and conducted the orchestra, by whom all the four overtures were played . . .'. This was followed in 1911 by *Freischütz*, 'an equally brilliant success', when 'the *Oxford Chronicle* commented: "It is to the orchestra and Dr. Allen that one comes back for the triumphs of the evening. The violins, led by Miss Mary Venables, did splendidly all through"'.[6]

The decisive event for opera in Oxford came in 1926 when the Oxford University Opera Club was launched following a production of Monteverdi's *Orfeo*, edited by Jack Westrup (then an undergraduate), and

---

[4] Cf. Bailey, *Oxford Bach Choir, passim.*

[5] See Crum, *Heather Professor of Music, 1626–1976*; and cf. Gouk in *HUO* iv and Shaw, 'Oxford University Chair'.

[6] Bailey, *Allen*, 60.

performed 'by members of the University and friends' in 1925. Under Westrup's conductorship from 1947 (when he returned to Oxford as Heather Professor) to 1962, the OUOC presented a series of works ranging from Scarlatti (*Il Mitridate Eupatore*, 1961) to Wellesz (*Incognita*, 1951), many of them in their British premières. (The Oxford University Orchestra originally grew out of the orchestral body formed, from 1947, to accompany the Opera Club performances: it was constituted as an independent concert orchestra in 1954.) Westrup was also prominent in the definitive transformation of music as an academic subject in the University. The modern Faculty of Music had been instituted under Allen in 1944, with premises in Holywell Street, next to the Music Room. The Honour School of Music was set up in 1950. Westrup as Heather Professor, together with such distinguished colleagues as Frank Ll. Harrison (from 1952), Frederick Sternfeld (from 1956), and Egon Wellesz (appointed to the University following his flight from occupied Vienna in 1938), presided over the teaching and examining of a new BA syllabus based on a wider view of musical scholarship. With these developments, music finally achieved 'that position in the University' which Ouseley and his successors had 'always hoped that it would one day attain'.[7]

[7] HCP 51 (1898), 43.

Acknowledgements and Sources
for Illustrations

PLATES

FIGURES

Bibliography

ADAMS, P., *Somerville for Women: An Oxford College, 1879–1993* (Oxford, 1996).

ANSON, H., *T. B. Strong: Bishop, Musician, Dean, Vice-Chancellor* (London, 1949).

ARGENT, M., ed., *Recollections of R. J. S. Stevens: An Organist in Georgian London* (London, 1992).

ARKWRIGHT, G. E. P., *Catalogue of Music in the Library of Christ Church, Oxford* (Oxford, 1915; corr. repr., 1971).

ARNOLD, D., 'Music Moves at Oxford', *MT* 123 (1982), 107–8.

BAILEY, C., 'Sir Hubert Parry and OUDS', *Oxford Magazine* (1918), 24–5.

——*Hugh Percy Allen* (London, 1948).

—— *A Short History of the Oxford Bach Choir* (Oxford, 1948).

BARKER, H., *Newspapers, Politics and English Society 1695–1855* (Harlow, Essex, 2000).

BARRETT, W. A., *English Glee and Madrigal Writers* (London, *c*.1877).

BASHFORD, C., and LANGLEY, L., eds., *Music and British Culture, 1785–1914: Essays in Honour of Cyril Ehrlich* (Oxford, 2000).

BELLASIS, E., *Cardinal Newman as a Musician* (London, 1892).

BENNETT, W., ' Hayes, Linley and the Three Choirs Festivals', *MMR* 67 (1937), 107.

BENOLIEL, B., *Parry before 'Jerusalem': Studies of his Life and Music with Excerpts from his Published Writings* (Aldershot, 1997).

BERGSAGEL, J., 'Music in Oxford in Holberg's Time', *Hvad Fatter gjør... Boghistoriske, litterære og musikalske essays tilegnet Erik Dal* (Herning, 1982), 34–61.

BILL, E. G. W., *Education at Christ Church Oxford 1660–1800* (Oxford, 1988).

BLAND, D., *Ouseley and his Angels: the life of St. Michael's College, Tenbury and its Founder* (Eton, 2000).

BLOXAM, J. R., *A Register of the Presidents, Fellows, Demies, Instructors in Grammar and in Music, Chaplains, Clerks, Choristers . . . of Saint Mary Magdalen College in the University of Oxford, from the Foundation to the Present Time*, 7 vols. (Oxford, 1853–81; index (W. D. Macray) Oxford, 1885).

BORSAY, P., *The English Urban Renaissance: Culture and Society in the Provincial Town 1660–1770* (Oxford, 1989).

BOYDELL, B., *A Dublin Musical Calendar 1700–1760* (Dublin, 1988).

BREWER, J., *The Pleasures of the Imagination: English Culture in the Eighteenth Century* (London, 1997).

BRIDGE, SIR FREDERICK, *A Westminster Pilgrim* (London, 1918).

BROWN, J. D., and STRATTON, S., *British Musical Biography: a Dictionary of Musical Artists, Authors and Composers, born in Britain and its Colonies* (Birmingham, 1897).

BRIDGE, J. C., *A Short Sketch of the Chester Musical Festivals, 1772 to 1829* (Chester, 1891).

BUCK, P. C., MEE, J. H., and WOODS, F. C., *Ten Years of University Music in Oxford . . . 1884–1894* (London, 1894).

BURCHELL, J., *Polite or Commercial Concerts? Concert Management and Orchestral Repertoire in Edinburgh, Bath, Oxford, Manchester, and Newcastle, 1730–1799* (New York and London, 1996).

BURDEN, M., and CHOLIJ, I., *A Handbook for Studies in 18th-Century English Music* (Edinburgh, 1987 ff.).

BURNEY, C., *An Account of the Musical Performances in Westminster-Abbey and the Pantheon . . . in Commemoration of Handel* (London, 1785; repr. Amsterdam, 1964).

——'An Account of an Infant Musician' [William Crotch], *Philosophical Transactions of the Royal Society of London*, 69 (1779), 183–206.

——*A General History of Music, from the Earliest Ages to the Present Period*, 4 vols. (1776–89); ed. F. Mercer, 2 vols. (1935; repr. New York, 1957).

The Letters of Dr Charles Burney, vol. i: *1751–1784*, ed. A. Ribeiro (Oxford, 1991).

BURNS, A., and WILSON, R., *The Balliol Concerts: A Centenary History* (Oxford, 1985).

BURROWS, D., 'Sources for Oxford Handel Performances in the First Half of the Eighteenth Century', *ML* 61 (1980), 177–85.

——*The Cambridge Companion to Handel* (Cambridge, 1997).

——and SHAW, H. WATKINS, 'Handel's "Messiah": Supplementary Notes on Sources', *ML* 96 (1995), 356–68.

BUXTON, J., and WILLIAMS, P., eds., *New College, Oxford 1379–1979* (Oxford, 1979).

CALDWELL, J., *The Oxford History of English Music*, 2 vols. (Oxford, 1991, 1999).

CHAN, M., 'A Mid-Seventeenth-Century Music Meeting and Playford's Publishing', in J. Caldwell, E. Olleson, and S. Wollenberg, eds., *The Well Enchanting Skill: Music, Poetry, and Drama in the Culture of the Renaissance. Essays in honour of F. W. Sternfeld* (Oxford, 1990), 231–44.

CHARLTON, P., *John Stainer and the Musical Life of Victorian Britain* (Newton Abbot, 1984).

Christ Church Cathedral School, Oxford: Register of Choristers, Probationers, Masters, Precentors, Organists from 1837–1900 (Salisbury, 1920).

COBBE, H., 'The Royal Musical Association 1874–1901', *PRMA* 110 (1983–4), 111–17.

COLLES, H. C., and CRUFT, J., *The Royal College of Music: A Centenary Record* (London, 1982).

CORDEAUX, E. H., and MERRY, D. H., *A Bibliography of Printed Works Relating to the University of Oxford*, 3 vols. (Oxford, 1968).

——*A Bibliography of Printed Works Relating to the City of Oxford*, OHS NS, xxv (Oxford, 1976).

CORFIELD, P. J., *The Impact of English Towns, 1700–1800* (Oxford, 1982).

COX, G. V., *Recollections of Oxford*, 2nd edn. (London, 1870).

CROSSLEY, A., ed., *The City of Oxford*, Victoria History of the County of Oxford, iv (Oxford, 1979).

CROTCH, W., *Specimens of Various Styles of Music, referred to in A COURSE OF LECTURES read at Oxford and London . . . by Wm. Crotch, Mus. Doct. Prof. Mus. Oxon.*, 3 vols. (London, *c*.1808–09).

——*The Substance of Several Courses of Lectures on Music, read in the University of Oxford, and in the Metropolis* (London, 1831; repr. (intr. B. Rainbow) 1986).

CRUM, M., 'Early Lists of the Oxford Music School Collection', *ML* 48 (1967), 23–34.

——'An Oxford Music Club, 1690–1719', *BLR* 9 (1974), 83–99.

——*The Heather Professors of Music, 1626–1976. Exhibition in the Divinity School, October 1976* (Oxford, 1976).

——'The Deneke Mendelssohn Collection', *BLR* 12 (1987), 298–320.

CUDWORTH, C., 'The Vauxhall "Lists" ', *Galpin Society Journal*, 20 (1967), 24–42.

DENEKE, M., *Ernest Walker* (London, 1951).

——*Paul Victor Mendelssohn Benecke, 1868–1944* (Oxford, 1954).

DEUTSCH, O. E., ' "Ink-Pot and Squirt-Gun", or "The Art of Composing Music in the New Style" ', *MT* 93 (1952), 401–3.

——*Handel: A Documentary Biography* (London, 1955).

DIBBLE, J., *C. Hubert H. Parry: His Life and Music* (Oxford, 1992).

DICKENS, C., ed., *A Dictionary of the University of Oxford* (London, 1884).

Dictionary of National Biography, 66 vols. (London, 1885–1901), reissued in 22 vols. 1908–9; further suppl. vols.

DOANE, J., *A Musical Directory for the Year 1794*, facs. repr. (London, 1993).

EDMUNDS, J., *New College Brats: A History of the Life and Education of the Choristers of New College, Oxford* (Oxford, 1996).

EHRLICH, C., *The Music Profession in Britain since the Eighteenth Century: A Social History* (Oxford, 1985).

——*First Philharmonic: A History of the Royal Philharmonic Society* (Oxford, 1995).

ELVEY, LADY (M.), *Life and Reminiscences of George J. Elvey* (London, 1894).

ENGEL, A. J., *From Clergyman to Don: The Rise of the Academic Profession in Nineteenth-Century Oxford* (Oxford, 1983).

FARMER, H. G., *Music-Making in the Olden Days: The Story of the Aberdeen Concerts, 1748–1801* (London, 1950).

FASNACHT, R., *A History of the City of Oxford* (Oxford, 1954).

FAWCETT, T., *Music in Eighteenth-Century Norwich and Norfolk* (Norwich, 1979).

FELLOWES, E. H., *Memoirs of an Amateur Musician* (London, 1946).

FELLOWES, E. H., *English Cathedral Music*, 5th edn., rev. J. A. Westrup (London, 1969).

FISKE, R., 'The "Macbeth" Music', *ML* 45 (1964), 114–25.

FLETCHER, REV. C., *A History of the Church and Parish of St. Martin (Carfax) in Oxford* (Oxford and London, 1896).

FORD, W. K., 'The Oxford Music School in the Late 17th Century', *JAMS* 17 (1964), 198–203.

FOSTER, J., ed., *Alumni Oxonienses*, 1st ser., 1500–1714, 4 vols. (Oxford, 1891–2); 2nd ser., 1715–1886, 4 vols. (Oxford, 1887–8).

FROST, T., 'The Cantatas of John Stanley (1713–86)', *ML* 53 (1972), 284–92.

GATENS, W. J., *Victorian Cathedral Music in Theory and Practice* (Cambridge, 1986).

GREEN, V. H. H., *A History of Oxford University* (London, 1974).

GRIERSON, M., *Donald Francis Tovey* (London, 1952, repr. 1970).

GROVE, G., *Dictionary of Music and Musicians*, 4 vols. (London, 1879–89).

Grove Concise Dictionary of Music, ed. S. Sadie, corr. repr. (London, 1994).

HADOW, W. H., 'Sir Hubert Parry', *PMA* 45 (1918–19), 135–47.

HALE, P., 'Music and Musicians', in Buxton and Williams, *New College, Oxford*, ch. VIII, 267–92.

HARGREAVES-MAWDSLEY, W., ed., *Woodforde at Oxford, 1759–1776*, OHS NS, xxi (Oxford, 1969).

HARPER, J., 'The Dallam Organ in Magdalen College, Oxford: A New Account of the Milton Organ', *Journal of the British Institute of Organ Studies*, 9 (1985), 51–64.

——'The Organ of Magdalen College, Oxford', *MT* 117 (1986), 293–6, 351–3.

HARRISON, C., ed., *John Malchair of Oxford: Artist and Musician* (Oxford, 1998).

HAVERGAL, F. T., *Memorials of Frederick Arthur Gore Ouseley, Baronet, M.A.* (London, 1889).

HAWKINS, SIR J., *A General History of the Science and Practice of Music*, 5 vols. (London, 1776).

HAYES, P., ed., *Cathedral Music in Score composed by Dr. William Hayes* (Oxford, 1795).

[HAYES, W.], *Remarks on Mr. Avison's Essay on Musical Expression* (London, 1753).

HEARNE, T., *Remarks and Collections*, ed. C. E. Doble *et al.*, 11 vols. OHS, ii, vii, xiii, xxxiv, xlii–xliii, xlviii, l, lxv, lxvii, lxxii (Oxford, 1884–1918).

HEIGHES, S., 'The Life and Works of William and Philip Hayes' (D.Phil. diss., University of Oxford, 1991).

HEIGHES, S., *The Lives and Works of William and Philip Hayes* (New York and London, 1995).

HIBBERT, C., and HIBBERT, E., eds., *Encyclopædia of Oxford* (London, 1988).

HIFF, A., *Catalogue of Printed Music Published Prior to 1801, now in the Library of Christ Church, Oxford* (Oxford, 1919).

HIGHFILL, P. H., Jr, BURNIM, K. A., and LANGHANS, E. A., eds., *A Biographical Dictionary of Actors, Actresses, Musicians, Dancers, Managers & Other Stage Personnel in London, 1660–1800*, 16 vols. (Carbondale, Ill., 1973–93).

HILLSMAN, W., 'Women in Victorian Church Music: Their Social, Liturgical and Performing Roles in Anglicanism', *Women in the Church*, ed. W. J. Sheils and D. Wood, *Studies in Church History*, xxvii (Oxford, 1990), 443–52.

HISCOCK, W. G., *A Christ Church Miscellany* (Oxford, 1946).

——*Henry Aldrich of Christ Church, 1648–1710* (Oxford, 1960).

The History of the University of Oxford, 8 vols. (Oxford, 1984 ff.).

HOGWOOD, C., *Haydn's Visits to England* (London, 1980).

—— and LUCKETT, R., eds., *Music in Eighteenth-Century England: Essays in Memory of Charles Cudworth* (Cambridge, 1983).

HUGHES, R., 'Haydn at Oxford: 1773–1791', *ML* 20 (1939), 242–9.

HUGHES, R., 'Dr. Burney's Championship of Haydn', *MQ* 27 (1941), 90–6.

IRVING, H., 'William Crotch on "The Creation" ', *ML* 75 (1994), 548–60.

INGRAM, J., *Memorials of Oxford*, 3 vols. (Oxford, 1837).

Jackson's Oxford Journal (1753–1928).

The John Marsh Journals: the Life and Times of a Gentleman Composer (1752–1828), ed., introd., and annot. by B. Robins (New York, 1998).

JOHNSTONE, H. D., and FISKE, R., *The Eighteenth Century*, Blackwell History of Music in Britain, iv (Oxford, 1990).

JONES, D. W., 'Robert Bremner and the Periodical Overture', *Soundings*, 7 (1978), 63–84.

JOYCE, F. W., *The Life of Rev. Sir F. A. G. Ouseley, Bart* (London, 1896).

JUDGE, R., 'May Morning and Magdalen College, Oxford', *Folklore*, 97 (1986), 15–40.

JUNG, P., *Guide d'Oxford* (Oxford, 1789; 2nd edn. 1805).

——*Concerts of Vocal and Instrumental Music, as performed at the Music Room, Oxford, from October, 1807, to October, 1808* . . . (Oxford, 1808).

KEMP, E. S., and MEE, J. H., *Ten More Years, 1894–1904, of University Music in Oxford* (London, 1904).

KLIMA, S., BOWERS, G., and GRANT, K. S., eds., *Memoirs of Dr. Charles Burney* (Lincoln, Nebr., 1988).

KNIGHT, F., *Cambridge Music from the Middle Ages to Modern Times* (Cambridge and New York, 1980).

KNIGHTS, F., 'Three Magdalen Organists', *The Organ*, 68 (1989), 137–45.

LANDON, H. C. ROBBINS, *Haydn in England, 1791–1795*, Haydn: Chronicle and Works, iii (London, 1976).

LANGFORD, P., *A Polite and Commercial People: England, 1727–1783* (Oxford, 1989).

LEVIEN, J. M., *The Singing of John Braham* (London, 1945).

LEWIS, D. M., *The Jews of Oxford* (Oxford, 1992).

LONSDALE, R., *Dr. Charles Burney: A Literary Biography* (Oxford, 1965).

LYSONS, D., *History of the Origin and Progress of the Meeting of the Three Choirs of Gloucester, Worcester and Hereford . . .* (Gloucester, 1812).

MACKERNESS, E., *A Social History of English Music* (London, 1964).

——*Somewhere further North: A History of Music in Sheffield* (Sheffield, 1974).

MCVEIGH, S., *Concert Life in London from Mozart to Haydn* (Cambridge, 1993).

MARTIN, G. H., and HIGHFIELD, J. R. L., *Merton College, Oxford* (Oxford, 1997).

MATTHEWS, B., 'The Musical Mahons', *MT* 120 (1979), 482–4.

MAURICE, P., *What shall we do with Music? A Letter* (Oxford, 1856).

MEE, J. H., *The Oldest Music Room in Europe: A Record of Eighteenth-Century Enterprise at Oxford* (London, 1911).

MORRIS, R. O., 'Hubert Parry', *ML* I (1920), 94–103.

MUSGRAVE, M., *The Musical Life of the Crystal Palace* (Cambridge, 1995).

Die Musik in Geschichte und Gegenwart (2nd rev. edn.), ed. L. Finscher, Sachteil 7 (Kassel, 1997).

New Grove Dictionary of Music and Musicians, ed. S. Sadie, 20 vols. (London, 1980; 2nd rev. edn., 29 vols., 2001).

NORTHCOTT, R., *The Life of Sir Henry R. Bishop* (London, 1920).

OUSELEY, SIR F. A. G., Professorial Lectures 1861–88 (Ob, MSS Tenb 1443–63).

The Oxford Chronicle (1837–).

The Oxford Magazine (1883–).

Oxford University Calendar (1810–).

Oxford University Gazette (1870–).

PACEY, R., and POPKIN, M., *The Organs of Oxford*: *An Illustrated Guide to the Organs of the University and City of Oxford* (Oxford, 1997).

The Parish Choir, 3 vols. (1846–51).

PARKE, W. T., *Musical Memoirs*, 2 vols. (London, 1830; repr. New York, 1970).

PICKERING, J. M., *Music in the British Isles 1700 to 1800: A Bibliography of Literature* (Edinburgh, 1990).

PIERRE, C., *Histoire du concert spirituel, 1725–1790* (Paris, 1975).

PONSONBY, R., and KENT, R., *The Oxford University Opera Club: A Short History, 1925–1950* (Oxford, 1950).

POOLE, R., 'The Oxford Music School and the Collection of Portraits Formerly Preserved There', *The Musical Antiquary*, 4 (1912–13), 143–59.

PREST, J., ed., *The Illustrated History of Oxford University* (Oxford, 1993).

Publications of the Oxford Historical Society (Oxford, 1884 ff.).

PULVER, J., *A Biographical Dictionary of Old English Music* (London, 1927).

QUILLER-COUCH, L., ed., *Reminiscences of Oxford by Oxford Men, 1559–1850*, OHS, xxii (Oxford, 1892).

REID, D. J., and PRITCHARD, B., 'Some Festival Programmes of the Eighteenth and Nineteenth Centuries, 2: Cambridge and Oxford', *RMARC* 6 (1966), 3–22 (addenda by G. Beechey, *RMARC* 7 (1969), 26–7).

REINAGLE, C. (née Orger), *A Few Words on Piano Playing* (London, 1855).

RENNERT, J., *William Crotch (1775–1847): Composer, Artist, Teacher* (Lavenham, Suffolk, 1975).

RIPPIN, J., 'George Butterworth 1885–1916', *MT* 107 (1966), 680–2; 769–71.

ROBINSON, B. W., and HALL, R. F., eds., *The Aldrich Book of Catches* (Novello, 1989).

Royal Commission on Oxford University: Evidence (Parliamentary Papers 1852).

RUMBOLD, V., 'Music Aspires to Letters: Charles Burney, Queeney Thrale and the Streatham Circle', *ML* 74 (1993), 24–38.

SADIE, S., 'Concert Life in Eighteenth Century England', *PRMA* 85 (1958–9), 17–30.

SALMON, T., *The Present State of the Universities and of the Five Adjacent Counties* ... (London, 1744).

SALTER, H. E., and LOBEL, M. D., eds., *The University of Oxford*, Victoria History of the County of Oxford, iii (London, 1954).

SCHOLES, P., 'Burney and Haydn', *MMR* 71 (1941), 155–6.

——*The Mirror of Music 1844–1944*, 2 vols. (London, 1947).

——*The Great Dr. Burney: His Life, his Travels, his Works, his Family and his Friends*, 2 vols. (London, 1948).

SHAPIRO, A. H., ' "Drama of an Infinitely Superior Nature": Handel's Early English Oratorios and the Religious Sublime', *ML* 74 (1993), 215–45.

SHAW, H. WATKINS, *The Three Choirs Festival: The Official History of the Meetings of the Three Choirs of Gloucester, Hereford and Worcester, c.1713–1953* (Worcester and London, 1954).

——ed., *Sir Frederick Ouseley and St Michael's, Tenbury: A Chapter in the History of English Church Music and Ecclesiology* (University of Birmingham, 1988).

——*The Succession of Organists of the Chapel Royal and the Cathedrals of England and Wales from c.1538* (Oxford, 1991).

——'The Oxford University Chair of Music, 1627–1947, with Some Account of Oxford Degrees in Music from 1856', rev. and ed. P. Ward Jones, *BLR* 16 (1998), 233–70.

SMITHER, H. E., *A History of the Oratorio*, vols. i–ii: *The Oratorio in the Baroque Era* (Chapel Hill, NC, 1977); vol. iii: *The Oratorio in the Classical Era* (Oxford, 1987).

SOUTHGATE, T., 'Music at the Public Pleasure Gardens of the Eighteenth Century', *PMA* 38 (1911–12), 141–59.

SPINK, I., *The Seventeenth Century*, Blackwell History of Music in Britain, iii (Oxford, 1992).

STAINER, SIR J., *The Present State of Music in England: An Inaugural Lecture delivered in the Sheldonian Theatre, Oxford, November 13, 1889* (Oxford, 1889).

——*A Few Words to Candidates for the Degree of Mus. Bac., Oxon.* (London and New York, [1897]).

STANIER, R. S., *Magdalen School: A History of Magdalen College School, Oxford*, OHS NS, iii (Oxford, 1940).

A Summary Catalogue of Western Manuscripts in the Bodleian Library at Oxford, 7 vols. in 13 (Oxford, 1895–1953), v (F. Madan).

TAPHOUSE Ltd., *The Story of a Music Shop, 1857–1957* (Oxford, *c.*1957).

TAUNT, H., *Oxford Illustrated by Camera and Pen* (Oxford, [1911]).

TEMPERLEY, N., 'Handel's Influence on English Music', *MMR* 90 (1960), 163–74.

——'Mendelssohn's Influence on English Music', *ML* 43 (1962), 224–33.

——*The Romantic Age, 1800–1914*, Athlone [later Blackwell] History of Music in Britain, v (London, 1981).

THEWLIS, G., Thewlis papers [Notes on the History of Music in Oxford], several vols., unpublished (Oxford, n.d. [*c.*1955]), Ob.

THORNE, G., ed., *The Oxford & Cambridge Musical Club: An 80th Anniversary History* (Oxford, 1979).

TOVEY, D., and PARRATT, G., *Walter Parratt, Master of the Music* (London, 1941).

TROWLES, T., 'The Musical Ode in Britain *c.*1670–1800' (D.Phil. diss., University of Oxford, 1992).

TUCKWELL, L. [S.], *Old Magdalen Days 1847–1877* (Oxford and London, 1913).

TUCKWELL, W., *Reminiscences of Oxford* (London, 1900; 2nd edn., 1907).

University of Oxford Commission: Evidence (Parliamentary Papers, 1881).

WAINWRIGHT, J., *Musical Patronage in Seventeenth-Century England: Christopher, First Baron Hatton (1605–1670)* (Aldershot, 1997).

WALKER, E., *A History of Music in England*, 3rd edn., rev. J. A. Westrup (Oxford, 1952).

WARD, G. R. M., *Oxford University Statutes*, 2 vols. (London, 1845–51).

WARD JONES, P., 'Elgar as amanuensis', *BLR* 8 (1989), 180–1.

WARRINER, J., *A List of Qualified Musicians Holding British Degrees or Diplomas, compiled from official sources* (London, 1888).

WEBER, W., *The Rise of Musical Classics in Eighteenth-Century England: a Study in Canon, Ritual, and Ideology* (Oxford, 1992).

——*Music and the Middle Class: The Social Structure of Concert Life in London, Paris and Vienna, 1830–48* (London, 1975; Oxford, 1998).

WENDEBORN, F. A., *A View of England towards the Close of the Eighteenth Century*, 2 vols. (London, 1791).

WESTRUP, J., 'Oxford', *NG* xiv. 36–8.

WILLIAMS, C. F. ABDY, *A Short Historical Account of the Degrees in Music at Oxford and Cambridge* (London, 1893).

WOLLENBERG, S., 'Music in 18th-Century Oxford', *PRMA* 108 (1981–2), 69–99.

——'Bishop and Music in 19th-Century Oxford', *MT* 127 (1986), 609–10.

——'Music in Oxford in the Time of Dorothy L. Sayers', *Proceedings of the Centenary Convention (1993)*, Dorothy L. Sayers Society (1994), 19–30.

——'Oxford', *MGG*, 2nd rev. edn. (ed. L. Finscher), Sachteil 7 (Kassel, 1997), 1255–63.

——'Malchair the Musician', in C. Harrison, ed., *John Malchair of Oxford: Artist and Musician* (Oxford, 1998), 33–43.

——'Music in Nineteenth-Century Oxford', in B. Zon, ed., *Nineteenth-Century British Music Studies*, vol. i (Aldershot, 1999), 201–8.

——'Oxford', *NG*, 2nd rev. edn. (London, 2001), xviii. 828–32.

——'The Oxford Exercises in the Eighteenth Century', *EM* 28 (2000), 546–54.

WOOD, A., *The History and Antiquities of the Colleges and Halls in the University of Oxford*, ed. J. Gutch (Oxford, 1786).

——*Athenae Oxonienses*, 2 vols. (London, 1691–2), ed. P. Bliss, 5 vols. (London, 1813–20).

——*The Life and Times of Anthony Wood, Antiquary, of Oxford, 1632–1695, described by himself*, ed. A. Clark (Oxford, 1891–1900).

WOODFORDE, J., *The Diary of a Country Parson*, ed. J. Beresford (Oxford, 1924–31).

WOODGATE, G. K., *The Oxford Chamber Music Society: A Brief History* (Oxford, 1997).

ZASLAW, N., 'An English "Orpheus and Euridice" of 1697', *MT* 118 (1977), 805–8.

Index